GUERNICA

GUERNICA

The Crucible of World War II

GORDON THOMAS AND
MAX MORGAN WITTS

STEIN AND DAY/*Publishers*/New York

First published in 1975
Copyright © 1975 by Gordon Thomas and Max Morgan Witts
All rights reserved
Designed by David Miller
Printed in the United States of America
Stein and Day/Publishers/Scarborough House,
Briarcliff Manor, N.Y. 10510

Library of Congress Cataloging in Publication Data

Thomas, Gordon.
    Guernica.

      1.   Guernica, Spain—Bombardment, 1937.
I.   Morgan Witts, Max, joint author.
DP269.27.G8T45   946'.63'081   75-11806
ISBN 0-8128-1839-3

Authors' Note

We have one advantage over historians who deal with earlier centuries. Two of our books (*The Day the World Ended* and *The San Francisco Earthquake*) dealt with events in the first decade of the twentieth century. Three of them (*Shipwreck, Voyage of the Damned,* and the present work) reconstruct dramatic events of the 1930s. All five of these books were done with the help of numerous men and women who survived the events and lived to tell us what they knew of them. It is our habit to arm ourselves with all of the available written and documentary material beforehand as a means of testing the veracity of the people we interview and hopefully obtaining the highest possible incidence of truth, particularly from those who view our exploration of the past as potentially dangerous to themselves and to the legends they would sustain as a curtain over the actual events. Some of the people, we find, are understandably alarmed. A few are hostile—at first. Perhaps a majority of them experience pain in the recollection of detail they would rather forget.

Thus, we must apologize to our interviewees and thank them in the same breath. In fact, no breath can be sustained long enough to thank the survivors of Guernica, the members of the Condor Legion, and the numerous others, including translators and research institutions, from whose minds and files and photograph albums we drew the raw material from which we were able to reconstruct an event that was the precursor of Rotterdam, Coventry, Hamburg, Dresden, and finally Hiroshima. The people we interviewed were so many, and the help we received so great, that we have devoted an Appendix of sources to naming all except those few who forty years later still live in fear.

When we started, Guernica was enshrouded in legend and controversy. Some people and governments claimed that the Basques blew up Guernica. Other people and governments claimed there were no military targets in the cultural capital of the Basque country, only innocent civilians. The facts we uncovered prove both views wrong.

We believe that most historians specializing in past centuries must envy our access to the people who lived through the events we describe. To them we say, Temper your envy. The books and archives that are your sources do not threaten you with imprisonment (as we have been in the course of our research for this book); your sources do not have hands that shake with emotion, eyes that shed tears over events no human being has heard before. Most of all, historians should temper their envy of our sources because in reconstructing this crucible of the Second World War, we are dealing with a chain of events that is still thrashing in the lives we lead today.

GORDON THOMAS

July 1975   MAX MORGAN WITTS

Contents

Illustrations

Guernica has the happiest people in the world, regulating their affairs by a body of peasants under an oak, and always conducting themselves wisely.

> —Jean Jacques Rousseau, eighteenth century

Your fight in Spain was a lesson to our opponents.

> —Adolf Hitler to German
> troops returning from Spain,
> June 1939

Spain gave me an opportunity to try out my young air force . . . and for personnel to gather experience.

> —Hermann Göring at Nuremberg
> War Crimes Trials, March 1946

The first squadron dropped their bombs, I saw them, but by the time I was over the target, the town was obscured by dust and smoke, so we had to drop our bombs as best we could . . . we couldn't tell what they were hitting.

> —Hans Henning, *Freiherr* von Beust,
> squadron leader over Guernica,
> April 26, 1937, as reported
> to the authors, 1974

It is impossible to give an adequate picture of the indescribable tragedy.

> —José Labauría, mayor of
> Guernica, on Radio Bilbao, May 4,
> 1937

Please induce Franco to issue an energetic and sharp denial that German fliers attacked Guernica.

—Joachim von Ribbentrop,
German ambassador in London,
to Foreign Ministry, Berlin,
May 4, 1937

Guernica was not bombed by my air force . . . it was destroyed with fire and gasoline by the Basques themselves.

—Press release from Franco
headquarters, May 5, 1937

An international investigation of Guernica is to be rejected under all circumstances.

—Adolf Hitler to Von Ribbentrop,
May 15, 1937

Guernica was . . . an experimental horror.

—Winston Churchill, in
The Gathering Storm, 1948

World War Two began in Spain.

—Claude Bowers, U.S. ambassador
to Spain, in *My Mission to
Spain,* 1953

Guernica can offer nothing of interest to anyone concerned with its past, nor is there any value in discussing what happened then with anyone here.

—Gervasio Guezuraga, mayor of
Guernica, to authors, 1974

Personae

THE NATIONALIST HIGH COMMAND:

General Francisco Franco, *Commander in Chief*

General Emilio Mola, *Commander, Nationalist Army of the North*

Colonel Juan Vigón, *General Mola's Chief of Staff*

General Alfredo Kindélan, *Commander, Spanish Air Force*

General Juan Yagüe, *Commander, Moroccan troops*

THE CONDOR LEGION:

General Hugo Sperrle, *Commander in Chief*

Lieutenant Colonel Wolfram, *Freiherr* von Richthofen, *Chief of Staff*

Major Klaus Fuchs, *Wing Commander, Flying*

Major Heinz Trettner, *General Sperrle's Adjutant*

First Lieutenant Rudolf von Moreau, *Leader, Experimental Bomber Squadron*

First Lieutenant Karl von Knauer, *Leader, No. 1 Bomber Squadron*

First Lieutenant Hans Henning, *Freiherr* von Beust, *Leader, No. 2 Bomber Squadron*

Captain Ehrhart von Dellmensingen Krafft, *Leader, No. 3 Bomber Squadron*

First Lieutenant Herwig Knuppel, *Leader, Messerschmitt Fighter Squadron*

Captain Franz von Lutzow, *Leader, Heinkel Fighter Squadron*

Lieutenant Hans Joachim, *Fighter Pilot*

Lieutenant Balthazar, *Reconnaissance Pilot*

Lieutenant Count Max Hoyos, *Bombardier*

Captain Klaus Gautlitz, *Chief Operations Officer*

Lieutenant Hans Asmus, *Assistant Operations Officer*
Lieutenant Heinz Raunce, *Assistant Operations Officer*
and some five thousand other unnamed officers and other ranks

THE PEOPLE OF GUERNICA

José Labauría, *Mayor*
Rufino Unceta, *Arms Manufacturer*
Luis Unceta, Augusto Unceta, *His Sons*
José Rodríguez, *His General Manager*
Father José Iturran, *Parish Priest, Santa María Church*
Father Eusebio Arronategui, *Parish Priest, San Juan Church*
Captain Juan Cortés, *Chief Medical Officer*
Teresa Ortuz, *Nurse*
Carmen Batzar, *Nursing Auxiliary*
Captain Juan de Beiztegi, *Garrison Commander*
Lieutenant Ramón Gandaría, *Staff Officer, Garrison HQ*
Lieutenant Juan Dominguiz, *Field Officer, Loyola Battalion*
Juan Plaza, *Farm Worker*
Mother Augusta, *Superior, Carmelite Convent*
Mother María, *Superior, La Merced Convent*
Juan Silliaco, *Bartender/Volunteer Fireman*
Isidro Arrién, *Restaurateur*
Pedro Guezureya, *Restaurateur*
Juan Guezureya, Cipriano Guezureya, *His Sons*
Julio Bareno, *Bank Manager*
Rafael Herrán, *Factory Manager*
Antonio Arazamagni, *Baker*
María Ortuza, *Housekeeper*
Faustino Pastor, *Soldier, Saseta Battalion*
and some twelve thousand unnamed townspeople, soldiers, and refugees

José Antonio de Aguirre, *President, Basque Government*
Francisco Lazcano, *Presidential Aide in Guernica*
Jesús de Leizaola, *Basque Minister of Justice*
Father Alberto de Onaindía, *Canon of Valladolid Cathedral*

Prologue

On March 28, 1975, four bombs rocked the ancient town of Guernica in northern Spain. It was not the first time, nor the last, that such incidents had occurred, and it provoked a not untypical reaction by the Franco regime. Next day, thousands of Spanish Civil Guards armed with machine guns virtually sealed off Guernica from the rest of the country.

Basque Nationalists had set off the bombs to commemorate an event that had occurred thirty-eight years earlier. This is the story of that event—and hopefully an explanation of why, even now, efforts are being made to distort what happened in Guernica on April 26, 1937, that has made it symbolize the horrors of war to millions of people, inspired Pablo Picasso to immortalize it in his most famous painting, and placed it apart in the annals of warfare.

For eight months after the Spanish Civil War began, the people of Guernica were hardly affected by the conflict. The fighting raged far to the south of them, leaving the spiritual home of the Basque people isolated behind the mountains of northern Spain.

When the fighting started on July 17, 1936, the seven thousand citizens of Guernica remained loyal to the government in Madrid, a hodgepodge of political parties ruling under the emblem of Republicanism. Although the townspeople had little in common with Spain's elected leaders, they had even less sympathy for the men who had plunged the country into civil war: the Nationalists, led by General Francisco Franco.

The origins of the conflict that split Spain were complex; it was not in the beginning a case of "the military" against "the peasants," or of fascism versus communism, as observers would later describe it.

In the five years of Republican government before 1936, the country had become increasingly unstable politically. During that time, Spain had had eleven prime ministers, and eighty other ministers had held office. As a result of the general election of February 1936, thirty-two disparate political parties were represented in the Cortes, the Spanish parliament.

Spain's Republican constitution collapsed because the peaceful coexistence of Right and Left on which it depended, alternating as government and opposition, proved unworkable. Right and Left agreed on only one thing: They could not work together. Gradually each became bent on the elimination of the other.

When the war began, Basque opinion was divided. In theory, as the region's politics leaned to the Right, it should have favored Franco. But Franco's Nationalists were for a unified Spain; Basque Nationalists were for an independent Basque nation. Soon after hostilities started, the government in Madrid granted the Basques "home rule," thereby guaranteeing their loyalty to the Republican cause. From then on, most Basques believed that if ever the conflict came to them, they would be fighting for their own country against an enemy that was the equivalent of a foreign aggressor.

Autonomy seemed only right to most Basques. Since records began, their three mountainous provinces of northern Spain had been the home of a distinct, recognizable culture, and their language, its origins unknown, was understood by few outsiders.

The Basques were among the most religious people in Spain, and the most strongly attached to Roman Catholicism. They practiced a form of democracy based on a stubborn tradition of strong local rights. For centuries, this combination of almost fanatical religious belief and strong political awareness had secured for the Basques a large measure of autonomy within the Spanish nation. Guernica was their sentimental capital, symbol of their independence, source of their inspiration.

Soon after the region became independent, Guernica's mayor declared himself a Franco supporter. He was promptly imprisoned, an example to other Nationalist sympathizers in the area.

The people of Guernica felt well protected by the three battalions of Basque troops based in the town. A few were worried by Guernica's booming armaments industry, but most agreed it was a small price to pay for what the war had given them—independence.

Until the end of March 1937, the struggle for Spain centered mainly around Madrid. Guernicans heard the radio bulletins, read the newspapers, and were relieved the war was being fought far away. They knew little of how the world had been caught up in the war; how twenty-seven countries had agreed to a Nonintervention Pact banning foreign help so that the conflict would not spread; how, even so, idealists—most totally untrained—from the United States, Great Britain, France, and many other countries had traveled to Spain without their governments' sanctions to fight against the Nationalists; how Hitler and Mussolini—also signatories to the pact—had sided with the Nationalists and officially, but secretly, seized upon the conflict to provide their armed forces with experience for a bigger war to come.

By March 1937, Germany had sent to Spain—while repeatedly denying it had done so—over five thousand troops, whose influence was out of all proportion to their numbers. They were the elite Condor Legion, handpicked to maintain and defend the largest and most powerful air armada until then ever assembled for any war. In firepower alone, the Condor Legion exceeded the combined air forces of World War I.

Although Germany had also provided a few tank units and naval specialists, it was the Legion that had secretly ferried Franco's feared Moroccan troops to Spain. It was the Legion that had air-dropped life-sustaining supplies into Franco's besieged fortress, the Alcázar. It was the Legion that had bombed Madrid.

And it was the Condor Legion that now looked northward to targets in the isolated Basque provinces. The mountains separating the Basques from the rest of Spain were a formidable natural barrier. But the Legion could fly over the jagged peaks and act as airborne artillery for the Nationalist ground troops.

The Legion's commander in Spain persuaded Franco to send his men north in support of a new offensive to be led by the Nationalist commander, General Emilio Mola. On March 30, 1937, Mola broadcast an ultimatum:

"I have decided to terminate rapidly the war in the north. Those not guilty of assassinations and who surrender their arms will have their lives and property spared. But if submission is not immediate, I will raze all Vizcaya to the ground, beginning with the industries of war."

Vizcaya was the most densely populated of the three Basque provinces. Because of its mineral wealth, it was the industrial fief of Spain. Iron ore, coal, and coke were mined around Bilbao, the region's seaport capital. Guernica, twenty miles east of Bilbao, was the province's spiritual center, with its historic Parliament Building and the oak tree, symbol of Basque culture and independence, growing on the Parliament grounds.

On March 31, Mola launched his offensive. Fifty thousand heavily armed troops, including the feared troops from Morocco, advanced on the Basque country. Air support was provided by the Condor Legion.

Opposing them was the Republican Army of the North. Poorly equipped with a few obsolete aircraft and fieldpieces, prevented by the Nonintervention Pact from procuring more modern weapons from Great Britain, France, or the United States, this army of forty-five thousand was further weakened by disagreements over strategy among its commanders.

Although the Republican troops put up a stiff resistance, gradually they were forced back. Guernica became a focal point for thousands of refugees fleeing from aerial bombing on a scale the world had never before experienced. They knew that after the planes dropped their death loads, ground troops would not be far behind. And they heard tales of a vengeful conqueror—that men were often shot after surrendering, and that women were sometimes forced at gunpoint to strip and submit to rape.

In spite of what the refugees told them, the people of Guernica felt little alarm. They believed Guernica to be inviolate; the town was, after all, world renowned as the capital of a region that had practiced a form of democracy, under which all men were accorded respect and dignity, long before the other countries of Western Europe. Even as the war came closer, and shortages of food, coal, and other supplies made the influx of refugees a serious problem, Guernicans told themselves that the enemy would surely respect their historic town. Even if Guernica were taken by the enemy, they thought, little violence would occur.

By April 25, 1937, the front line was twenty miles from Guernica. Between its inhabitants and the enemy was a rugged terrain; thousands of Basque troops provided protection.

Or so the people of Guernica thought.

SUNDAY
April 25, 1937

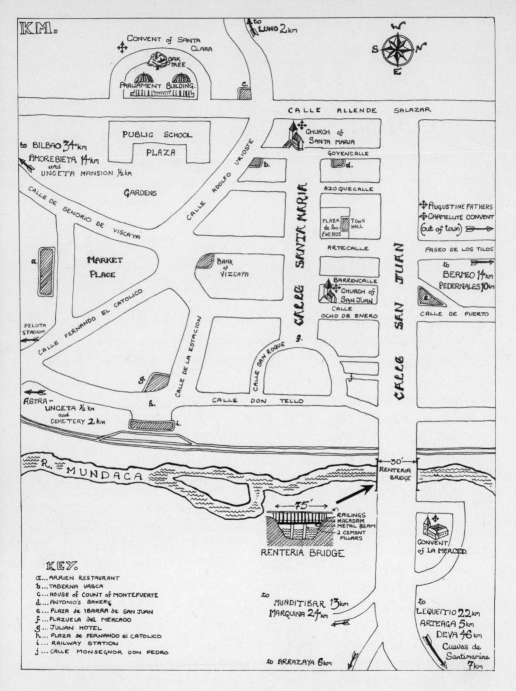

KM.

Convent of Santa Clara

OAK TREE

PARLIAMENT BUILDING.

c.

to LUNO 2km

CALLE ALLENDE SALAZAR

PUBLIC SCHOOL

PLAZA

Church of Santa Maria

GOYENCALLE

b.

d.

to BILBAO 34km
AMOREBIETA 14km
and
UNCETA MANSION ½km

CALLE DE SEÑORIO DE VISCAYA

CALLE ADOLFO URIOSTE

GARDENS

AZOQUECALLE

✝ Augustine Fathers
✝ Carmelite Convent
(out of town) ⟹

PASEO DE LOS TILOS

MARKET PLACE

a.

Bank of Vizcaya

CALLE SANTA MARIA

PLAZA de los FUEROS

TOWN HALL

ARTECALLE

BARRENCALLE
Church of SAN JUAN

CALLE SAN JUAN

to
BERMEO 14km
PEDERNALES 10km

CALLE DE PUERTO

PELOTA STADIUM

CALLE FERNANDO EL CATOLICO

CALLE DE LA ESTACION

CALLE SAN ROQUE

f.

CALLE OCHO DE ENERO

g.

ASTRA-
UNCETA ½km
and
CEMETERY 2km

h.

CALLE DON TELLO

i.

R. MUNDACA

30'
Renteria Bridge

75'

RAILINGS
MACADAM
METAL BEAM
2 CEMENT
PILLARS

RENTERIA BRIDGE

CONVENT of LA MERCED.

KEY:

a... ARRIEN RESTAURANT
b... TABERNA VASCA
c... HOUSE of COUNT of MONTEFUERTE
d... ANTONIO'S BAKERY
e... PLAZA de IBARRA de SAN JUAN
f... PLAZUELA del MERCADO
g... JULIAN HOTEL
h... PLAZA de FERNANDO el CATOLICO
i... RAILWAY STATION
j... CALLE MONSEGNOR DON PEDRO

to
MUNDITIBAR 13km
MARQUINA 24km

to
LEQUEITIO 22km
ARTEAGA 5km
DEVA 46km
Cuevas de Santimarine 7km

to ARRAZAYA 6km

Central Guernica (not to scale) before it was destroyed on April 26, 1937

Midnight—6:00 A.M.

•1•

Two sounds made Teresa Ortuz pause in her task. The first was dull, like a hammer blow on an anvil bedded in earth. It was artillery fire, coming closer to Guernica.

The second sound was nearer. Something alive was with her in the mortuary.

Teresa lifted her lantern. Its light barely carried to the open door at the opposite end of the morgue. Beyond, dim illumination from the main hospital building cast shadows on the flagstone courtyard outside this long, low, windowless room.

Teresa heard the footsteps of the patrolling sentry. Around her were the sheeted forms, each a dead soldier. She replaced the lantern on the floor. Then, kneeling beside a naked body still warm after its journey from the operating room, she wiped away the blood and dirt of the battlefield, closed the eyes and mouth, and folded the arms.

The only signs of violence on the body were the surgical sutures that ran from gullet to abdomen. Behind the stitches were the man's intestines, bundled back into his abdominal cavity following his death.

Teresa heard the sound again, a crunching noise.

She rose to her feet and moved toward the door, holding the lantern higher for more light. Ahead of her, something was tugging at a corpse. As she watched in horror, a huge, lean dog backed away, dragging the body outside.

Teresa screamed. The animal growled and tugged more fiercely. Hearing its teeth grind against bone, Teresa screamed again.

The sentry appeared in the doorway, raised his rifle, and shot the animal. Then he dragged it outside by its tail.

He returned and stood in the doorway. "They are getting a taste for human flesh. It is bad. . . ."

Teresa thanked him, assured him she was no longer frightened, and went back to her work. She could sense he was still standing there, puzzled at the sight of a dark-haired nurse laying out corpses at this witching hour. She explained this was the only free time she had, and added, "It has to be done."

Teresa Ortuz was nineteen years old. This Sunday was the two hundred seventieth day of the war she had spent in the convent of the Religiosas Carmelitas de la Caridad, one of the oldest religious orders in Europe. On July 27, 1936, the barracklike convent on the northern outskirts of Guernica had been requisitioned as a military hospital.

In the convent nearly five hundred wounded were now cramped together, many close to death. To tend them were twenty nuns and as many lay nurses. Five surgeons, led by Captain Juan Cortés, the chief medical officer, operated in shifts for eighteen hours a day.

Teresa divided her time between wards and operating room, where she had been assigned to work with Captain Cortés. Theirs was not a comfortable partnership. She recognized his surgical skill but deplored his personal habits. He drank, reeked of garlic, and swore volubly. He refused to change his surgeon's apron, while insisting she be spotlessly garbed for every operation.

Twice in the past Teresa had asked Mother Augusta, the Superior in charge of the nursing staff, to switch her to another surgical team. Mother Augusta believed Teresa was one of the few nurses strong enough to manage Cortés. She explained there was no one else available to work with him and coaxed Teresa to stay with a promise to have yet another talk with the irascible surgeon.

Teresa doubted whether another of Mother Augusta's appeals would have any effect. Previous ones had produced no change in

Cortés. He still worked prodigious hours, performed great surgical feats, and drove his staff mercilessly.

Most of all, Teresa was upset that Cortés was irreligious. She marveled that Mother Augusta continued to believe he would change. The Mother Superior's faith somehow strengthened Teresa's resolve eventually to become a nun.

She knew her decision to take holy vows disappointed her father. He wanted her to be, like him, a doctor. When she had told him of her ambition, he had asked her to wait a further year before embarking on the life of self-sacrifice. Secure in her belief, she had agreed to wait.

Soon afterward, the war had started and Teresa had enrolled on the hospital staff. In the nine months that followed, she had devised several self-imposed "tests," as she put it, to "prove I still had the willpower necessary to become a nun."

One of her "tests" was to give up her midnight coffee break to go to the mortuary and lay out the dead.

Teresa completed her task and returned to the main building. Its ground and two upper floors were filled with beds. The normal living space of the convent was limited to the chapel and a small wing where the nuns slept; lay staff were never allowed into this private world.

Mother Augusta once said it was "God's will" the convent had been occupied. Captain Cortés was quick to offer a more practical explanation: The building's yard-thick walls could withstand all but the most sustained ground attack. From the air, only a direct hit by a large bomb would do any real damage. But, the surgeon had warned, the red cross painted on the convent roof was no guarantee of safety. On the contrary, he pointed out, in other theaters of the war the emblem had acted as a magnet, drawing both aircraft and artillery fire.

Bolts of black cloth, originally intended for nuns' habits, were used by Mother Augusta to black out windows; only a few on the ground floor facing into the courtyard remained exposed when the cloth ran out. Screened spaces were prepared to hide ambulances discharging wounded. An overhead covering of grass laid on wire netting was rigged to camouflage surgical linen being laundered.

Each nun gave up a portion of her free time during the day to sit on the roof of the convent and scan the sky for aircraft. Others patrolled the road, ready to stop transport from approaching the building if an air raid occurred. Several ambulance drivers had been gently admonished for driving too quickly near the hospital; dust clouds from their vehicles could provoke the interest of aircraft.

Teresa had also acted as an aircraft lookout. A few days ago, she had seen tiny specks crawling over the mountains in the south, heading in the direction of Bilbao. That night she heard the port had been bombed.

Next day, following air attacks on the Basque front line, the hospital had received its first victims of incendiary bombs. All but one of the soldiers had soon died from the terrible phosphorus burns.

The sole survivor lay in a cubicle on the ground floor. His scalp was singed, his lips were seared, and a wide bandage covered his sightless eyes. His arms and chest were yellow with blisters and weals. He had been kept alive by blood and saline transfusions.

Passing the cubicle, Teresa saw that the drips had been removed. She hurried in search of Captain Cortés. He was about to begin a ward round; he preferred the nocturnal hours to pad from one bed to another, inspecting his patients. In response to her demand for an explanation, the surgeon told Teresa he had stopped the transfusions because the man was going to die anyway, and he would not waste blood on a doomed case.

Teresa was horrified. "Only God knows for sure when a person will die," she protested.

Cortés blinked and replied, "The dead do not interest me. It is then, if at all, that they become a matter for God."

Teresa returned to the cubicle. The man had died.

At that moment she despised Captain Cortés almost as much as she hated the enemy pilots who had dropped the incendiary bombs.

•2•

Thirty-five flying miles south of Guernica, across the mountains at Vitoria, Lieutenant Colonel Wolfram, *Freiherr* von Richthofen, was taking his usual pre-bedtime tour around the airfield. As he did so, he detected the first signs of a "bomber's sky." The air was getting drier, the breeze was just strong enough to clear smoke from a target, cloud was breaking up to provide the right mixture of cover and visibility for his pilots. Like him, the air crews had been frustrated by long periods of bad weather that kept them grounded. Some passed the time in the Vitoria brothels. Others simply drank the strong local wines and brandies.

Von Richthofen was proud of his self-control. Partly through training and partly because of his nature, he refrained from showing emotion of any kind in public. Although he had once felt physically ill when a Spanish general greeted him with a kiss on the cheek, he had successfully concealed his feeling.

The chief of staff of the Condor Legion was forty-one, almost twice the average age of his pilots. Nevertheless, in stamina and flying ability he could match the best of them. He was impressive without being tall: firm-muscled, lithe, with a hunter's swift reaction. He reminded many people of his cousin Manfred, the German flying ace killed in World War I.

Von Richthofen's blue eyes and pursed mouth came from his father; his aristocratic snub nose had been a family characteristic for four hundred years. His strong legs were developed in boyhood through constant physical exercise over the family estate in Silesia. Even in the heat of Spain he never missed his morning pushups, running in place, bending-and-stretching exercises. And at the end of each day he walked among the airplanes he cherished almost as much as he did his wife and young son back in Germany.

Not all the aircraft were at Vitoria. Seventy miles southwest, at Burgos, were three squadrons of Junkers bombers, the new Heinkel-111s, and the workhorses of the task force, the Dornier-17s. Here, at Vitoria, were the fighters: the HE-51s, the still secret ME (BF)-109s, and four HE-23 Stuka dive bombers whose distinctive whine produced a special terror in its victims on the ground. Also dispersed around the airfield were the reconnaisance HE-70s and HE-45s. Finally, there were the Legion's two W-34s, which rose awkwardly into the air at dawn and dusk each day so that their crews could study cloud density and windspeed. The weather forecasts were based on their flights.

Recently the forecasts had turned out to be more unreliable than usual, due to the rapid weather changes over mountainous northern Spain. The pilots blamed the luckless weather crew not only for being wrong, but for actually causing the bad weather; it was a sign of the frustration everyone felt.

Now, to the north, over the mountains, the sky was light enough to silhouette the trees and the aircraft parked under and around them. Von Richthofen paused by each aircraft, listening as the breeze rustled through the wire stays. There was no doubt in his mind: The wind was from the south, a sure sign of fine weather on the way.

Well clear of the aircraft, surrounded by a high fence, was a large compound guarded by Spanish soldiers. Inside, canvas-covered irregular mounds concealed bombs and ammunition cases.

Continuing his walk, Von Richthofen strode past the tents where the fitters stored their tools. He had once surprised a group of mechanics by reciting the exact sequence they must follow in stripping down an engine. It earned him further respect—but he had never gained the affection of his officers and men. Von Richthofen was too preoccupied with results to ever achieve more than a casual relationship with those he commanded.

As a child he had amused himself by dismantling old farm machinery. While a cadet in the Prussian Army, he spent much of his time alone, digesting technical magazines. After flying with his cousin Manfred's squadron, he ended World War I with seven "kills." Some said he had shot down more enemy aircraft than he was officially credited with; that the cousin of the Red Baron allowed them to go to others to avoid any charge of nepotism.

After Berlin University, where he earned an engineering doctorate in 1929, he went into the diplomatic service. For three years he served as air attaché at the German embassy in Rome. Late in 1932 he returned home. Within months Hitler was in power.

Initially, Von Richthofen had had doubts about Hitler. Von Richthofen was, after all, an aristocrat with a title going back to the sixteenth century; he felt nothing in common with the Nazis and their beerhall manners. Finally, however, Von Richthofen came to believe Hitler would regain for Germany "her rightful place at Europe's table after the shameful *diktat* of Versailles."

Among those who came to power in the Nazi takeover was Hermann Göring, who had also flown in the Red Baron's squadron. The intervening years had done nothing to soften Von Richthofen's dislike of Göring, with his gaudy uniforms, his childish vanity and greed. Von Richthofen despised Göring's undisciplined drinking habits and suspected him of being a drug addict.

When they met in 1934, Göring was building the Luftwaffe in secret. Von Richthofen, motivated by patriotism, and fearing Göring "would bungle things," saw an opportunity "to be in on the ground floor of Germany's military rebirth." He accepted Göring's offer of a planning job in the new Air Ministry. He rejected Göring's suggestion he join the Nazi party. That matter was never raised again.

Von Richthofen's work behind the impressive columns of the main Defense Ministry building in Berlin involved devising secret war games to play in Bavaria. But he yearned to see whether his theories really worked.

The Spanish Civil War was to provide that opportunity.

Within days after the war began, General Franco sent a personal message to Hitler. The Führer was on his annual pilgrimage to Bayreuth for the Wagner festival. On the night of July 25, 1936, after the curtain rang down on *Siegfried* at 9:50 P.M., Hitler met with colleagues to consider "the Spanish question," and decided "immediately to fulfill this appeal for help." Göring was delighted: Here was the perfect opportunity to test the Luftwaffe's men and machines in action.

Lieutenant Colonel von Richthofen arrived in Spain with the Condor Legion in November and was made its chief of staff at the beginning of 1937. The early months were difficult for him. There were the Spanish to contend with; their belief in mañana made him impatient. But he was also learning how to control his bombers and fighters in a way that would serve him well—not just in Spain, but later, in World War II.

In the years ahead, Von Richthofen's reputation would outstrip that of his famous cousin, the Red Baron, and bring additional glory to a family already prominent in German military history. For he would be credited with perfecting the aerial blitzkrieg—a sudden, unexpected, devastating attack delivered with precision at thunderbolt speed. It was a tactic he would use with ruthless efficiency in France, Yugoslavia, Greece, and Crete. Later he would lead an armada of over seven hundred fighting planes to Russia, creating terror at Sevastopol, Leningrad, and Stalingrad. He would rise to the rank of field marshal, eventually joining Adolf Hitler's personal staff.

But as Von Richthofen completed his midnight inspection of Vitoria airfield, all that lay ahead. Soon he would apply his unique qualities of ambition and invention to take a major step toward his future successes: deciding the fate of the most revered town in northern Spain.

•3•

At 1:30 A.M. an ambulance arrived at Guernica's Carmelite Convent. It carried corpses. Teresa Ortuz overheard Captain Cortés tell the driver he should be shot for wasting fuel to transport the dead.

The surgeon glanced at the bodies and walked past Teresa into the hospital.

An orderly emerged and helped the ambulance driver unload the bodies. Teresa concluded that they had been dead for some time: Rigor mortis had passed and the muscles were again relaxed. She hoped death had been instantaneous.

Teresa returned inside to the sterilization room, where Cortés was checking the record book she was detailed to keep. The last entry, for Saturday, April 24, showed that twenty-two major operations had been performed and six patients had died. Cortés remarked it was "about average."

Icily, Teresa asked if he were referring to the number of operations or the dead. Cortés laughed, then closed the book and left the room.

Teresa realized she had touched a weak spot—Cortés did not like to be reminded that any of his patients died.

Since childhood she had witnessed how patients respected her father. He was a venerated figure, accorded the same status as a priest. In turn, her father had lived up to his image. Cortés, however, seemed to her to relish his own intemperate behavior: "He enjoyed shocking people," she later said.

Teresa had come to the conclusion that the only way for her to survive professionally in Cortés's company was to stand up to him. His response had shown her it was the right policy, for she had also recognized something else: "Captain Cortés could show a perverse delight in being challenged."

Now Teresa made her nightly check of the sterilization room, ensuring everything was ready for another eighteen hours of surgery, due to begin at 6:00 A.M. The *poupinelle,* a copper sterilizer the French had sent, was loaded with surgical instruments. She moved around the room, reflecting that its contents showed the international involvement in the war—despite the Nonintervention Pact.

In the deep cupboards along one wall were instrument boxes from Russia, linen drums and barrels of compresses from Belgium. The instrument and swab tables were from Holland. The anesthetist's trolley had been manufactured in England; its metal flasks of ether and rows of phials came from Poland and the United States.

The previous day's surgery had made further inroads on their supplies. Boxes and bottles stood empty on the shelves, the prospects of refills diminishing each day that the Nationalist blockade of Bilbao continued.

By the time she finished her checks, Teresa knew that the hospital was facing a crisis. By the end of the coming week there would not be enough ether to anesthetize a single patient.

The thought kindled anew an emotion that she had struggled to subdue for weeks: hatred of the enemy. She knew that if an enemy soldier appeared this moment in the room, she would try to kill him with her bare hands. The thought made her tremble; stifling that hatred was another of the "tests" she had set herself to prove she was worthy of taking holy vows.

When she had regained her composure, she took a compress, dampened it with water, and left the room to walk through the wards guided by her lantern. In rooms to one side of the central passageway on the ground floor were patients who had recently undergone surgery. On the other side were those waiting, each classified by a colored gummed sticker on his sleeve: red for acute, blue for less acute, yellow for nonurgent cases. She could not remember when she last saw a yellow label, but in the last week there had been an alarming proliferation of red ones.

Teresa went from ward to ward, from cot to cot, offering soothing words and a cool compress. She took care to appear oblivious to the smell of sweat, urine, and feces.

One room housed the preoperative thorax cases, with great bandages around their stomachs, chests, rising and falling in painful breathing. Most slept, sedated by morphine.

One man lay awake, watching Teresa as she approached for any hint that might relieve or confirm his fears. She smiled at him, holding up her lamp so that he could see her face.

The man was scheduled for a splenectomy in the morning. But Teresa knew that wounds of the spleen seldom occurred alone; his liver and large and small intestine were probably damaged. His eyes opened wider as he pleaded for water.

Teresa was about to explain he could not have any, then changed her mind. The man's face was ashen, his lips like clay. Death, she guessed, was close. In the morning, if he was still alive, he would be moved to a ward where the prolapsed cases, those beyond aid, waited to die.

She let the man drink.

During the early days of the war, some of the doctors had performed "compassionate surgery," operating on patients who were without hope, and afterward prescribing massive doses of morphine until death. In this way a man died without pain, and in hope.

Captain Cortés had ordered a halt to such surgery soon after Mola's northern offensive began. Much later, Teresa would recall his sardonic comment: "Even if we are in a convent, we are not going to waste time working on terminal cases and trying for a miracle."

It was the only time Teresa had seen Mother Augusta angry. She had turned on the surgeon and reminded him that miracles were not expected of him; they were the province of God. Cortés had not been moved.

Only afterward, when the hospital's surgical case load had grown overwhelming, did Teresa wonder what her father would have done in the situation. She could not ask him. Three weeks earlier he had volunteered for medical service in the Republican Army.

Several times during her ward rounds, she paused at the sound of distant shellfire. Some of the patients were frightened by it; she guessed they were the ones who had heard the rumor that the enemy slaughtered wounded soldiers in their beds. Teresa calmed their fears by saying it was Basque artillery laying down a barrage. The gunfire did not disturb Teresa; she knew there were still twenty thousand troops between the town and the enemy.

Nevertheless, to satisfy one patient, she went outside to see if she could spot any artillery flashes. The mountains were now silent. As she turned to go back inside, she noticed a group of people on the road approaching the convent. It was too dark for her to identify them; she assumed they were refugees.

They were soldiers.

Some of the troops Teresa Ortuz and the other people of Guernica believed were defending them had slipped out of their excellent positions and retreated across the mountains to the town, leaving a fifteen-mile hole in the front.

Behind this collapse was a sorry story of poor leadership in the field and political chicanery at the rear. The Republican Army in the north, at best tenuously commanded, had by this Sunday morning become disorganized and dispirited. Two battalions manned by passionate trade unionists were withdrawn from the battlefield by their political paymasters in a crude attempt to persuade the Basque government to give them representation. A general retreat had begun because units feared being cut off.

The group Teresa mistook for refugees comprised more than one hundred soldiers who had entered the town from the east, over the Rentería Bridge. Foot-weary and dejected, they shuffled into Guernica seeking shelter. Instinctively, they avoided the open squares around the marketplace, public school, and railway station that lay to their left. The soldiers knew from experience that such places were ideal targets for fighter planes to strafe.

They also avoided the churches of San Juan and Santa María, knowing enemy bombers regarded churches as suitable targets; the Nationalists claimed the Republicans often stored ammunition in crypts.

Finally, the troops passed the Carmelite Convent; a hospital was no place for soldiers who weren't wounded. They chose instead to spend the rest of the night in the gardens of the monastery of the Augustine Fathers, just beyond the convent, on the main road to Bermeo. The ancient monastery marked the northern boundary of the town.

The soldiers fell asleep almost immediately upon lying down, their rifles at their sides. Beside one group of three men was the company's prize possession: a modern machine gun. It had been dismantled for easier carrying, and now its crew used the ammunition belts as pillows.

The soldiers' arrival did not go unnoticed. Refugees saw them and passed the news along to the railway station plaza where hundreds more refugees waited, their eyes intent on the freight train being loaded from one of the town's armament factories, the Talleres de Guernica.

Stevedores, moving carefully, grunting under the loads they carried, were emptying the factory. Once a man stumbled and his companions froze as he struggled to hold onto a box of hand grenades and mortar shells, the factory's main products. One of the sentries guarding the train ran and hoisted the box back on the man's shoulder.

After the explosives were loaded, the plant's tools and machinery were placed in the freight cars. The Talleres de Guernica was being gutted of everything movable and would be reassembled behind Bilbao's "ring of iron," the defensive shield of antiaircraft guns, field artillery, rifle trenches, and barbed wire the Basques had built around their industrial capital. When the loading was completed, the soldiers closed the boxcar doors.

In the station plaza, men holding an assortment of clublike weapons edged toward the train.

"It's moving!" The shout, from one of the refugees, was nearly lost in the hiss from the engine's valves. In a concerted rush, the refugees ran toward the train.

Startled, the soldiers swung around, uncertain of what to do. An NCO bellowed at them.

"Aim!"

The soldiers moved their rifles to their shoulders.

"Warning volley. Fire!"

The bullets whistled over the heads of the mob.

"Reload!"

The click of the rifle bolts being opened and closed was heard.

"Aim! Shoot to kill on command!"

The soldiers swung their rifles directly on the refugees.

"Stop!"

From the Talleres de Guernica a young officer ran to place himself between the soldiers and the mob.

Lieutenant Ramón Gandaría deliberately turned his back on the refugees and ordered the soldiers to lower their weapons. When they had done so, he complimented the NCO for his swift action, then turned to walk toward the mob. He stopped in front of the biggest man he could see, reached forward and took the man's club, then contemptuously flung it aside.

"All of you," said Gandaría sharply, "throw down your sticks."

They did as he ordered.

A voice at the back of the mob shouted they should still storm the train to get to Bilbao.

Gandaría swiftly elbowed his way through the group and yanked the speaker to the front. Holding the man by the scruff of his neck, Gandaría again addressed the crowd.

"Even if you somehow managed to take this train to Bilbao, your fate there would be a certain one. You would be shot. This train is vital to the war effort. You are not."

He shook the man by the neck.

"Do you wish to die?"

The man stirred uneasily.

"Then get out of here. And take this rabble with you!"

Gandaría thrust the man from him. The mob melted away.

Adjusting his cap, with its red, five-pointed star of the Republic, Gandaría watched the freight train begin its forty-five-minute journey to Bilbao. Then he turned to the NCO and said how much he sympathized with the refugees' desire to leave. Ignoring the man's confusion, Gandaría walked away.

Ramón Gandaría had been born twenty years earlier in the squalor of Barcelona's dockland. He was the youngest of fourteen children; his mother died bearing him. He learned later it had been a struggle to raise money for her burial. His father was a political militant who weaned his children on slogans. A passionate, inarticulate man, he died when Ramón was eleven. The child was brought up by an elder sister. Educated by nuns, he had by his teens renounced orthodox Catholicism. He flirted briefly with communism, found it wanting, but became a fervent supporter of Spain's

Popular Front, the alliance of left-wing parties that won the last election before the country was plunged into civil war.

Gandaría had taken to the streets of Barcelona at the familiar cry of "Barricades!" Troops loyal to Franco in the city fired on the demonstrating workers, killing a woman beside him. The mob hurled itself upon the troops, driving them to their barracks, where they could later be killed at the workers' leisure.

Sickened by the violence, Gandaría had trekked over the Pyrenees to visit a sister living in San Sebastián. He arrived on that August day in 1936 when the Nationalist Navy was shelling the port. His sister was killed by a salvo.

Her death, more than anything else, turned Gandaría into a tough fighter. He joined the Basque militia and fought in a dozen bloody battles. In January 1937, he was promoted to lieutenant. Two months later, at the start of the Nationalists' northern campaign, he was sent to the headquarters staff of the Loyola Battalion in Guernica. This lean, war-scarred veteran, just twenty years old, had been entrusted with the task of instilling battle readiness in the HQ staff.

A few days earlier he had received new instructions—to turn Guernica into a defensive fortress and to supervise the evacuation to Bilbao of the town's two armaments factories.

He had dispatched the Talleres de Guernica on that freight train. Apart from the incident with the refugees, there had been no difficulties. Gandaría doubted it would be so simple with the Astra-Unceta complex, which he planned to move this coming Tuesday. He was sure that its owner, Rufino Unceta, would put up a determined fight. Gandaría relished the thought of outwitting the most powerful citizen in a town which he had disliked from the moment of his arrival.

He had been in Guernica nearly a month. Each day his resentment toward the townspeople had increased: "They were complacent. They seemed to think a divine right would ensure the war passed their town by. They thought themselves superior."

And in no one had he found that superiority more marked than in Rufino Unceta. Gandaría, with his Barcelona accent and harsh upbringing, looked on people like Unceta as one of the "fundamental reasons why there had to be a war." In Gandaría's eyes, the arms merchant, with his mansion and personal fortune, belonged to "that class of rich who grow richer by owning the poor."

On impulse, Gandaría walked back to his battalion headquarters along a route that took him past Unceta's home at the southern end of the town. The mansion was in darkness. Gandaría studied the yellow-stone building carefully. When the time came he would commandeer it as part of his fortification plan for Guernica.

At 3:00 A.M. a soldier patrolling near the Rentería Bridge saw flames coming from a lodging house near the River Mundaca. It took him three minutes to run to the fire station beside the Bank of Vizcaya on Artecalle, one of the main streets in the center of the town. He roused the stable lad, who ran to the homes of the ten volunteer firemen and woke them. By 3:30 A.M. the town's only fire cart, pulled by two dray horses, was outside the rooming house and the 600 gallons of water it carried were hissing onto the flames. With additional water drawn from the river, the fire was soon extinguished.

Fireman Juan Silliaco had never known a better turnout; the years of practice had paid off. A dark-eyed man of forty-five with powerful biceps, a bushy moustache, and a hard, lean body, Silliaco knew more about firefighting than did any of his colleagues. Even the fire chief—an elderly man who nowadays rarely attended a fire—knew that Silliaco was effectively the group's leader.

At the outbreak of the war Silliaco had been asked to join the Bilbao fire brigade to gain further experience. After a week in Bilbao, he had been offered a permanent post. He declined, preferring to return to his job as a bartender in the Bar Catalán on Calle Don Tello, one of Guernica's longest and drabbest streets, and to his respected position among Guernica's volunteer firemen.

Tonight's call had been their first in six months, and the volunteers had reacted well. But Silliaco wondered how they would cope with a serious blaze. Much of their equipment was outmoded. Hose pipes had been carefully patched, yet still leaked; the water pump was unreliable; some of the couplings to the main supply were misshapen. Two weeks ago he had written to fire headquarters in Bilbao cataloging the faults. He was awaiting a reply.

On the way back to the fire station the horses shied at gunfire coming from the mountains east of Guernica. It confirmed what Silliaco had suspected for days: The fighting was creeping closer.

The time had come for him to make a painful personal decision.

The distant, intermittent shelling and the volley of rifle shots from the railroad station ensured that baker Antonio Arazamagni would go short of sleep. He lay in bed listening to the ticking of his alarm clock, waiting for its bell to ring at 4:30 A.M., his normal hour for rising. He lived over the bakery, at No. 11 Goyencalle, a narrow, cobbled street on the western slopes of the town.

As the twenty-one-year-old baker turned restlessly in bed, he heard low voices from below his window. For such a well-built man, Antonio moved surprisingly quietly and quickly down the stairs and into the bakehouse. Pausing only to pick up a wooden rolling pin, he slipped open the front door.

Farther up the alley two men were stalking a cat, trying to entice it with scraps of meat. The cat was suspicious, but eventually its natural caution was overcome by hunger. As the animal darted for the meat, one of the men grabbed it by the neck; the other prepared to slit its throat.

Antonio hurled the rolling pin, hitting the second man in the back, forcing him to drop his knife. Clawing and spitting at its captors, the cat wriggled free and raced down the alley.

The two men turned, saw Antonio's strong figure, clad only in underwear, bearing down on them, and they, too, fled.

Picking up his rolling pin, Antonio knew that one cat had been at least temporarily spared from the clutches of the gangs who nightly hunted the animals, killed and skinned them on the spot, and sold the carcasses as rabbits.

A passionate animal lover, Antonio waged constant war against the gangs; as a consequence Goyencalle was one of the few streets in Guernica where cats were safe. Several of them lived in his bakery.

Just as Antonio was debating whether to go back to bed, the alarm clock rang. He got dressed.

The trade in cat meat was another sign that the Nationalist blockade had proved effective. Public transport had almost ceased to exist. Domestic coal was hard to obtain. Antonio managed to heat the bakery ovens with strips of old newspapers wadded into balls and sprinkled with water. But in one way he was better off than most people. In a hungry town he could always eat bread—or use it to barter.

Later today, the baker intended to reap the benefits of a month's delicate negotiations. The talks had centered on his 1929 Ford, now parked outside his bakery, which he polished until it gleamed like the limousines whose pictures he culled from magazines and posted on the bakehouse walls.

For months he had been able to afford only enough fuel for his bread rounds. Then the owner of his garage had indicated there might be a way he could purchase more gasoline. Day after day the pair haggled before reaching an agreement: Antonio would provide at reduced price an extra loaf and an apple pastry every day for a month; the garage man would provide a full tank of gas at the prewar price.

Antonio planned to collect the gas when the garage opened later this Sunday morning. Then, free for the rest of the day, with his week's wages—the equivalent then of 75 U.S. cents—jangling in his pocket, he would set out to visit cousins in Marquina, some fifteen miles across the mountains to the east. In particular he hoped to further his friendship with a pretty eighteen-year-old friend of the family. On his last visit to Marquina she had teased him about his ability as a baker; now, proof of his skill, an appetizing fruit pie, stood on a table in the bakery.

Excited at the prospect of the day ahead, Antonio loaded up his car and set out on his rounds. Even at this hour, 5:00 A.M., many of his 650 regular customers waited for him on their doorsteps. The sight of Antonio at the wheel of the old Ford, its seats stacked high with still-warm loaves, was reassurance that life, after all, had not changed that much.

Antonio pressed the car's klaxon and greeted his customers with cheery banter. He had known many of them all his life. His family had been the town's main bakers for centuries, making bread long before the present tree of Guernica, the sacred oak symbolizing Basque independence, had been planted in 1860. Antonio even claimed a forefather had baked bread for the great festival of 1766 that marked the town's four-hundredth birthday.

This morning several customers mentioned they had heard gunfire during the night. Antonio assured them there was no cause for concern. On his journey through the town he had seen no roadblocks, few soldiers patrolling, nothing to suggest the authorities feared an attack.

Every morning his route took him across the broad plaza before the railway station in the center of the town. It was the only part of his journey he disliked; the plaza was a meeting point for refugees. Hundreds now stood in line waiting for the booking office to open at 6:00 A.M. so that they could buy a ticket for the next passenger train to Bilbao.

Uprooted, salvaging what they could carry or load on a donkey cart, sometimes driving a cow before them, the refugees had begun entering Guernica soon after Mola's offensive started. Nobody knew exactly how many there were. Some put the figure as high as four thousand.

They were a drain on the town's depleting larder and a strain on the nerves of the local people. Refugees told how the Moors, the Moroccan shock troops now in the service of Mola, murdered, looted, and raped as they advanced. It was said nuns had been ravished and then made to walk naked through the streets, priests had been castrated and disemboweled; in Zaragoza the Moors were said to have nailed the tongues of some women to a table.

Antonio wished the refugees would leave Guernica. He did not believe all they said, and he disliked their Gypsylike behavior. He watched with satisfaction a group making its way down the road to Bilbao.

Whistling cheerfully, the baker continued on his rounds, delivering the last loaf to a family who lived on the northeast edge of the town, beside the Rentería Bridge.

•4•

At 5:00 A.M. Von Richthofen jumped out of bed and performed his morning exercises. Then he scrubbed under a cold shower, dried himself briskly, and dressed in the khaki uniform that two months earlier had been issued to each member of the Condor Legion. His was identical in every way to those worn by the five thousand men he commanded, apart from the colonel's pips on his epaulettes.

He briefly checked his appearance in a mirror and took his usual quick look around the bedroom: Everything was in place.

Von Richthofen occupied a suite on the top floor of the Frontón Hotel in Vitoria. At his bedside was a framed portrait of his wife. On a shelf was his flute. At the foot of his bed was a trunk filled with books. His reading included belles lettres and volumes on the lives of the fox and eagle. In a smaller chest was his "war library": a study of Bismarck, two slim manuals on air tactics in World War I, and a well-thumbed edition of *Command of the Air*. Its author, an Italian strategist named Giulio Douhet, argued that the best way to break an enemy's resistance was to launch air strikes against targets well behind the front line, and even against the civilian population itself. It was a theory already interesting many of the more forward-thinking officers of the major air forces in the world.

But so far, Von Richthofen's experience in Spain had led him to reject this theory. The chief of staff favored using the Legion's air power in direct support of the ground troops, attacking the enemy's supply routes and soldiers near the front line.

The question of how best to use the Legion had led to further tension between Von Richthofen and his immediate superior, General Hugo Sperrle.

Discord had been there since those days back in Berlin when

both men had formed part of Germany's new military elite. Sperrle disliked Von Richthofen's naked ambition, relentless drive, and seeming disregard for anything, or anybody, who barred his path. Further, Sperrle looked on Von Richthofen as a *Hochwollgeboren,* a snobbish Prussian. Von Richthofen, in turn, resented Sperrle's coarse witticisms and rough table manners. He believed Sperrle was given command of the Legion largely because he was an officer from the old Reichswehr, the small military force Germany had been allowed to keep after World War I.

Publicly, the two men maintained a civil front. Privately, they avoided each other. Sperrle, talking to colleagues, would often prelude a waspish comment with "What would the fancy *Freiherr* say to this?" Von Richthofen rarely wasted time on such personal remarks, though once he referred to "our coffeehouse commander."

Although commander of the Condor Legion, Sperrle was not its driving force. While the more energetic Von Richthofen made the day-to-day decisions about the Legion's operations, Sperrle spent most of his time with General Franco. The Generalissimo liked him, and respected the German's advice.

Now, as Von Richthofen left the Frontón Hotel, he was relieved to see that Sperrle's coupe was in the parking lot, its Spanish driver asleep at the wheel. Von Richthofen hated those mornings when the monacled Sperrle accompanied him to the airfield. Climbing into his Mercedes, Von Richthofen wondered if the latest Spanish intelligence report that would await him at Vitoria airfield would be accurate.

On March 31, the first day of the northern offensive, Spanish intelligence had led the Legion to launch a massive air attack on the town of Durango, a road and rail center with an important arms factory, situated behind the Republican line. Durango was to be the key that opened the northern front.

It was General Sperrle who had ordered the raid, after discussions with General Mola. Spanish intelligence had reported troops in the town, and the German, without checking, had accepted the information. The decision was communicated to Von Richthofen, who implemented Sperrle's order with vigor.

But his enthusiasm for the assault turned sour when he learned, some hours after the bombers had returned to base, that the enemy soldiers had fled the town well before the Legion struck. Bombs killed fourteen nuns in their chapel and the Jesuit church received a direct hit at the moment when the priest was communicating the Body of Christ. In the town's parish church, a priest died while elevating the Host. By the end of the attack, 127 civilians were dead; 121 others died later from their injuries. Another 525 were wounded. No soldiers were reported among the casualties.

Even so, Durango continued to be a military objective; the town's armaments factory was still intact. The Legion carried out a second air strike. Again their victims were civilians, again they missed the arms factory. Another attack was carried out on April 2. Two nuns were machine-gunned to death; not a bomb fell near the arms factory. On April 4 the Legion tried again. More houses were destroyed; more civilians died. But they still failed to destroy the factory or make the roads in the town impassable.

Von Richthofen, though incensed that the Legion had failed to kill enemy troops, nevertheless regarded the Durango attack as successful. His bombers had forced the troops to retreat farther and had demoralized the civilian population by its indiscriminate bombing. The Legion had cut its teeth in the "Durango affair" and had drawn blood—even if it had been only the blood of priests, nuns, women, and children.

Von Richthofen drove as fast as he dared over the poor roads in the Mercedes that had been shipped to him from Germany at the express orders of Hitler. In ten minutes he parked outside the white stucco building that housed his office at the airfield. For a moment he paused to look at the sky. The wind was still blowing from the south, gusting at times. The cold, rainy front was passing. He hurried into his office and checked the barometer: It was rising. Everything pointed to a few days of fine weather for his fliers to again pound the enemy.

He turned to his desk: One of his aides had prepared maps, situation and intelligence reports. Now, at nearly six o'clock on this Sunday morning, he began to read the Daily Intelligence Summary signed by Colonel Juan Vigón.

Vigón was chief of staff to General Mola, and as such, was Von Richthofen's opposite number on the Spanish side. Whereas Mola was something of a dilettante, Von Richthofen saw in Vigón someone much like himself: dynamic, decisive, enthusiastic for battle. It was Colonel Vigón, not General Mola, who had first encouraged Franco to agree to the campaign in the north.

Even so, since the "Durango affair" Von Richthofen had mistrusted the Spanish intelligence reports. Vigón, he knew, could only rubber-stamp information from agents in the field.

The latest summary—ASSESSMENT AND INTENTIONS OF ENEMY PROJECTED TO MIDNIGHT SUNDAY, APRIL 25—claimed that although the fall of Durango was "imminent," the Republican line was still intact and held by some "26,000 troops, armed with machine guns and mortars of 81 mm. They also have about 35 guns of calibers varying from 7.35 to 15.5 cm. Their intention must be to continue to hold their defensive line running due south from just east of Bermeo. Little enemy air force activity need be expected."

The summary was just six hours old, but in part was already outdated. Many hundreds, if not thousands, of Republican troops were now in general retreat, falling back toward Bilbao.

Von Richthofen suspected as much. He consulted his map of the territory north of Durango. He noticed that three main roads leading toward Bilbao from eastern Vizcaya converged at one point: the Rentería Bridge at Guernica.

On one corner of his desk was the polished butt of a shell case, a souvenir from World War I. It would have made a fine ashtray for anyone who dared smoke in his office. Instead, it was filled with colored pencils. Von Richthofen selected a yellow one and drew a circle. Yellow was the color for "possible target."

Von Richthofen had encircled the Rentería Bridge in Guernica.

Then he turned to matters requiring his more immediate attention.

6:00 A.M.—Noon

•5•

Masked, gloved, and gowned, ready to respond to the commands of Captain Cortés, a tired Teresa Ortuz unexpectedly found herself assisting during the first surgery of the day. At 5:30 A.M. the nurse who normally took the early-morning session with Cortés had reported sick. Mother Augusta asked Teresa, due to go off duty at 6:00, to stand in.

The walls and ceiling of the operating room were draped with white sheeting, its floor covered with several layers of sacking in an attempt at asepsis. Twin tables stood a few feet apart, their white oilskin surfaces glistening under a 300-watt scialitic light on a stand that could be wheeled from one table to another. This arrangement allowed Captain Cortés to begin a new operation while his assistant finished up the previous case.

As usual, all Teresa could see of Cortés was a pair of red-rimmed eyes above his surgical mask. He expelled overwhelming odors of garlic and wine with each grunt he gave as he explored the man's damaged areas. The spleen had been smashed, there was a constant flow of blood caused by a large hematoma. Unable to locate the source of the bleeding, Cortés delicately moved to one side the colon with its peritoneum and vessels still attached.

Standing across the table, her head bent close to Cortés, Teresa was repelled by his breath. She inched back from the table. He looked up at her sharply. She edged forward again as Cortés turned once more to the man on the table.

The anesthetist reported the patient's blood pressure was falling.

Working calmly and quickly, Cortés made exploratory incisions through the posterior peritoneum. He told Teresa to monitor the flow of plasma; too quick a transfusion would be fatal.

She checked the bottle of blood on its stand at the foot of the table and adjusted the flow. Then she returned to her position.

The anesthetist reported the patient's blood pressure was dangerously low. The respirator bag was barely inflating.

Cortés continued to probe. Suddenly a fountain of blood frothed upward. He had dislodged a metal fragment deep in the gut. He attempted to halt the hemorrhaging by applying tamponage and manual pressure. As the spuming subsided, he bent over the patient, listening intently. After a moment he told Teresa to stop transfusing. The man was dead.

The anesthetist disconnected his apparatus from the body and moved to the adjoining table to prepare for the next patient.

As Teresa began to gather together the instruments that would be needed, Cortés asked her why she had moved away from the table during the operation. When she told him, he seemed taken aback. He asked why, in all the months they had worked together, she had not raised the matter before. There was a mocking note in his voice that Teresa found distasteful, but another of her "tests" was not to overreact in such situations.

He pressed her for an answer. She sidestepped the question, saying that it might be best if she asked for a transfer to other duties. But Cortés "just stared at me and laughed. Then he said he would take more care in the future with what he ate and drank when I was working with him."

In speaking out, Teresa recognized for the first time her own importance to Cortés as a member of the surgical team. In the nine months they had worked together, there had been little cause for him to find fault; she had been quick to learn his ways, anticipating every cut, clamp, and stitch he made. In that time she had also witnessed many examples of his quick temper toward other nurses. He had once thrown a kidney tray at one who had laid out the wrong box of instruments for an operation. That nurse never came near the operating room again.

Now Teresa helped him wheel the scialitic stand light across to the next table. She waited while he studied the patient, naked, harshly lit by the lamp, stomach colored with red dye around the torn flesh. She could see the fear in the soldier's eyes as he watched orderlies remove the body from the other table.

Cortés took the young man's hand and talked reassuringly until the anesthetist's mask covered the patient's face. Then he set to work.

Rufino Unceta, the fifty-one-year-old owner of the Astra-Unceta arms factory, maker of Spain's most famous pistol as well as submachine guns and rifles, quietly pushed open the shutters of his bedroom window and walked out onto the balcony. The bells of the Church of Santa María tolled five-thirty.

In more peaceful days the sound would have reminded him to cross himself and offer a prayer for all the blessings he had received: a good wife, five handsome children, success in business. Today his mind was busy with the thought that this might be the last day his factory would be occupied, and that at last he might end the dangerous double life he had been forced to lead since the war broke out.

He scanned the hills around Monte San Miguel, anxious for any sign to confirm his hopes. Nothing stirred. But after the long months of waiting, he knew the end was approaching. The Nationalist troops were out there, in the hills, and in this Republican town Rufino Unceta and his family were among the few who longed for them to arrive.

It was a feeling he could share only with his family and closest friends. Only they knew how deep ran his pro-Franco feelings. And they were glad that the wealthiest and most powerful of Guernica's seven thousand citizens supported the Nationalists, because they believed Franco would now repay that loyalty by sparing the town.

Rufino Unceta knew just one man who could destroy his hope. If

Lieutenant Gandaría even suspected how passionately he supported the Nationalist cause, Gandaría would kill him. And then, Unceta reasoned, there would be no reason for Franco to spare the town.

If anything, the war had increased Unceta's standing with the townspeople. He had given generously to support widows and orphans; he had built a massive air-raid shelter for his workers. His fellow Guernicans viewed these acts as signs of opposition to the Nationalist threat to Basque independence. Unceta was content that people should think he was sympathetic to the Republican cause; it was not a time "to make noble, pointless gestures. Running up a flag for Franco," he had told his family, was "the quickest way to the firing squad."

To those few who dared press him for a political opinion, as Lieutenant Gandaría had done, Unceta had one stock answer: "Business and politics do not mix. I am a businessman."

Ever since his father had handed him the business twenty-four years ago, Unceta had cultivated a deliberate aloofness from the daily life of Guernica. It was his father who had first seen the potential of Guernica, close to the steel mills of Bilbao, situated on a river and railway. But it was he who had planned the impressive factory as the first step toward establishing an industrial dynasty.

Rufino had persuaded the municipal authorities to sell him the factory site for "a few pesetas." In turn he had promised to raise the town's standard of living and to attract other business. That had been in 1913, when Guernica had had no bank and only a few cafés and taverns set among architecture going back five centuries. Within a year Unceta had convinced the Bank of Vizcaya to open a branch in the town, offering his company account as an incentive. The railway was cajoled into increasing its services after he gave them the exclusive right to freight his guns to Bilbao. Finally a hotel, the Julián, had opened to cater to the increasing number of arms buyers who came to Guernica.

From his bedroom balcony, Unceta could see a large part of the old town, which had been burned and sacked several times in its six hundred years. In its streets worked tailors, shawl makers, pot

menders, purveyors of lotions and potions, and a dozen other ancient crafts. From dawn to dusk the district sounded its voice in
argument, anger, and laughter; shrill and continuous, ebbing and
flowing amidst the creak and squeal of ox-cart wheels.

Rufino Unceta felt a sense of history about Guernica. Its three
convents, one monastery, and two churches marked the town as an
important religious center. The pilgrims of the Middle Ages had
come to Guernica to lecture about their travels; some were buried in
the local cemetery. Later, Guernica became the place where the
coach from San Sebastián stopped to change horses before continuing to Bilbao. Shipowners once recruited local youths to crew their
voyages of discovery; it was said Christopher Columbus took with
him to America deckhands from Guernica.

The town had grown and long ago gobbled up the small boat-
yards along the Mundaca. Now there were apartment houses in
their place, and a candy factory near the Rentería Bridge provided
work for nearly fifty townspeople, mostly young women. The industrial zone at the other end of the town contained the Astra-Unceta complex and the now-empty Talleres de Guernica factory.
Beyond the zone were fields where medieval knights were supposed
to have jousted; little boys still combed the area for spearheads.

Unceta himself had become a local legend following that day in
1914 when the Spanish government had asked him to design a new
Army pistol. It was a modest contract for a thousand weapons, but it
marked the beginning of Unceta's connection with governments,
monarchs, and heads of state throughout the world. As Spain's
pistol maker, Unceta had promised King Alfonso XIII he would
never sell a gun "which might be turned against Spain, or used by
Spaniards to kill Spaniards." His promise held true until the Civil
War.

Then, Rufino Unceta had privately pledged his loyalty to
Franco. He believed the general could save Spain from communism,
and that the Basque country should remain part of a united Spain.

But promptly at 7:00 A.M. on the morning of July 28, 1936,
Republican troops had arrived at Unceta's home. An officer had

politely requested he accompany him to the factory. When Unceta refused, the officer had replied that if he persisted he would be shot on his doorstep.

The walk to the factory had given Unceta time to compose himself. By the time he reached his office he had come to a decision. He informed the officer: "I am, above all, in business. Business has nothing to do with politics. Accordingly, I will meet any reasonable demand that comes within that framework."

In the following months his factory had made thousands of weapons for the Republican Army. An appalled Unceta could do nothing.

Lieutenant Gandaría had arrived on the day Mola launched his northern offensive. The young officer was at first coldly polite, but he insisted on one production increase after another. Unceta had been secretly impressed, yet frightened, to discover one day that Gandaría had been painstakingly learning the intricacies of gunmaking. With a tight smile, the officer had told him, "Soon, I will know if this place is working to full capacity. For your sake I hope it is."

Throughout the occupation of his factory, Unceta had maintained one sound business principle: He insisted on full payment for everything. By Friday, April 23, 1937, just two days ago, the factory had produced 11,658 pistols and machine guns and received 1,116,000 pesetas from Republican coffers.

Recently, Unceta had noticed increasing anxiety among the troops guarding the factory. Then he had learned from Gandaría that the plant was to be shipped to Bilbao. Unceta had immediately begun plotting to block the move. He had protested there were no workers in Bilbao capable of operating the machines. His objection had been brushed aside. Then, with a flair for technology that baffled Gandaría, Unceta had argued it would be impossible to dismantle and reassemble the equipment without specialist help. The nearest experts were in Madrid, a city now separated from Guernica by hundreds of miles of Nationalist-occupied territory.

Lieutenant Gandaría had left Unceta's office angrily. On April

21 he had reappeared, smiling triumphantly. Russian experts would arrive in Guernica on the morning of Tuesday, April 27, to supervise the dismantling.

That was still two days away. As if in answer to the prayers of the man standing on the bedroom balcony, there came a rumble of artillery fire from the hills. Rufino Unceta hurried into the bedroom and shook his wife. "Wake up," he whispered to her, "Franco's on our doorstep."

•6•

From his office window Von Richthofen watched the pilot of the reconnaissance plane settle himself in the high-backed bucket seat. For a moment longer, nothing disturbed the quiet of the airfield. Then, at 7:30 A.M. precisely, as it had every morning of this war in the north, the plane's starter motor whined. Blue flame escaped from the exhaust, followed by a roar as the propeller blades spun. The aircraft rocked on its tires, straining against the wheel blocks.

In his mind Von Richthofen ran through the checks the pilot would be making. Flaps up, mags on, undercarriage locked, full fuel, instrument checks. Chocks removed, brakes released, the HE-45 taxied to the end of the runway, then roared across the grass and was airborne.

Von Richthofen hoped the reconnaissance pilot would return with information to confirm what he had read earlier in the Daily Intelligence Summary. When the Heinkel disappeared over the nearest mountain, he gathered into a canvas bag the reports and maps on his desk. Then, at his usual high speed, he drove back to operations headquarters at the Frontón Hotel.

His route took him past the newly painted villa housing the Legion's officially approved brothel. Girls had been recruited from all over Spain to staff its twenty bedrooms. A corporal—"old enough not to take advantage"—watched over them. Weekly, the Legion's medical officer checked the girls for venereal disease.

Von Richthofen tolerated the brothel as the most efficient way of controlling syphilis and gonorrhea. Doubtless he would have been surprised had he known that when the Legion had moved from the previous base to Vitoria, the girls had been airlifted along with all the other equipment.

On the veranda of the Frontón Hotel a number of young officers breakfasted. Most were about twenty-two years old, many from aristocratic backgrounds. Indeed, the leader of the second squadron of the heavy Junkers-52 bombers, Baron von Beust, had the same senior hereditary title, *Freiherr,* as Von Richthofen.

He paused for a moment as they read out items from week-old German newspapers, checked the financial columns for their stocks, and indulged in the latest gossip. The chief of staff had no time for such talk. His only concern was that the young fliers justify the trust placed in them and acquire the expertise necessary to fight the Reich's "inevitable enemy, the Bolshevists."

Von Richthofen's sojourn in Spain had strengthened his view that ultimately Germany must fight Russia. They were, he told his men, already at war with "the Reds" here in Spain. Virtually to a man, the personnel of the Condor Legion believed they had come to Spain to stop the spread of communism. Few, if any, of Von Richthofen's pilots knew that the Basque country was not Communist-oriented; although some were Communists, the majority of Basques were motivated to fight by a desire for separatism.

Von Richthofen nodded curtly to the men on the veranda, hurried into the hotel and up to his suite. There he took down his flute, sat on the edge of the bed, and began to play. He played well. Then, refreshed by his break, he went to the operations room to continue what he was even better at: waging war.

·7·

A small group of exhausted men flopped down on the pine-needle carpet of the forest. Above them the wind tugged at the treetops; below in the distance they could make out the road from Durango to Amorebieta. In recent days traffic along the road had been mainly one way—westward, toward Bilbao and away from the advancing Nationalists.

Now the road was empty. The last of the carts carrying household goods and crated livestock had passed by; so had the columns of refugees who had survived the air attacks on Durango.

The Nationalists, supported by the Condor Legion and heavy artillery bombardment, had swept into the mountains north, south, and east of the town. Farther south, in the village of Ochandiano, the Republican stand had broken after fifty planes of the Condor Legion had attacked the village in a daylong raid. Fearful of encirclement, the Republicans had withdrawn, leaving an estimated six hundred dead and four hundred wounded.

Under cover of the heavy rain that had then grounded the Condor Legion, the Basques had force-marched deeper into the mountains, scattering into small units in an attempt to avoid detection.

It was one of those units that now rested on the slopes of Monte Oiz, north of Durango. Wearing mud-spattered dark-gray trousers and rope-soled shoes, the men could be recognized as members of the Eighteenth Loyola Battalion only by the insignia on their jackets. Until a few months ago most of them had never left Bilbao. Now their battalion headquarters was in Guernica.

Their unit commander, Lieutenant Juan Dominguiz, studied

the surrounding countryside. Then he focused his binoculars on a small road that led north to Marquina. Though little more than a dirt track, it appeared inviting to soldiers whose legs ached from trekking through the mountains. But for the moment, Dominguiz was content to let his men lie in the forest and watch the clouds scurrying in the sky.

For nearly a month now, the tall, striking Dominguiz and his men had been fighting a rearguard action. Their retreat had begun when they were ordered out of Durango shortly before the Condor Legion bombed the town on March 31. From a hillside vantage point, Dominguiz had watched the air attack. Afterward, in a notebook he carried in his map pouch, he had jotted his observations: "Durango was bombed and machine-gunned indiscriminately. It is a terrible example of the destruction that can befall all our homeland. It gives good reason why we must resist."

Dominguiz was the eldest son of fairly prosperous parents. They owned a men's clothes shop in Bilbao, regularly attended Mass in the city's cathedral, and encouraged their son in his aspirations to become a journalist. In January 1935, he had taken a position on the staff of a Bilbao newspaper.

Soon he began to take an interest in Basque affairs. He became an active campaigner for separatism, epitomized by the slogan: "Basque Government for the Basques, by the Basques." In the general call to arms, Dominguiz had volunteered. His education and a natural aptitude for leadership had earned him his officer's pips.

In October 1936, Dominguiz was posted to the Loyola Battalion headquarters in Guernica. There he met and fell in love with an attractive local girl, Carmen Batzar. The bitterness Dominguiz felt toward the enemy was expressed in a letter he had written to Carmen following the first air attack on Durango:

It is disgusting the way our generation on both sides is being systematically destroyed while the real power is in foreign hands. There is a sinister and yet uncompleted phase: the invasion of our country by the Italians and Germans. Do they not realize we are not Communists? Do they not realize we are not even Spanish, but Basque? They have come at the bidding of Franco, that part of the Church loyal to him, and the landowners who are jealous of our industrial wealth here in Euzkadi [the Basque region]. And because we refuse to join Franco by betraying the constitutional government of Spain, he is allowing particularly cruel reprisals to be exacted against us. There have been many examples of how the Germans, the Moors, the Italians are all doing Franco's bidding—and all that carried on under the blessing of the Nonintervention Pact. How can England, France, America, any country, justify such an agreement when it is being so clearly ignored by Hitler and Mussolini in order to butcher us?

Now Dominguiz lowered his military map to the forest floor and examined it carefully. He knew there were Nationalist troops very close. Although the route through the mountains would be hard for his tired men, there was no real choice.

Dominguiz decided to let the soldiers rest a little longer. He took the opportunity to write in his notebook a thought that had worried him for some days: When would the Republican International Brigades come to the aid of the Basques? Their exploits in the defense of Madrid were known around the world. With their help the Italian advance at Guadalajara had been turned into an ignominious rout, a blow to Franco and Mussolini. That had happened a month before. Dominguiz noted: "If only the French, American, and British International Brigades were here, everything would be different."

His writing was interrupted by the sound of an aircraft engine. With a high, hammering noise, the Heinkel reconnaissance plane flew close to where the men lay hidden. They did not move until it had passed well clear of Monte Oiz.

Dominguiz refolded his map and ordered his troops to continue their trek through the mountains. They would follow the road to Marquina. They might be lucky enough to get a lift. In that way Dominguiz hoped they might still reach their headquarters, the Convent of La Merced in Guernica, by nightfall. There he would be given new orders, perhaps equipment to replace that lost in the retreat from Ochandiano.

But what really excited the young officer was the knowledge that

Carmen would be waiting for him. Weeks before, when they were last together, they had chosen the date for their wedding in Guernica's Church of Santa María. Now, April 30 was just five days away.

Father José Domingo de Iturran was the parish priest of the Church of Santa María. But on this Sunday morning he was in no way concerned about a future wedding. His mind was occupied with thoughts that had troubled him for weeks.

In the gloom of the church, he rose from his morning devotions in the side chapel of Our Lady of Begonia. At sixty-one, the tall, stooped priest could look back on nearly a quarter of a century in Guernica.

During the early period he had kept loneliness at bay by nurturing his interest in history—he had even kept a diary—and by maintaining his scholarly pursuits. But he had made no real contact with the townspeople. He had had a secret hope of higher office, of perhaps one day working in the Bishop's Palace in Bilbao. But as time passed, he had realized he would probably end his living in the Church as he had begun—a parish priest.

The acceptance had changed him. Soon he became a popular figure in the town's life; his influence was felt in many quarters and his advice was sought on almost every kind of problem. His standing in the community was now paramount, and Father Iturran was aware of the responsibility it gave him.

For this very reason, until now he had not spoken publicly about the war.

Privately, he was sure that Franco would eventually win. The belief gave the priest no pleasure; he thought many of the Nationalists no better than "barbarians." But for him to say as much publicly would bring him into the conflict that already divided the Church in northern Spain. On August 6, 1936, the bishops of Vitoria and Pamplona had broadcast a pastoral letter to "roundly condemn the adhesion of Basque Catholics to the Republican side. Theologically it is not allowed, *non licet*, for Basque Catholics to make common cause with the Republicans."

The vicar-general of Bilbao had rejected the pastoral letter on a number of grounds: It might be a forgery; it had not been promulgated with "due formality"; it might have been written under coercion. Further, certain papal encyclicals were interpreted to mean that the sort of rebellion proclaimed by the Nationalists could never be legal. From then on, many Basque priests openly endorsed the Republican cause.

Father Iturran preferred to wait for clear-cut guidance from Pope Pius XI. But as the Vatican remained silent, doubts crept into Father Iturran's mind. He wondered if, after all, the young parish priest of the town's other church, San Juan, was right. When they last had met, Father Eusebio de Arronategui had angrily argued that "the Vatican regards us as unworthy of concern. Rome has declared for Franco because everyone else is regarded as Communist."

Father Iturran was shocked by such talk. Yet all over Nationalist-occupied Spain, bishops, canons, and priests offered prayers for a Nationalist victory. Some priests actually fought with the armed forces; the parish priest of the village of Zafra was said to have buried alive four Republican militiamen and a wounded girl in graves that they themselves had been forced to dig.

Father Iturran agonized in private. In his presbytery, he used colored pencils to mark the changing fronts on a map. By April 1937, it showed that, apart from the isolated area facing the Bay of Biscay that included the Basque country, the Nationalists controlled all of Spain west of a line north from Granada to Badajoz, to Toledo, through Guadalajara, and on up to the French border; almost two-thirds of the country.

Now, as Father Iturran leaned back in his chair and looked at that map pinned to the wall, he remembered the enthronement of the boy-king, Alfonso XIII, in 1902, and his abdication into exile twenty-nine years later, leaving Spain a republic. During the next five years Spain had slipped inexorably into chaos. Father Iturran could recall word for word the end of a speech made by the leader of the Catholic Party on July 16, 1936:

"A country can live under a monarchy or a republic. It can live under a parliamentary or a presidential system. It can live under communism or fascism. But it cannot live in anarchy. Now, alas, Spain is in anarchy. And we are today present at the funeral service of democracy."

The Civil War had broken out the next day.

Father Iturran knew from the newspapers that among the Nationalist forces now outside Guernica were Italian and German troops. He wondered whether the German planes had brought to the north the Moors now also approaching the town.

The thought of the Moors horrified him. Like everyone else, he had heard reports of their barbarous behavior. Many of the stories he presumed to be exaggerated. But in the last few days he had heard from the town's doctors that they were having to treat an increasing number of women refugees who had been violated.

Among Father Iturran's many duties was that of spiritual adviser to the local public school's five hundred pupils. Half of them were girls. If they remained in Guernica, they faced great danger. But how could he tell over two hundred young girls they might soon be raped?

Father Iturran left the presbytery and walked back up the steps and into his church. He had made his decision. He would speak out, regardless of the pain it would cause him.

Juan Silliaco looked at his young son, still asleep at nine o'clock, and also came to an agonizing decision. He would break the news to the boy at breakfast. It would not be easy for either of them.

Silliaco had recently heard many tales that the Moors were pederasts who raped and murdered young boys. And the latest rumor he had heard was that the Moors would be in Guernica within a week. The thought that twelve-year-old Pedro might be in danger of sexual assault from the Moors gave him nightmares. Silliaco determined that his son must leave Guernica.

The boy was stirring. Back in October, Pedro had been one of the lookouts during an occasion of historic importance, when the Basque leaders, the *Procuradores,* dressed in their morning suits and wing collars and top hats, had walked in solemn procession to Guernica's famous Parliament Building, unused for fifty years. Inside, Father Iturran had conducted a religious service. Within the circular debating chamber they had all prayed for divine guidance, and had then elected as their president José Antonio de Aguirre.

Aguirre had led the dignitaries outside. Under the revered oak tree, he had then recited in the Basque language: "Humble before God, on Basque soil, standing in memory of our ancestors, under the tree of Guernica, I swear faithfully to fulfill my trust."

The Basque statute of autonomy gave the president the right to choose his own cabinet. Aguirre's was a mixture of Basque Nationalists, Socialists, and one Communist. All were considered moderate Republicans; apart from the Communist, all were devoutly religious.

After the service, Juan Silliaco had met his son and with him hurried home to tell his wife the news. He had found her in bed, wan and shivering. A doctor had diagnosed acute pneumonia. Two days later she had died.

Now he prepared to part with his son. The boy could travel to Bilbao by the special bus that had taken children from Guernica to the Basque capital each morning for the past week. It would mean he would have to live alone. He himself could not vacate his responsibility in the town's fire brigade.

As Pedro opened his eyes, his father smiled. He had, he told him, something to discuss.

Carmen Batzar was ensuring that the chapel altar in the Convent of Santa Clara would have the most elaborate floral decorations in all Guernica, just as she had done every Sunday for months. The convent was in the group of buildings on Guernica's western slopes that included the Parliament Building and its oak, the handsome mansion of the count of Montefuerte, and the Church of Santa María, where in five days Father Iturran would marry Carmen and Juan Dominguiz.

For a hundred years members of the Batzar family had decorated this altar, but none had ever shown as much loving care as this comely, copper-haired nineteen-year-old. Earlier, in the cool dawn, she had walked through the fields, picking wild flowers. Then, her arms full, Carmen had entered the chapel, the only part of the convent open to the outside world.

The twenty-nine nuns who lived in the cloisters behind the chapel were Sisters of Penance of the Order of Santa Clara, the strictest of all the religious enclaves in Guernica. Founded in 1221, the order had settled in the town in 1422. In 1618 it had become a closed order, and from that moment the sisters had never stepped outside the building.

Carmen had seen them pass their shopping lists through a small, grilled peephole in the convent door. Tradesmen later left the goods outside the door and were paid through the same peephole. Even death did not free the sisters; generations of them were buried in a cemetery inside the convent walls. Each new nun was given a number belonging to a sister who had died. For five centuries the numbers had rotated as they were reassigned for the life span of one nun after another.

That was one of the more unusual rituals Carmen had learned about during her regular visits to dress the altar. Unfailingly, when she finished, from behind the grilled door a nun's voice would thank her. Over the months Carmen had come to distinguish the voices. She had become friendly with several of the sisters whom she could hear but could not see, and they had patiently answered her questions about their way of life. At the end of each discussion, through the grille, a forefinger would gently trace the sign of the cross on Carmen's forehead.

During these talks with the sisters, Carmen had also confided the exciting milestones in her life: her successes at school, her first job, and more recently, her engagement to a dashing young officer. The nuns seemed to know nothing about the war, and once when Carmen had told one of them of a Basque victory she had heard about on Radio Bilbao, the sister had gently changed the subject.

Six Sundays ago one of the older nuns had suggested that if Carmen were agreeable, the convent would help make her wedding dress. She had eagerly accepted the offer, for the Sisters of Penance were famed for their needlework.

Carmen chose a bolt of white brocade from the haberdashery

where she worked. The following Sunday she left it outside the grilled door with a note of her measurements. Three Sundays ago, after decorating the altar, she had been directed to a private anteroom at the rear of the convent. Set in one of its walls was a long drawer with two shiny brass handles. From behind the wall a muffled voice had told her to pull out the drawer. Carmen had done as she was told. In the drawer was her pinned-together dress with instructions to take it away for a fitting. Carmen's mother had made some adjustments, and the bride-to-be had then returned the dress to the drawer. She had watched, fascinated, as the drawer disappeared into the wall. It reminded her of what she had been told by one of the nuns: Unwanted babies were sometimes left in the drawer. They were brought up by the sisters, who had no way of knowing who the children's mothers were. Later they were taken in by an orphanage.

Now Carmen was again alone in the anteroom. She crossed hesitantly to the drawer, and without speaking, drew it open. There, as promised, was her wedding gown, complete with veil. She carefully placed them over her arm and shut the drawer. She knocked on the wall, but there was no response, no one to thank.

A little uneasy, she left the anteroom. Once outside, she turned to thoughts of her fiancé. Carmen could hardly wait until Thursday, when Lieutenant Dominguiz was due to get his leave of absence for the wedding.

The operations room of the Condor Legion was in the lounge of the Frontón Hotel at Vitoria. Leather-covered sofas and armchairs had been augmented by trestle tables; wall prints replaced by maps and charts. The curtains were permanently drawn and on a door was stenciled: ENTRY FORBIDDEN TO UNAUTHORIZED PERSONNEL.

Captain Klaus Gautlitz, the thin-faced, round-shouldered operations officer, had posted the notice in an attempt to reduce the number of people who visited the operations room, but nothing could stop the young fliers who wanted to watch the nerve center of the Legion at work.

Lieutenant Hans Asmus, a twenty-three-year-old pilot who had been transferred to operations, understood the fascination the room had for the airmen. It reminded him of a classroom back in his old school in Hamburg. There was a blackboard on an easel alongside a dais and desk. Gautlitz had sat behind that desk since nine o'clock this Sunday morning.

Asmus and the other assistant operations officer, Lieutenant Heinz Raunce, were seated at one end of a long trestle table that ran the length of the room. Every inch of its surface was crammed with papers that aides were continually updating: weather maps, operations orders, intelligence summaries, instructions about payloads and servicing—everything the men in the room needed to know to wage war.

Among the papers pinned to a bulletin board was an order signed by Von Richthofen on March 31, 1937, the day Durango was first bombed. It reminded "all concerned" that although the Legion would only attack military targets, it should do so "without regard for the civilian population."

Nearby hung a thick wad of papers listing the daily expenditure of bombs and machine-gun bullets since the campaign in the north had begun. During the first twenty-four hours, 70 tons of bombs had been dropped and 35,350 rounds of ammunition fired. After that, the rate had increased. But the chief of staff was outspoken in his criticism of the slowness of Mola's troops to advance. He had told one of his officers: "This large expenditure is out of proportion to the ground gains."

There was also a memo reminding squadron leaders to brief their pilots on the "golden rule" of bombing. If, for any reason, the original target could not be attacked—because of poor weather or smoke hiding the target area—the bombs were to be dropped "blind," anywhere over enemy territory, again "without regard for the civilian population."

At the far end of the room Von Richthofen sipped coffee and studied the aerial photographs the early-morning Heinkel reconnaissance flight had taken. Clearly visible in the pictures were Republican troops on the roads around the small town of Marquina, east of Guernica.

Scooping up the prints, Von Richthofen walked briskly to Gautlitz's desk. The two men studied them. The operations officer called an aide to bring an expanded map of the area. Von Richthofen jabbed his finger at the three roads leading into Marquina. "Here, here, and here," he said.

The wall clock showed 9:30 A.M. Lieutenant Raunce logged the time in the DOR, the Daily Operations Register, which recorded the orders the Legion received and the missions they carried out.

Lieutenant Asmus and the meteorological officer joined Von Richthofen and Gautlitz. They all moved to the weather map pinned to the blackboard. In a few sentences the met officer explained the map's squiggles and lines: The weather favored attack.

In a knot, the group then moved to the central trestle table to study copies of the Daily Intelligence Summary the Spanish had provided. This moment always reminded Asmus of a film he had once seen in which a group of doctors had gathered around to discuss a particularly difficult diagnosis.

Von Richthofen asked Gautlitz a one-word question: "Availability?"

The operations officer reported the Legion was almost at full strength. Eighty bombers and fighters were awaiting command.

"Use the three squadrons of Junkers with strong fighter support," ordered Von Richthofen. "Save the Stukas and the experimental squadrons for later, perhaps Bilbao."

Lieutenant Raunce entered the decision in the DOR.

The last question to be settled was the bomb mix, the calculated balance between high-explosive, incendiary, and antipersonnel splinter bombs.

Von Richthofen glanced briefly at the papers on the table. The aerial reconnaissance photographs showed no antiaircraft guns with the retreating enemy; indeed, the troops appeared to have no heavy artillery at all. In a precise voice Von Richthofen gave his orders.

There would be no incendiaries. The first squadron of nine Junkers-52 bombers would carry 500-pound bombs for blocking the roads. The remaining bombers would use an equal mix of 100-pound explosive bombs and 20-pound antipersonnel bombs, capable of shredding a man to pieces at thirty yards.

To achieve maximum effect, the bomber squadrons were to attack at twenty-minute intervals; each subsequent wave would compound the damage caused by preceding formations. During the intervals, the Legion's fighter planes would carry out their usual strafing of the enemy troops, pinning them down for the bombers to hit again.

Raunce entered the bomb mix in the DOR.

Von Richthofen had one further instruction: "Tell the fighter pilots to take along a few hand grenades for dropping over the side."

Gautlitz nodded.

"And tell everyone to attack anything that moves on the roads around Marquina."

With that, the Legion's chief of staff left the room.

By the time he was through the door, Asmus was on the telephone to the bomber base at Burgos. There, awaiting instructions, was the Condor Legion's wing commander, Major Klaus Fuchs.

With his usual enthusiasm, Asmus dictated the orders. It would be another action in a campaign he considered *"viel Spass,"* a real picnic.

•9•

Teresa Ortuz, near exhaustion, had been on duty for twelve hours, the last four in the operating room, and had not eaten since leaving home the night before. On an empty stomach, the smell of ether combined with fumes from Captain Cortés was sickening. Mechanically, she passed scalpels, hemostats, and needles in the sequence the surgeon required.

Once, she dropped some scissors. Cortés glanced at her irritably but said nothing. Then, toward the end of the operation, his blood-shot eyes signaled emergency. The patient was hemorrhaging. While he fought to control the bleeding, he shouted at Teresa to give a transfusion.

Normally he would have done that. Now there was no time. Teresa worked the transfusion needle into the patient's arm vein, trying to keep her own hand steady.

The anesthetist monitored heartbeat and color changes in the patient's face. Teresa watched the blood begin to flow, acknowl-edged the anesthetist's nod, and returned to her place opposite the surgeon. She reached for the needle tray; thicker needles for deep sutures were on one side, finer ones for veins on the other. Both types had been threaded with catgut.

The surgeon called out and she handed him a needle, her scissors ready in the other hand. As he stitched and tied, she snipped and obeyed his calls for needles. Stitch, tie, snip, call; stitch, tie, snip, call; it was part of the orchestrated precision of the operating room that she had come to like so much.

Finally, the skin was sutured, the area dressed. Captain Cortés straightened up with a satisfied grunt. "He'll live."

He looked at Teresa and realized how tired she was. "You're no good to me or anyone else in that state," he said. "Go and get some rest."

Without waiting for an answer, he walked out. Teresa had never before heard him express concern of any kind for his staff. The anesthetist shrugged.

Normally, by ten on a Sunday morning, Teresa would have had a few hours' sleep at the end of her night shift and would be preparing to go to Santa María Church.

This morning she was far too tired to attend Mass. Instead, she decided to make her devotions in the convent's chapel and then go home to sleep. She joined some of the nursing staff, mostly nuns, in their meditation, slipping into a rear pew to offer up her prayers for the salvation of her country.

Afterward she went to the staff common room where nuns and nurses drank coffee at a long refectory table. The only thing in the coffee's favor, a nurse remarked, was its warmth. But even without milk or sugar, the black liquid helped to revive Teresa.

At the far end of the table, Mother Superior Augusta rose to her feet. She looked around her flock, and it seemed to Teresa that she was "saying a silent prayer that God would guide her."

Then the Superior spoke. "The Nationalists are close by. Many of you no doubt have heard stories about how some of their troops treat prisoners, especially women. I fear there is some truth in what has been said."

Still speaking softly, her voice betraying no fear, the Superior warned against panic. "No one, for whatever reason, is to leave her post. Our sole preoccupation must continue to be the welfare of our patients. Even if the enemy actually reaches this convent, this attitude must prevail."

Teresa marveled that Mother Augusta's voice remained calm, without inflection. The Superior concluded, "It is the responsibility of us all to show courage and fortitude and make others follow our example. God loves and will take care of us. Whatever happens will be His will."

Watching the Superior walk from the room, Teresa wondered whether she would ever acquire the same serenity. She felt a flush of admiration for Mother Augusta, for it was said in the convent that the Superior's two sisters had been raped when the Moors occupied Badajoz in western Spain last August. The thought suddenly made Teresa fear for the safety of her mother and younger sisters. Impulsively, she decided she must persuade them to move to Bilbao. They would not want to go, but she was sure they must.

She pushed back her chair, and without a word to her colleagues, hurried out of the room. In the corridor, she overtook Mother Augusta. The Superior called to her, reminding her this was the Sabbath, that it was unseemly for nurses to rush, and that she should go quietly home to relax, for it "may be the last chance for some time."

Mother Augusta explained she had received a message from Bilbao designating the convent "a hospital of first urgency." The war was now less than a two-hour ambulance journey away.

The Superior had another item of news: The Second Basque field surgical unit would arrive in Guernica in a few days. Teresa felt sudden excitement. Her father was one of the unit's doctors. But she knew, too, that once her mother learned the news, nothing would make her leave the town.

Grim-faced, Lieutenant Ramón Gandaría stood in the communications room of the Eighteenth Loyola Battalion, listening to the voice of the officer at the other end of the field telephone line, fifteen miles away in Marquina.

Gandaría had been awakened after five hours' sleep to take this call. He timed it at 10:15 A.M., scrawling it in the daily log beside the telephone. Captain Juan de Beiztegi, the battalion's commanding officer, insisted that proper records be kept of everything that happened while he was away in the field, or as he now was, reporting to the Basque GHQ in Galdacano near Bilbao.

In his absence he had made Gandaría duty officer, effectively responsible for all the other officers and two hundred soldiers garrisoned in the battalion headquarters in the Convent of La Merced on the northeast side of Guernica, just across the Rentería Bridge.

Though the telephone link was poor, Gandaría detected the officer's dismay as he reported, "We are pulling back."

Gandaría was shocked. "Does Bilbao know?"

"Yes."

Gandaría replaced the telephone. A limited retreat could mean only one thing: falling back to a new front.

It was more imperative than ever that the Astra-Unceta arms complex be moved on schedule to Bilbao this coming Tuesday. Once that was done, he could concentrate on his other task: fortifying Guernica.

The two duty clerks looked at him anxiously, their faces pale under the bare lightbulb. There was nothing to show that nuns had once received their visitors in this room; now it was festooned with telephone lines and a portable switchboard. The Spartan furnishings were completed by some old straight-backed chairs and plain wooden tables. The dark-green-painted walls were covered with maps.

Gandaría ordered the telephonist to "Get GHQ."

While he waited for the call, he studied the largest of the maps. The overall picture looked bleak; the front was moving closer. Still, Gandaría was confident that Bilbao's "ring of iron" could withstand enemy attack. Within the perimeter was a sizable army. The hilly terrain around Bilbao offered ideal conditions for Republican heavy artillery. From the heights they could slow the Nationalists as they moved forward. Those who got through would be caught at the barbed wire.

The telephone call to GHQ in Galdacano interrupted his thoughts. A colonel told Gandaría that "the situation around Marqina means a new front must be formed before Guernica." Troops were expected to defend a line east of the town. The Loyola Battalion headquarters would coordinate the defense, and "nothing must obstruct that aim."

Shaken, Gandaría listened to the colonel's final words. "The war is coming to you, my friend. Every hour you resist means more time for reinforcements to be called up."

Gandaría looked at the switchboard telephonist. The soldier had listened in to the conversation. The lieutenant overlooked the offense, saying simply, "So now you know."

From inside the convent, as if in counterpoint to his words, a score of voices started to sing. *Las Mercedarias,* the Sisters of Mercy, who had insisted on remaining in their convent even after it was occupied by the battalion on July 28, 1936, were singing Terce, the third Hour of that timeless world they had continued to maintain in their chapel, refectory, and cells. All the other rooms had been taken over by the soldiers, although most were now empty as the troops had gone to the front.

Leaving the communications room, Gandaría wondered how the soldiers still in the convent would feel when they realized the prospect of dying for their country was close. Would they be prepared, as he was, to sacrifice themselves for their beliefs? He hoped so. More than once he had wished his soldiers would display the same single-minded dedication as did the nuns whose singing now grew louder as he walked toward their part of the convent.

Grandaría was fascinated by the life-style of *las Mercedarias.* He had listened to their prayers and now knew the difference between their exquisite daybreak chant of the Office of Lauds and the intimate way they rendered Compline every night at eight o'clock. He knew, too, the time of Prime, the early-morning blessing of the day ahead; it was followed by Terce, the "third Hour." Then came Conventional Mass, followed by Sext at midday, the "sixth Hour." There were no sung prayers at the "ninth Hour," three o'clock in the afternoon, as this time was for silent meditation to mark the death of Christ. Singing started again with evening Vespers, and the nuns' day ended with Matins, the quiet prayer for the night. Then came the Great Silence, which no sister would break except in grave emergency.

Once, before the Great Silence had descended, Gandaría had heard the convent's Superior, Mother María, reminding her flock they were to pray that the soldiers would leave, that God would return the convent to the nuns.

But Gandaría had decided it was the nuns who must now leave.

The decision troubled him. The only truly happy memories he had of childhood were of his schooldays with the nuns in Barcelona; they had been gentle, understanding, and had encouraged him to become a teacher. Instead he had chosen the Army, where he had taken care to conceal the hopes the nuns had once had for him; he believed then that "soldiering and religion had nothing in common." Instead he had developed a rough, cynical front, relishing the fact that people like Rufino Unceta marked him as a "hard fellow."

Now, as he opened the stout wooden door into the area where the nuns lived, he was relieved no soldiers were near to see how nervous he was.

Carefully closing the door behind him, he found himself in a dim, flagstoned corridor. He had been here before to listen secretly to the nuns' chanting. At the far end of the corridor, beyond another door, their singing rose and fell in unison, high and sweet.

He paused in the corridor to let the sound envelop him. Abruptly, it stopped. He walked toward the door, opened it, and entered the chapel.

Ahead of him, kneeling on the cold slab floor, *las Mercedarias* were praying before the gaunt Christ suspended on the Cross before the altar. Each nun was in the same humble, folded-down position.

He knew there were young and old in the community. But from where he stood, looking at their backs, there was no way of telling their ages, for they had all achieved perfect immobility. Not one spine sagged, no shoulder drooped, no muscle moved to disturb the marblelike folds of their habits.

Lieutenant Gandaría walked toward them. One of the figures rose, genuflected to the altar, and turned to meet him. He thought it uncanny that she had known he was there.

The pinched face of Mother María did nothing to prepare him for her voice. It was remote and lonely and seemed to come from a great distance.

"What do you wish of us?"

"Reverend Mother, the time has come for you all to leave."

The Superior remained silent.

"The convent is no longer safe," continued Gandaría.

The distant voice came again. "For whom? For you or for us? This has been our home for three hundred years."

"Reverend Mother, soon there may be fighting. Many more troops will arrive."

"Where shall we go?"

"Bilbao, Reverend Mother. You will be safe there."

"We cannot move today."

"Reverend Mother, you must—"

The Superior silenced him, saying the nuns would leave the following day, after Vespers on Monday evening.

Grateful for her agreement, Gandaría turned to leave.

"Wait!"

He felt her scrutinize his face, looking into his eyes. A warm flush came to his cheeks, as it had years before whenever a teacher had stared at him.

"You are only a child."

The Superior made the sign of the cross over him and murmured her benediction. Then she turned and rejoined the ranks of kneeling nuns.

To most of the people in Guernica, their forty-six-year-old mayor, José Labauría, was a little-known figure. Though he had now been *alcalde* for nine months—having replaced the pro-Franco mayor at the beginning of the war—he still kept very much to himself.

Labauría was a former sea captain who had spent most of his life in command of a large fishing ship. On land, he found it difficult to adapt. Rather than mix with the townspeople, he preferred the privacy of his first-floor office in Guernica's Town Hall. Even this Sunday, before going to church, he was there, sifting through his papers.

He walked across to the balcony and looked down on the Plaza de los Fueros. Children were playing, dressed in their Sunday best. He waved to them; they waved back.

Labauría knew the townspeople did not consider him their *real* mayor; that honor was still reserved for Severo Altube, an old man who had retired to France. Altube had worn Guernica's chain of office for five years, leaving in 1935 when the pro-Franco mayor, Amurrio, had taken over.

It was Altube who had first formed, and then coached, the town band of which everyone was so proud. Indeed, it was said that Altube had had no interest in political affairs, that he had cared only about the cultural activities of the town. Perhaps that was the reason his memory lingered on so long after he had gone: The people of Guernica wished everything was as it had been during Altube's time, before politics had split Spain.

Labauría returned to his papers. It was clear from them that food and fuel were in short supply, and the situation was likely to get worse. One of the town's councilors who had complained had already been sharply reminded by the mayor that there was a war on. Such deprivations were to be expected, maintained the mayor, and borne stoically. Labauría discounted the opinions of those who predicted that unless Guernica's refugee population could be substantially reduced, mass hunger would result, and looting. That, he said, was scaremongering.

The air-raid shelters in the town, such as they were, had been built not through any mayoral decree, but out of the initiative of individuals. After the bombing of Durango, residents in some of Guernica's streets had got together and superficially strengthened the cellars of various houses with sandbags and wooden supports. Their locations in the town became known by word of mouth, and the entrances to most had *Refugio* scrolled artistically on a piece of cardboard nailed to their doors.

The mayor had, however, given the town clerk permission for the records normally kept in the Town Hall basement to be moved elsewhere, so that the large room could be used as a shelter. Now it stood empty. The ceiling above the eighty-by-sixty-foot area was covered by a double layer of bags filled with sand dredged from the Mundaca estuary. This ceiling, twelve feet high, was supported by strong wooden pillars. It was one of the best-built shelters in the town. The clerk estimated that four hundred people could be crammed into it.

Labauría had permitted the Town Hall's underground shelter to be constructed because he knew it would be unseen, and so would not remind people of the war he had hoped would never touch his town. But he disapproved strongly of the unsightly *refugio* that had been constructed aboveground on a nearby street. Apart from its ugliness, he thought it totally unsuitable for the purpose for which it was intended. He had not objected to its construction, however, guessing that if he did, he would be accused of interfering with the safety of his citizens.

The shelter had been erected on Calle Santa María, a narrow street leading up from the town's center, past the Town Hall, to the Church of Santa María. Now, anyone who walked up Calle Santa María to the church had to pass the grotesque structure nearly blocking the street.

The shelter was made from a series of heavy wooden supports about six feet high, joined by similar beams across the top. Its overall length was about twenty feet. On top of the roof beams were piled sandbags. This incredibly ugly box stood in stark contrast to the elegant buildings on Calle Santa María.

As the war drew closer, José Labauría felt increasingly impotent. The military commanders in the town seldom consulted him, and kept him ignorant of the military situation. If Guernica was to be overrun, he concluded ruefully, he might well be the last to know.

Twenty miles away in Bilbao, the thirty-six-year-old chain-smoking president of the Basque Republic, José Aguirre, knew that José Labauría was not the strong leader Guernica needed. Aguirre, also his government's minister of defense, was aware that the town was in grave danger. He placed a telephone call to one of his most trusted ministers, Francisco Lazcano, and requested him to proceed urgently to Guernica to "take charge of the town." Lazcano said he would be there within twenty-four hours.

Baker Antonio Arazamagni checked his fob watch. It was just after 10:30 A.M., time for him to leave Guernina for Marquina. The fruit pastry he had baked earlier this morning for his eighteen-year-old friend was carefully wrapped and placed on the passenger seat of Antonio's old Ford. The car's tank was filled with the prewar-priced gasoline, and the garage man had received his first payment, an extra loaf and a pastry.

Antonio decided to take a last look into the shed where he stored his flour. And as he opened the door and entered the shed, he realized at once that he had been robbed. While he was away, someone had stolen a sack of flour, enough for a day's baking.

Antonio was a victim of the increasing number of thefts in the town. A black market had developed, as yet ill-organized, but for those who could afford it and knew whom to approach, an egg could be purchased at up to twenty times its prewar price, and a kilo of coffee could fetch more than a man earned for three months' labor.

The young baker guessed the flour would be hoarded by whoever had stolen it, and used for private consumption. Many families in Guernica baked their own bread. And many families in Guernica were hungry.

At the police station, the details of the theft were written down. When Antonio asked whether his flour would be found, the overworked policeman at the desk shrugged. Too many ordinarily law-abiding people were now taking to theft; the most likely suspects, the refugees, were a transient population. Those among them who had committed crimes could be on the way to Bilbao before they were missed. Besides, added the policeman, it was difficult to search and question people who had already suffered so much.

Unhappy with what he had been told, Antonio drove across the Rentería Bridge, and then, just beyond at a junction, took the right-hand road to Marquina, his spirits, at last, rising.

Juan Dominguiz, leading his small group through the mountains with care, occasionally paused and listened to the Nationalist artillery. At times, hearing an approaching shell, he ordered his men to throw themselves facedown on the ground.

Farther back in the mountains, salvos of heavy shells hurtled over their heads. They came from the enemy's larger guns, capable of stripping a tree of its branches or slicing a man in half.

As they retreated farther from those guns, Dominguiz and his men saw the result of the bombardment: corpses, recently blown apart.

Dominguiz's men forced their feet to take them away from the intermittent sound of heavy fire. They retreated toward Marquina, the last town of any importance they would see before turning west for Guernica.

Antonio Arazamagni was now also approaching Marqina. He had traveled eight miles since leaving Guernica. As he passed through the hamlet of Múnditibar the road narrowed and climbed through the hills, forcing him to reduce speed. Suddenly, the car began to shudder and swerve. The fruit pastry fell off the seat and broke. Cursing, Antonio pulled to the side of the road.

A front tire was flat.

The operations officer at Condor Legion headquarters in the Frontón Hotel at Vitoria put down the telephone. He had just been

Above left: Guernica's mayor, José Labauría. Formerly a sea captain, he lacked the administrative skills to deal with the war's civilian problems. *(Photo: Authors' Collection)*

Above right: The Town Hall and its plaza. Mayor Labauría allowed the records normally stored in the basement to be moved so that an air-raid shelter, or *refugio*, could be prepared. *(Photo: Studio Pepe)*

Below: The Convent of La Merced. Since the outbreak of the Civil War, it had been used as a Basque garrison headquarters; soldiers and nuns lived uneasily under the same roof. *(Photo: Sister Auxilo De María Alcíbar)*

Above: Guernica, isolated for centuries by the mountains of northern Spain, was the cultural and religious center of the Basque region. *(Photo: Authors' Collection)*

Left: The sacred oak tree of Guernica, symbol of Basque independence, bloomed late in 1937—a bad omen, some said. At left is the Basque Parliament Building. *(Photo: Studio Pepe)*

Left: Father Eusebio Arronategui, the twenty-seven-year-old parish priest of the Church of San Juan. On the Sunday before the bombing, he urged the young men of his congregation to take arms in defense of Basque independence. *(Photo: Authors' Collection)*

Below: The church of San Juan. Small and simple, it drew its congregation from working-class people in the poorer part of town. *(Photo: Ataxi)*

Right: The fifteenth-century Church of Santa María. A continuous pealing of the church bells would signal an air raid. *(Photo: Studio Pepe)*

Below: The main altar of Santa Maria. Forty feet high and veneered with several pounds of gold leaf, it reflected the church's more well-to-do congregation. *(Photo: Studio Pepe)*

Above: The plaza in front of the railway station, with the Hotel Julián at left. On April 26, 1937, the square was filled with refugees waiting for the train to Bilbao. *(Photo: Ataxi)*

Below: The opposite view, looking down Calle de la Estación to the station. The first bombs fell here. *(Photo: Ataxi)*

Above: José Rodríguez, general manager of Astra-Unceta. He contrived to delay the Republicans' plan to move the arms factory to Bilbao. *Photo: Augusto Unceta)*

Right: Rufino Unceta, probably the most influential man in Guernica. When his factory was occupied by Republican troops, he kept his Nationalist sympathies well concealed. *(Photo: Augusto Unceta)*

Below: Astra-Unceta, one of two major weapons plants in Guernica, was not damaged in the attack. *(Photo: Augusto Unceta)*

Antonio Arazamagni, twenty-year-old baker and proud possessor of one of the few cars in Guernica in 1937. *(Photo: Antonio Arazamagni)*

Above: The public school plaza. A traditional meeting place for young lovers, it was also the site of open-air dancing on Sunday and Monday evenings. *(Photo: Studio Pepe)*

Below: The town band, its members sporting their Basque berets. They provided music for dancing at the Plaza Las Escuela. *(Photo: Ataxi)*

told that the bombers at Burgos had taken off; the fighter planes from Vitoria were already in the air. He logged the time: 10:40 A.M.

Juan Dominguiz and his troops were now within sight of Marquina. It lay below them, in a hollow, surrounded by fertile farmland.

Dominguiz surveyed the scene through his binoculars. He could see a road entering the town from the east, and on it, hundreds of retreating men. The road from the north was also crowded. In the surrounding hills soldiers moved singly and in groups, picking their way. There were even a few on the road leading west out of Marquina toward Guernica.

This was no orderly retreat, but a rabble falling back without order.

He lowered his glasses and looked again at Marquina. Its church—massive, ancient, nobly proportioned of weathered stone —rose majestically. He turned back to the mountains. As the sun shone between banks of cloud, the hills changed color, from dark green to rose to copper. The shade reminded him of his fiancée's hair.

Down the mountain slopes the soldiers continued to stumble toward Marquina. Dominguiz looked again to the town. High above its bell tower, he saw what appeared to be a flock of birds. The lieutenant reached for his binoculars, and after a moment's pause, turned to his men.

"Bombers!"

·10·

At 10:45 A.M. Father Iturran nodded to the three youths in the circular room and each tugged at a rope that disappeared through a hole in the ceiling. From far above, in the bell tower, the three bells of the Church of Santa María began to peal out the summons to the main Mass of the day.

Father Iturran hurried through the church, pausing to make the sign of the cross before the main altar. Covered with several pounds of pure gold, the altar was twenty feet wide at the base and towered sixty feet into the gloom of the Gothic curved ceiling.

Behind him the pews were filling, mostly with women and children; many of their men had gone to the war. The families sat in their best clothes, watchful and grave. Father Iturran nodded and smiled at the children as he went back into the presbytery.

He now had less than ten minutes to read through his notes before delivering the most important sermon of his life. The elderly priest wondered what Father Eusebio would say when he heard about it. Perhaps the sermon would lead to a rapprochement; the past weeks had been lonely since the young priest had stopped calling. But before that, the tension between them over the war had become unbearable. Father Iturran had preferred silence, Father Eusebio unreserved militancy.

What the parish priest of Santa María intended to say this Sunday morning was not planned to impress his younger colleague. Father Iturran's only concern was that his parishioners know what he thought about the war, the attitude of the Church hierarchy in Rome, and in particular, the threat facing all the women and children who now sat patiently waiting in the congregation for High Mass to begin.

As he scanned his notes, he was filled with a feeling of excitement.

Half a mile away, in the Church of San Juan, Father Eusebio Arronategui lit the altar candles. The church was situated close to the Rentería Bridge, its congregation made up largely of the working-class people who lived in the poorer part of the town, that maze of cobbled streets between the bridge and the railway station. It was a rough-and-tumble area of taverns, tiny shops, and humble homes. But Father Eusebio had accepted every challenge of this, his first ministry.

At twenty-seven, he didn't mind that his presbytery was cramped, that its walls were damp for half of the year. Nor, like some of his predecessors, did he feel uncomfortable ministering in the shadow of Santa María. In April 1936, when Father Eusebio had first arrived in Guernica, the previous incumbent of San Juan had cautioned him to "beware of the Pope in the church on the hill."

Even in his cassock Father Eusebio looked a countryman, short, muscular, with dark hair and windburned face. His rope-soled shoes made him appear a rustic in holy orders. But his voice, incisive and commanding, was that of a born preacher. And this Sunday morning he meant to use it to maximum advantage.

As he waited for Mass to begin, his mind turned to Father Iturran. He liked the priest of Santa María, but every sermon he preached had widened the rift between them. He could remember the night the war began. They had been in Father Iturran's presbytery indulging their common interest in the Basque language and its origins when Radio Bilbao had interrupted its program to report that fighting had broken out. Father Iturran had suggested that they both pray "for the Church in this time of strife."

Soon afterward, Father Eusebio had launched an impassioned attack from his pulpit, condemning the Nationalists, "who fight in the name of God, but are the agents of the Devil." He had tried to convert the old priest to his point of view, but Father Iturran was not to be persuaded. Their evenings together had become bitter debates. On Sundays, Father Eusebio had continued to lambast the Nationalists. Finally, after an especially outspoken sermon a month ago, Father Iturran had warned that if such talk continued, he would have to report the matter to the Bishop of Bilbao.

On this Sunday morning, the young priest had no doubt that when Father Iturran heard what he had said, he would carry out that threat.

The Santa María bells were a warning to pretty María Ortuza that she was behind her usual Sunday morning timetable. By now she should have finished lunch preparations. But the constant demands of her mistress, the autocratic Señora Dolores de Arriendiara, had disrupted María's schedule.

Twice during the morning she had been summoned to the drawing room to explain why the household budget had risen again this week. The old lady had questioned the cost of some fish and demanded to know why María had bought a kilo of corn. Patiently, the young housekeeper had explained it was for the hens that every morning produced two eggs for the señora's breakfast.

With her mistress's warning to be "more careful" still in her ears, twenty-two-year-old María tried to make up for lost time. She toyed with the idea of not going to Mass, but she knew Señora Arriendiara would regard it as a serious matter if any of her staff missed church.

María put the Sunday lunch, a rabbit, in a dish and placed it in the oven. She would add the vegetables when she returned from church, and she hoped the fastidious señora would not notice they had not been marinated in the meat juice.

María slipped a coat over the black smock each of the maids wore when on duty. After straightening her thick lisle stockings, she removed her white cap and placed a mantilla over her dark hair. Then she hurried out of the servants' door at No. 8 Calle Allende Salazar and joined the other worshipers walking toward Santa María Church.

Only after she had entered the church and was seated in a pew reserved for the Arriendiara household did María remember that in her anxiety not to be late for Mass she had forgotten to heat the oven.

For a moment she thought to flee the church. But just as she was about to move, Señora Arriendiara arrived to occupy the end seat of the pew, effectively blocking her escape.

Juan Silliaco had still not settled the question of his son's going to Bilbao to escape the Moors. When they discussed the matter over breakfast, the boy cried, begging not to be sent away. Silliaco did not press the point; instead, he intended to raise the subject again later in the day, when Pedro might be more willing to anticipate the excitement of a trip to Bilbao.

In an attempt to cheer him up, he decided to take Pedro walking through the town before church. They paused periodically for Silliaco to explain the plans he and the other volunteer firemen had devised to fight a blaze in this shop or that apartment house. At the end of each little lecture he used one of his favorite phrases: "Anticipation is half the battle."

He was careful to hide from his son his fear that large parts of Guernica were virtual firetraps, especially in the commercial center through which they now walked.

Constructed principally from timber dry with age, the wood frame buildings were a fireman's nightmare. The situation, in Silliaco's opinion, was made worse by the narrow streets that could act as wind conductors during a fire, fanning the flames along their length. Danger was further compounded by the behavior of the refugees; they had camped with their open fires and braziers almost throughout the square. A spark from one of them could bring the catastrophe he most feared.

His mind filled with such thoughts, he and his son reached the fire station. Silliaco glanced at his watch. There was still time. Together, they slipped through a side door into the silence of the station. Thirteen years of handling the equipment still had not blunted Silliaco's fascination for the polished brass couplings, the coils of hose pipes, the steel axes, and the gleaming horse-drawn truck. During a fire his place was beside the driver.

Pedro looked at the truck. Then he turned to his father and asked, "Papa, are the ones in Bilbao bigger?"

"Much bigger."

The boy looked wistful. In silence they left the fire station and walked the remaining few yards to the Church of San Juan, each alone with his thoughts. As they entered, Juan Silliaco knew now that his son would go to Bilbao.

On the other side of the town, Rufino Unceta had perfectly timed his arrival with his family at the Church of Santa María. They settled themselves in the first pew immediately beneath the pulpit at precisely the moment the church bells stopped tolling. The Uncetas knelt on their stools, closed their eyes, and offered up their private prayers. Then, when the bells struck the eleventh hour of the morning, they resumed their places on the polished bench.

In the pew immediately behind the Uncetas, diminutive José Rodríguez looked at his wife and smiled. It had been close, but they had reached the church ahead of the Uncetas. To have arrived after the ruling industrial family of Guernica had taken their seats would have been unthinkable, even for Rodríguez, who played such a part in the Unceta fortunes.

Thirty-six years old and barely five feet tall, Rodríguez was Unceta's troubleshooting general manager. Nowadays he carried on his shoulders the daily burden of coping with, and sometimes outwitting, the troops guarding the factory. Even now, in church, Rodríguez was hatching new plans to delay moving the Astra-Unceta complex to Bilbao on Tuesday.

His object was somehow to safeguard the factory, so that it could be handed over in working order to the Nationalists when, and if, they took Guernica. He was hampered in his plans because he could not be sure when the Nationalists would strike. If they attacked before Tuesday, he would have the delicate task of hiding as many of the factory's vital machine parts as he could, in order to thwart any plans Lieutenant Gandaría might have for sabotaging the factory before the Nationalists arrived. On the other hand, if the Nationalists were to launch their attack against the town after Tuesday, Rodríguez would have the equally delicate job of causing those same vital parts to break down. Then, he hoped, Gandaría would not think it worthwhile to remove them to Bilbao.

Rodríguez was still considering the matter when the procession led by Father Iturran moved down the central aisle and the High Mass was sung.

The Low Mass in the Church of San Juan was said without music. Father Eusebio felt this simpler form of worship was more in keeping with the church itself, which had few of the outward trappings of Spanish Christianity. There were no Virgins who wept tears of real emeralds, few gold-covered altars and blood-streaked Christs; none of the "overpowering feeling of religion" Father Eusebio disliked so much in the Church of Santa María.

Turning from the altar, bare except for the mandatory three

cloth coverings, the cushion for the Missal, the two flickering candles, and the crucifix, the young priest looked at his congregation. Most were poorly dressed, the children hungry-looking, their parents anxious and drawn.

As he entered the pulpit he knew this was not the time to fail them. In the resounding voice that he knew thrilled them, Father Eusebio began. "Today, there are some of you who should not be here. You should be out in the fields, in the mountains, out everywhere the enemy is, resisting him and protecting your families, your homeland. . . ."

Father Iturran began his sermon by reminding his congregation that in all the years he had preached to them, he had constantly said it was sufficient to know who God was and what He was. Knowing that, he told them, was enough for them to be able to receive the full and comforting benefits of their religion.

Carmen Batzar was disappointed. After arranging the flowers in the chapel of Santa Clara convent every Sunday, she came to church and waited for Father Iturran to speak on the issue that most concerned her—the war. She wanted him to tell her that her fiancé, Lieutenant Juan Dominguiz, was right to risk his life for the separatist cause.

At the rear of the church, sixteen-year-old Juan Plaza stifled a yawn as Father Iturran began to develop another thread familiar from past sermons: Life on earth was like a bird, passing, but eternal life was everlasting.

Rufino Unceta and his family looked up at the pulpit. Father Iturran was talking along well-worn lines, and the familiarity of the words was comforting.

Several more sentences passed before they, and the rest of the congregation of some five hundred, realized that their spiritual adviser was veering in a direction both new and disturbing.

"For months I have failed you by speaking only of abstract things—and not what must passionately concern you all. That does not mean I have not shared in my heart your feelings about the war. But the time has come for you all to know that your anger has been my anger at brother fighting brother. Your sorrow has been my sorrow at the Church divided. Your revulsion has been my revulsion at the atrocities committed 'in the name of God.' It is enough to shake one's faith. That must not be shaken. But your faith in me, your priest, would be shaken, perhaps even has been shaken, if I did not now speak out and warn you of the evil that is coming closer to our community. . . ."

Gasps came from various parts of the nave. In his pew, the mayor stirred uneasily and looked at Father Iturran, willing him to stop. But the priest continued to talk of impending disaster.

Carmen Batzar felt a surge of excitement. Her silent plea had been answered.

Later, many would remember how Father Iturran paused once in his sermon to sweep his eyes over the congregation, then fix his gaze on Rufino Unceta.

People would also recall how the two men stared briefly at each other, how Unceta "seemed to hunch into himself," like "an armadillo taking shelter from impending attack."

In fact, Father Iturran had settled upon Unceta for a quite different reason—he hoped for some sign of approval from the powerful industrialist. Instead, he saw only an unblinking face.

Drawing again upon his reserves, the elderly priest continued his sermon.

"Life," thundered Father Eusebio in the Church of San Juan, "is sacred. To take life is a crime."

He, too, swept his eyes over his congregation. Then he went on: "But to give your life in defense of all you hold dear in the name of God—your wives, your children, your homes—then, I tell you, it is permissible to give your lives. And if need be, to take life in defense of those things!"

Juan Silliaco shifted uncomfortably as Father Eusebio reminded his parishioners of the agony of St. Agnes.

"She was a child, twelve years old. They took her, stripped her naked, and violated her, and finally, when they had had their way, they murdered her. St. Agnes was sustained in her agony by her faith. We must also be sustained in belief. But we must not let our children be molested because we did nothing to defend them. We must not let our wives be taken because we did nothing. There have been many instances in this war similar to the rape of St. Agnes. Such violations can only be halted by firm action. Go, I say, you young people here, go and defend all that is precious to you, to all of us!"

Father Eusebio lowered his voice and ended, "God will not judge you guilty, because in His eyes you cannot be guilty for defending that which is right."

There was silence. Then, in various parts of the nave, one young man after another rose and left the church.

In the Church of Santa María, Father Iturran's voice was rising, stronger than it had ever been. He cried out, "In Spain men and women and children are being killed in the barbaric name of the Nationalists in a manner we cannot have considered possible. They dare to commit their crimes in the name of God. God would never sanction their wickedness. It is tragic that the Church, by the silence of its leaders, appears to be condoning this evil. I must say to you that I cannot for one moment believe the Holy Father, if he knew what was happening here, would condone it. By speaking out, I hope others who have chosen the path of silence will now also come forward, so that the Holy Father will know of the dreadful things being done in God's name."

He paused, waiting for his words to register, looking down at his notes. Written on the paper was: "Parish priest of Eunari."

The terrible story of that priest had come to Father Iturran secondhand. He had questioned its authenticity, but in the end he had been forced to conclude it was true: The story was too chilling, too outrageous to have been invented.

He knew it would shock, even revolt, many in his congregation. But he had decided to use it because it would help his congregation to realize he knew what was happening in the war, and also to learn where he, personally, stood.

Father Iturran glanced up at the huge statue of the Virgin Mary and Christ built into the main altar, then turned back and faced the congregation

"The Moors arrived as the priest was saying Mass. They cut off his nose and skewered it to his tongue. Then they chopped off his ears and left him to die suspended from the church bell tower. That is why I have urged that at least the women and children should depart in the next few days before the Moors come."

Father Iturran left the pulpit, aware of sobbing among the women.

Shortly before noon, Lieutenant Gandaría was called from the communications room in La Merced Convent to see the young men from the Church of San Juan. They told him they wished to enlist. When he asked if they could each handle a rifle, all said they could. He told them to report back on Monday morning. Then Gandaría returned to the communications room and tried again to contact the command post in Marquina. The line was dead.

Gandaría then telephoned GHQ in Galdacano. He was told to "stop bothering" them unless he had information to impart. Gandaría reminded GHQ of the three trains he had been promised to evacuate the Astra-Unceta complex on Tuesday. He was informed the matter was "in hand."

Not for the first time, Gandaría felt the General Staff were displaying a dangerous laxness in their pursuit of the war.

He told the telephonist to keep trying to raise Marquina, even though it was probably a waste of time. He guessed the line had been broken by an artillery shell. For once he was wrong.

·11·

The telephone line between Marquina and Guernica had been severed by one of the 500-pound bombs Von Richthofen had ordered his bombers to drop.

From his vantage point in the hills, Lieutenant Juan Dominguiz heard the downward rush of the bombs and saw the sudden quiver of the earth. Then came the vast roar of the explosions, blasts of air, and dark, heavy smoke climbing into the sky.

After the droning of the bombers, flying high overhead, Dominguiz heard the propeller howls of the Heinkel-51 fighter planes as they swept downward. There was a barrage of machine-gun bullets before the planes soared skyward, "leaving on the ground the limbs of dead men still twitching."

Before the wounded could be collected, another swarm of bombers arrived, and after they had loosed their bombs, the fighters came again. This time they, too, dropped bombs. Some pilots threw grenades from their open cockpits. And then, as the fighters disappeared, Dominguiz saw a third wave of bombers approaching.

On either side of the road into Marquina he could see hundreds of men throw themselves facedown when the bombs fell. Cracked rock and earth spattered high into the hillsides, and the air resounded with the cries of the wounded.

From below, Dominguiz heard the firing of a Lewis machine gun. It was a futile gesture, for the bombers were well out of range.

Cautiously, Dominguiz raised his head. He was about to shout at the gunner to stop wasting ammunition when a fighter burst through the clouds, followed by two more planes. Dominguiz saw them heading in his direction. He heard the bullets hit overhead, tear through the tops of the trees behind him, rattle down twigs into the clearing where he and his men sheltered.

He closed his eyes, put his arms over his face, and waited, facedown, as the planes kicked up earth-clouds ahead of them. Then a stream of bullets stitched across his body, killing the men on either side of him and leaving Dominguiz critically wounded.

His fiancée, Carmen Batzar, lived with her mother in the cobbled triangle of roads that surrounded the marketplace. She had grown up with the aroma of fruit, vegetables, and fish brought from the port of Bermeo. Early this Sunday afternoon, the lingering smell wafted through the open window of Carmen's attic bedroom to the table where she sat writing.

Carmen was committing to paper as much of Father Iturran's sermon as she could recall, trying to remember the exact words before writing them down in an exercise book.

There were several such books on the table, all filled with her neat penmanship. They were a detailed daily record of her life and thoughts these past weeks. It had been Juan Dominguiz's idea that she keep the diary. On the first page he had written: "Write down everything that is important to you while I am away. It will also be important to me."

Father Iturran's sermon presented a special challenge to Carmen's skill as a chronicler. She wrote: "I do not want to recall only his words, but also to try to convey the effect they had on everyone."

She remembered how the mayor had left the church "downcast, like a person who had been told he has an incurable disease." According to Carmen, the Unceta family left Santa María "showing nothing." Others, mostly older women, walked away sobbing.

She paused to look through the window at the Church of Santa María, where the banns of her wedding were posted. There was, she had once written, a "great beauty about the building. Its stained-glass windows have been carefully designed to let in as much of our northern light as possible. The buttresses are like anchor chains stretched tight by a strong Biscay tide."

Carmen closed the exercise book and changed out of her church clothes into the plain smock she wore for her regular Sunday afternoon shift at the Carmelite Convent hospital. Shortly before one o'clock she left her home and began the quarter-mile walk to the convent.

Coming down the road toward her was a group of soldiers who had just come out of the monastery gardens of the Augustine Fathers; they were the troops who had slipped into the town in the early morning. Refreshed by sleep, they were looking for food. The men had come only a little way along the road before they were besieged by urchins, begging: *"Un pan, un pan. Un poco de pan, camarades."*

Carmen guessed by their clothes the children were refugees. The soldiers had no food for them. As Carmen passed by, she watched the beggars try a new tack. Undaunted, they formed up in a squad under the command of an older boy, who started to strut along the road, shrilling out the drill command: "Halte-oop! Halte-oop!"

The soldiers laughed. One of them tossed some cigarettes among the marching children. There was a wild scramble for the bounty.

Carmen felt saddened by what she had seen. But not until she reached the hospital did she wonder who the soldiers had been; they were too unkempt to be members of the battalion stationed at La Merced Convent.

Inside the hospital Mother Augusta brusquely told her they were the "fortunate ones. We have just been told to expect heavy casualties from an air attack this morning in the Marquina area."

The Superior looked at her, then consulted a piece of paper. "No ward work for you today, my child. Have you enough experience to handle the *poupinelle?*"

"Yes, Reverend Mother."

"Then see to it that the operating room does not run short of instruments."

Carmen hurried to load the sterilization oven with surgical instruments. In the room beyond, she could hear the operating staff making its preparations. All those undergoing surgery would first pass through the room where Carmen stood.

María Ortuza did not know how to break the news to Señora Arriendiara that lunch was not ready. Might her temperamental mistress use this excuse to terminate her employment? Recently the señora had become irritable, showing no understanding of the problems María faced with the rising cost of food and the limited choice available.

María knew that now would be the worst possible time to be unemployed. The household staffs of the local aristocracy, the Count of Montefuerte and the Count of Arana, had already suffered cutbacks, and she had no doubt that other prominent families would follow their lead. Dismissal could mean María would be forced to work as an ordinary domestic helper, or in one of the town's cafés. The thought was not appealing.

As soon as Mass was finished, María hurried from the church, taking care to avoid her mistress, and rushed home to her kitchen.

For a moment she considered preparing something cold for lunch. But she knew the señora would not accept that: Sunday lunch had to be hot and it had to be good, whatever the difficulties. María looked at the rabbit, still in its dish in the cold oven. She then opened the damper flue that heated the oven, set the table, and went to the kitchen window, looking down the tree-lined Calle Allende Salazar to the Church of Santa María.

She could see a small group of people clustered together in the road between the church and the Parliament Building. Señora Arriendiara was among them. The longer she stayed there, thought María, the more chance the rabbit would be at least partially cooked before her return. She had no doubt that Father Iturran's sermon was the topic of the group's conversation. María had found the priest's words shocking, though not for a moment did she intend to take his advice and leave the town. She thought few people would do that.

The group in the road started to break up. Señora Arriendiara walked slowly up the hill; as she came closer, María could see she looked unhappy. It was a bad omen.

María opened the door and took the señora's hat and coat. Neither spoke, neither looked at the other.

Screwing up her courage, María started to explain about lunch. Señora Arriendiara silenced her. "I have no interest in lunch after what we heard in church. I should think nobody would want to eat after that sermon."

The old woman climbed the stairs to her bedroom.

María returned to the kitchen, unable to believe her lucky escape. She turned down the damper flue; she would serve the rabbit for dinner. She guessed that by then Señora Arriendiara's hunger would overcome all other considerations.

From outside came the sound of laughing and whistling. Past the kitchen window trooped a group of soldiers carrying rifles. María did not recognize any of them. Then she remembered the report of one of the other staff members earlier that morning that troops had been seen sleeping in the grounds of the monastery of the Augustine Fathers.

Obviously, thought María, these men were a few of those troops, and they were out for a good time. Sunday was the one evening of the week María had free. She liked to spend it dancing. The sight of the soldiers made the pretty twenty-two-year-old feel this day, which had begun so badly, might end altogether differently.

Through the restaurant window, Isidro Arrién watched the soldiers wander aimlessly across the marketplace, then head in his direction. He had nothing against soldiers, but the Arrién Restaurant was the most exclusive and expensive in the town. Soldiers were bad for business, with their loud voices, noisy eating habits, and demands for the cheapest wine and food. Fortunately, they seldom came in. Only the officers billeted at La Merced Convent could afford to dine at the restaurant with any regularity. This Sunday lunchtime, as normal, the Arrién was full.

Isidro, a corpulent man, turned from the window and walked

from table to table, greeting his customers, inquiring after their health, smiling at their jokes, acknowledging their praise for the cooking. In addition, he found himself having to display suitable concern about Father Iturran's sermon.

The mayor, José Labauría, dining alone at his customary corner table, mumbled it was "quite wrong" for the priest to "alarm people." Then Labauría gave full attention to a dish of hake served in a thick parsley sauce garnished with asparagus and fat clams. Here in the Arrién there was no evidence of a food shortage. The mayor was able to follow his first course with the specialty of the day, *cordero asado*, roast lamb basted in brandy and lemon sauce.

The lamb was also the choice of the man and boy seated opposite each other at a table near the kitchen. They had not made a reservation and were lucky to get even that table. Isidro, who prided himself on knowing all his customers, could not immediately place the man's face. Then he remembered: Silliaco, the fireman who months before had complimented him on having one of the few buildings in town that was not a fire risk. Isidro poured a glass of wine and presented it to Silliaco. It gave the restaurateur great pleasure to make such gestures, though few customers were as appreciative as Silliaco.

Isidro smiled at the fireman's son, and the boy informed him this was a "special occasion. Papa's sending me to Bilbao. He's promised I can go and see the fire engines there."

Isidro looked at Silliaco. The fireman explained, "It's better in Bilbao."

Isidro wondered whether he was right to keep his own children in Guernica. His wife, the stout, round-faced Victoria, had left the decision to him. Now, after Father Iturran's warning, Isidro was uncertain. Bilbao, he knew, was being bombed almost every other day; Guernica had yet to see an airplane.

Even if the town were captured, Isidro did not think the Moors would be allowed to rape and pillage as they had elsewhere. He believed the Nationalist leaders were well aware of the historic significance of Guernica, and would take special care to "liberate" it in a safe and proper manner. On balance, he believed he was right to keep his four sons and five daughters with him, working in the restaurant.

This Sunday, as usual, his children were either in the kitchen or waiting on table. He watched his eldest daughter, Isabel, carrying a steaming salver of baked bream to a table, and heard one of the diners ask her how the restaurant continued to serve such delicacies when every day the war produced new shortages.

That question always angered him. Implicit in it, Isidro believed, was the suggestion that he dealt on the black market, an allegation he was tired of denying. He and his family knew that the restaurant was able to continue to offer high standards solely through Isidro's foresight.

When the war had started, he had anticipated shortages. Prudentially, he had laid in a vast stock of wines and sherries from southern Spain, an area now occupied mainly by the Nationalists. He had stockpiled other basic raw materials before they, too, had become unavailable. To maintain his all-important supply of fish, every morning before dawn he traveled from one Biscay port to another, collecting mussels for *mulago a la vasca,* hake for the traditional Basque dish of *cochochos.* By daybreak, Isidro would be back in Guernica; soon afterward, Victoria and the children would join him in the kitchen, peeling, blanching, stewing, roasting, and occasionally sampling.

Now Isidro was satisfied to hear his daughter give the reply he had taught all his family to give in such a situation: "Surely, señor, the only question worth asking is, 'Why shouldn't it be possible for us to give you what you expect?' "

Isidro looked toward the window. The soldiers were peering in. He moved to the door, reaching it as they entered.

The restaurant, he said, was full. Then, said one of the soldiers, they would wait for a table. Isidro apologized; there was no more food available. One of the soldiers protested that they had not had a proper meal for a day, and began to describe their long march back from the front line.

On impulse, Isidro told them to go to the back of the restaurant. There he served them a meal and listened as they discussed the bitter fighting they had taken part in.

"It isn't the enemy troops or artillery that is beating us. It's the planes," one said.

Another soldier imitated the whine of a diving plane. Another provided the sound effects: *"Rat-tat-tat-rat-tat-tat."* A third fell theatrically off his chair and onto the floor.

Although amused by the scene, Isidro was reminded of the offer he had accepted from Rufino Unceta. Months ago, the industrialist had said that in the event of an air attack, Isidro and his family could shelter in the special cement bunker he had had built at the rear of his arms complex. At the tme Isidro had thought Unceta rather overcautious to construct such a shelter. Now he was not so sure.

Punctually at 1:20 P.M., José Rodríguez said good-bye to his wife and walked the 400 yards from his modest home at No. 3 Calle de la Estación to the Unceta mansion, as he did every Sunday.

Rodríguez had once measured the distance, just as recently he had paced the 410 yards between his home and the bunker behind the Unceta complex. He had told his wife that if ever there was an air attack, she could run to the shelter in under four minutes.

This Sunday afternoon Rodríguez was strongly aware of the possibility of a sudden air attack. Usually an intensely practical man, Rodríguez, for once, was disturbed by his own imagination. The feeling, he would later recall, was "without any foundation. It was just something nagging in my mind."

For fear he would be laughed at, Rodríguez was careful to put his foreboding to the back of his mind before seating himself in one of the overstuffed armchairs in Unceta's drawing room. On the other hand, Rodríguez knew that Unceta liked him to express any concern he had about the business; it confirmed that the general manager was a loyal company man.

Rodríguez received almost as much satisfaction as his employer from the way the business had prospered. Astra-Unceta had been steadily nibbling at the markets of Krupp and Armstrong before the war had stopped its expansion.

The general manager deeply resented the Republicans who had occupied the factory—especially Lieutenant Gandaría. Once, when the officer had demanded an increase in output, Rodríguez had flared, "You may know how to fire a gun, but you have no idea how to make one!"

Now he and Unceta reviewed the events of the past week and discussed the days ahead. Unceta argued that the Nationalists "could be here in a matter of hours."

Luis, Unceta's eldest son, the solemn-faced twenty-three-year-old heir apparent to the business, voiced a fear. If the Nationalists did attack, he asked, what guarantee was there that their artillery would not shell the factory?

Rodríguez answered with conviction. "The Nationalist commanders know where the factory is. They know where our loyalties lie. Most important, they know they need our weapons to help finish the war. We have nothing to fear from Nationalist gunners."

Rufino Unceta nodded agreement. Then, in his soft, low-pitched voice, he spoke. "There is another matter. The Germans who fly for Franco are here in the north. If the Germans attack the town, will they also have been told of our importance?"

Antonio Arazamagni changed the punctured tire, ate the broken fruit pastry meant for the girl in Marquina, and set off again down the twisting mountain road to Marquina. From time to time he had to pull to the side to let an ambulance hurtle past. Otherwise, the road was empty.

Now, as he turned another bend, Antonio was once more forced to let a column of ambulances pass. One of them stopped beside him and an officer in its cab ordered the young baker to "take your car up this road fast and bring back as many wounded as you can."

Antonio pulled up in front of a lime-washed stone house that was being used as a first-aid post. Beyond, in the distance, he could see Marquina. Streaming out of town was a mass of people. His last hopes of reaching Marquina today were dashed with the sight of this evacuation; he could only hope his relatives and girl friend were somewhere among those winding out of the town. He could sense the indecision of the refugees from the way they would sometimes stop and look around, as if wondering whether they were safe.

For the first time, Antonio "could smell the fear war brings." It made him very frightened.

An officer ordered the young baker to turn his car around and wait. Smoking nervously, Antonio sat behind the wheel, taking in a scene totally foreign to him. His idea of soldiering was based upon the officers and men garrisoned at La Merced Convent, whom he had seen drilling and marching to and from the Unceta complex.

The men now slumped around the stone house were slow to obey commands, moved lethargically and littered the ground with equipment they didn't bother to reclaim: filthy knapsacks, mess tins, cartridge belts of ammunition, even rifles. Their air of defeat and demoralization increased Antonio's anxiety.

From out of the house an orderly led three men with bandages around their heads and arms. In silence two of the wounded soldiers got into the back, the third slumped on the seat beside Antonio. The orderly thumped the side of the car and pointed down the road.

Slowly, anxious not to exacerbate the men's pain, Antonio drove back to Guernica.

•12•

At 2:00 P.M., after the last fighter plane had landed and its pilot reached the Frontón Hotel, debriefing began in the operations room. In Burgos, the bomber crews were questioned under the watchful control of Wing Commander Fuchs, but here at Vitoria, Von Richthofen himself supervised.

The debriefing officers sat on one side of the long trestle table;

the fliers stood on the other side. Von Richthofen had chosen to question the fighter squadron's commander, Captain Franz von Lutzow. Although Von Lutzow had only recently arrived in Spain, he already had two "kills" to his credit. Now the tall, fair-haired, twenty-two-year-old still bore the red marks of his flying helmet on his face. His voice was a shade higher than usual. When he spoke, he flexed his fingers; a short while ago they had pressed the firing button. Von Richthofen recognized the special excitement aerial combat produced.

The chief of staff was a meticulous debriefing officer. His questions were sharp, incisive, designed to exclude anything but the essential facts. In turn, Von Lutzow's answers were short, factual, devoid of opinion.

Swiftly, the chief of staff established the facts. The fighters had rendezvoused with the bombers on time and at the correct height. The raid on Marquina had been pressed exactly as planned.

"Resistance?"

"Little, sir. Some machine-gun fire."

"Enemy aircraft?"

"None, sir."

"Casualties?"

"None. The enemy was surprised. Conditions were ideal. Troops bunched on the roads. Others caught on open hills."

Von Richthofen rose and nodded for the young officer to join him at a wall map showing the area around Marquina. Von Lutzow pointed out the enemy positions. Then Von Richthofen indicated the road west of Marquina and asked how far down that road the enemy had retreated.

"No more than two kilometers, sir, before the bombers closed in."

The chief of staff seemed surprised. Had Von Lutzow seen the bombs falling?

"No, sir. But the craters were plainly visible."

Von Richthofen turned back to the map. On which side of the town was the greatest concentration of troops?

"East, sir."

"Heading?"

Von Lutzow hesitated. Then, in a confident voice, he said, "West, sir."

Von Richthofen studied the map. West of Marquina the road divided into two that wound their way across desolate mountain country. Farther west, the roads joined again at Múnditibar, continuing as one until just outside Guernica. There the road merged with two others near a point where the River Mundaca was crossed by the Rentería Bridge.

The chief of staff resumed questioning. "West of Marquina, the enemy are in retreat. Which way?"

Von Lutzow indicated a broad area of the map: The troops were fanning out as they retreated, seeking the shelter of the wooded hills.

"And the roads?"

"No appreciable traffic, sir."

"Gut!" Von Richthofen turned away.

By 2:30 P.M., the last questions had been asked, the last answers written down. Captain Gautlitz, the operations officer, beckoned his two aides, Lieutenants Asmus and Raunce, to join him and Von Richthofen around the dais desk.

Every afternoon at this hour, the operations room staff and Von Richthofen would meet to discuss future targets. Sometimes the meetings were lengthy as they debated a choice and all the parameters associated with it: weather, enemy defenses, bomb mix, fighter cover, bombing altitude.

Years later, Hans Asmus would say that this particular meeting was "a piece of cake. The target was obvious."

Nevertheless, military protocol and Von Richthofen's presence dictated that the Target Selection Committee follow well-established procedures.

In silence the group studied a large-scale map of northern Vizcaya. Asmus confirmed that all the pilots he had debriefed said that the enemy looked as if it would continue retreating beyond Marquina. Raunce said he had been told the same.

"They could form a new line in the hills beyond Marquina," said Gautlitz.

Von Richthofen said he thought that unlikely because of the supply problems involved.

"There's only one place they could hold, sir, and that's here," said Asmus.

He pointed his finger at a blue spot on the map that marked Guernica.

"Check the target files," Gautlitz ordered Raunce.

Raunce kept the buff-colored folders locked in a metal filing cabinet in a corner of the room. Inside them were population figures, industrial descriptions, aerial reconnaissance photographs, and intelligence reports describing the defenses for individual cities and towns. Some files, like the ones for Bilbao and Madrid, were bulky; others contained little more than the information available in any tourist guide.

Raunce riffled through the cabinet. There was no file on Guernica.

Von Richthofen looked at the men around him. "Do any of you know anything about Guernica?"

All shook their heads.

Gautlitz studied the map once more and delivered his assessment. Guernica looked like a potential defensive position, hemmed in as it was by mountains. If the enemy chose to make a stand there, it would be hard to dislodge them, so they must not be allowed to retreat into the town and establish themselves. The best way to stop that happening was to smash the one vital artery leading into the town from the east. If the enemy could be bottled up there, thousands might be taken prisoner.

Asmus remembered afterward how the chief of staff then looked at them. "It was the usual ritual. First Raunce and then I pointed at the map where all the roads joined together at Guernica, forming the artery that led across the bridge into the town. Then Gautlitz drew a circle around the spot in red pencil, to signify a 'most probable target.' We had chosen the area round the Rentería Bridge."

They went on to discuss other suitable targets. Bilbao was

marked down for another concerted pounding; the mountains around Marquina were to be strafed and bombed again.

"The whole object," Asmus would recall, "was to keep the enemy on the run—and nobody was better at that than Von Richthofen."

At three-thirty the session ended. Asmus telephoned Burgos to instruct Wing Commander Fuchs to put up against Bilbao the new Heinkel-111 bombers of the experimental squadron. Raunce began to reread the target file on the seaport in case there was any useful new information.

Gautlitz walked Von Richthofen to his Mercedes. Von Richthofen placed his map case on the seat and said to him, "Don't do anything about Guernica until I've learned what Vigón is planning."

Von Richthofen then set out on the seventy-five-mile drive to Spanish military headquarters in Burgos to confer with the Spanish leaders.

·13·

Early in the afternoon, the injured began arriving at the hospital in the Carmelite Convent. Most of their wounds were from shrapnel, some from machine-gun fire. One of the stretcher-bearers explained to Carmen Batzar that the soldiers were "easy targets."

Carmen buried her thoughts, concentrating on putting soiled instruments in the *poupinelle* and taking out those that had been sterilized. She worked with her back to the center of the room, facing the wall, hoping to avoid the unpleasant sights. Around her was a growing pile of boots and clothing that the doctors had cut away, along with bloodied field dressings.

By midafternoon the injured lay on stretchers in a line extending from the sterilization room back down the corridor. Once, Carmen was ordered to go to the dispensary at the end of the corridor to get an urgently needed piece of equipment. Carmen was glad the corridor was dimly lit; it meant she did not have to look at the wounded. But she could tell that some of their injuries were very bad. Men had died where they lay on their stretchers, and some, she guessed, wished they were dead.

A few, like the man now lying on a stretcher inside the door of the sterilization room, tried to speak. Carmen turned from the *poupinelle*, forcing a smile to her lips. She would write later: "The man had been shot through the thighs. His trousers and underpants had been cut away and the blood-washed flesh coated with a thin, transparent red varnish." He asked Carmen for a cigarette. She nodded and went out into the corridor, looking for an orderly. When she returned, the man had been taken into the operating room.

In his place was a large man, shrapnel-wounded in a number of places. He was crying. A doctor came out of the operating room and plunged a needle into the man's arm. His sobbing stopped. Two orderlies lifted the stretcher and carried the man in to take his place on one of the twin tables.

Carmen turned back to the *poupinelle*. Behind her, she heard the orderlies lay another stretcher on the floor. This time, fearing she could no longer control her distress, she was determined not to turn around.

"Nurse! Clamps!"

Carmen took the tray of surgical clamps from the sterilizer and gave them to the nurse waiting in the doorway of the operating room. She averted her eyes from the man lying on the floor.

But on her return to the *poupinelle* she could not avoid looking at him. His arms were folded across his chest; his body was swathed in field dressings, his head also bandaged. Other than a trickle of dried blood at the corner of his mouth, his handsome face was unmarked.

Carmen slumped to the floor, fainting at the sight of her fiancé, Lieutenant Juan Dominguiz.

Following their leisurely lunch in the Arrién Restaurant, Juan

Silliaco and his son decided to continue their walk. It was a pleasant, sunny afternoon. Like all the other patrons in the restaurant, and indeed most of the people in town, the Silliacos were unaware of the ambulances that had arrived in Guernica during the past hour.

They crossed the Calle de Ferial in front of the restaurant and walked through the marketplace. Many people were out strolling, encouraged by the first fine weather for some days. Silliaco nodded at the men and touched his black beret to the ladies.

Leaving the marketplace, he and his son walked up the broad steps that led to the Plaza Las Escuelas, the town's main square. There Silliaco's benevolent mood evaporated. A screen had been set up on the bandstand; the mobile cinema from Bilbao was showing a Communist propaganda film. Silliaco sniffed and turned away. He was glad to hear the audience jeering.

The boy paused to look at the public school he had attended these past five years; tomorrow he would be going to a new one in Bilbao. Silliaco quickly moved his son on, suggesting they call at the Residencia Calzada to see whether any of the children living there would like to join them on their walk.

The Residencia, at the southern end of town beyond the Unceta mansion, was a home for the elderly poor of the area and for orphans. It was a large stone building, constructed, like so many of Guernica's large buildings, around three sides of a square. Silliaco noticed a newly painted red cross on its roof. About forty persons now lived in the Residencia, including the children. They were looked after by six nuns belonging to a charitable religious order, and a small domestic staff.

Silliaco explained to a nun the purpose of their visit. She thanked him but said the children were too young to go. All were around six years old, except for one girl about his son's age, and she was away until Tuesday.

The Silliacos retraced their steps and eventually reached the jai-alai, or pelota, court, in the town's commercial district. On Monday afternoons, after the market ended, crowds would pour into the stadium to see some of the world's best players; the *frontón* had a seating capacity of almost one thousand. Even during the war, players managed to come here from abroad, for the Basque country was the home of the game.

The Silliacos paused to watch some local players having a friendly match. All four players were dressed in white. Each wore strapped to one hand the long, banana-shaped scoop used to sling the rock-hard ball against the stone floor and walls at speeds over a hundred miles an hour. Spectators were on the open, fourth side of the court, shielded by a heavy net curtain.

Father and son watched as the ball shot around the court like a bullet, alternately caught in a scoop and ricocheting off the floor and walls. Every man in the crowd seemed to be betting. As the game progressed, touts shouted and changed the odds on which pair of players would win.

The game over, the Silliacos continued walking. In the railway station plaza, the fireman saw refugees cooking over small open fires. They made him angry, and when he reached the Bar Catalán, where he worked, he gave vent to his feelings. "The time has come to sort out these refugees once and for all," he told some of the regulars.

Pedro asked his father not to be angry on this, their last day together, and Silliaco calmed down. Encouraged, Pedro asked whether, as a special treat, they could visit the caves of Santima-miñe. Silliaco hesitated. It was nearly four o'clock and the caves were over four miles away. But the pleading look in the boy's eyes persuaded him. Silliaco turned to one of the men at the bar, a farmer from Arteaga, a small village to the northeast of Guernica. The man agreed to give them a lift in his truck on his way home.

The caves had been discovered in 1916 by a group of boys. Later, archaeologists had arrived to investigate an apparently endless succession of interlinked caverns whose walls were covered with prehistoric drawings—bison, deer, horse, and bear, many of them in color. By April 1937, the first half-mile had been made safe for the public.

Inside, the Silliacos found themselves in total darkness, feeling their way down steep slippery stone steps. Silliaco held his son's hand. From below came echoing voices, magnified and hollow.

Abruptly they emerged into an enormous cavern lit by oil lamps, high and majestic, like the inside of a cathedral. From its hidden ceiling hung long, golden-colored, translucent stalactites. The steady dripping from these massive columns, the eerie lighting effects, the cavernous roof made Juan Silliaco and his son gasp in awe.

They walked along a narrow companionway with ropes on either side, toward the next large cavern. Water could be heard rushing past below them. They looked over the side of a low parapet: It was like peering down into a bottomless canyon.

Here Pedro decided he did not want to proceed farther. Silliaco could see his son was becoming frightened by the awesome spectacle nature had provided. As they retraced their steps, the boy asked his father why the men of the olden days had ever chosen to live in such a place. Juan Silliaco explained it was a sanctuary, offering both peace and safety. He nodded as his son added, "I know, a sort of *refugio.*"

Five hours after leaving the hospital in the Carmelite Convent, Teresa Ortuz was back on duty. In the morning she had gone home to find her mother and sisters out. Too tired to eat, she had fallen asleep on the sofa, and was awakened by an ambulance driver hammering on the front door. All off-duty personnel were being called in to help deal with the victims of the air attack near Marquina.

The clock inside the hospital entrance chimed four as Teresa hurried past. She arrived in the sterilization room as Mother Augusta was leading away a sobbing Carmen Batzar. The Superior explained the girl had just seen her fiancé among the wounded. He was now in the operating room.

Teresa liked Carmen. A few days earlier, she had contributed to a wedding gift for the couple from the hospital staff. She tried to comfort her, saying, "Captain Cortés is a good surgeon."

Just at that moment Cortés appeared, and told Mother Augusta to take Carmen away. "This isn't the place for hysterics." Then he snapped at Teresa, "The government doesn't pay you to waste your time out here. There's plenty of work to do."

He returned to the operating room.

Mother Augusta said Cortés had been operating for almost ten hours nonstop, and asked Teresa to be understanding.

Still angered by the surgeon's rebuke, Teresa scrubbed up. An orderly shook out her clean gown and cap. She raised her hands and worked the rubber gloves onto her fingers.

Dominguiz was in position on the table. Teresa heard Cortés mumble, "They bring them in half-dead and expect miracles."

She found her anger at Cortés subsiding. He was right. With the fighting coming closer, she said, the wounded would probably arrive sooner. The surgeon asked her if she had forgotten the dire state of their supplies. "Perhaps the Reverend Mother will pray for them to be delivered from heaven."

"Perhaps," suggested Teresa, "we should all pray."

While Cortés injected Dominguiz in the arm, Teresa hurried to the *poupinelle* to collect the sterilized trays containing scalpels, artery forceps, scissors, towel clips, clamps, needles, probes, glass gallipots, lint rolls, lintine packs, and dressing towels. She laid them out on the instrument trolley.

The anesthetist picked up the black Ombredan mask, a metal globe containing a rubber facepiece. In the mask, air was passed through the cloth soaked with ether. The anesthetist carefully measured out four ounces of ether, sufficient to keep Dominguiz "on the table" for two hours. Then, satisfied that the ether had saturated the cloth, the anesthetist placed the mask over Dominguiz's face and squeezed the rubber bladder attached to the mask, encouraging him to inhale.

While Dominguiz became more deeply unconscious, Captain Cortés was peeling away the field dressings, revealing injuries of the arm, leg, and abdomen. Next, he removed the head bandage. It had served its purpose: The lieutenant's hemorrhaging had stopped.

Cortés then exposed the leg vein, inserted a needle into it, joined the needle to a length of tubing that, in turn, he connected to a bottle of blood on a stand. He released the clamp on the tube and blood began to flow through it.

Cortés now swabbed the abdomen with a soapy solution, working steadily downward. When he held out a gloved hand, Teresa slipped a scalpel into his palm. Using the blunt end, he drew the scalpel tightly across Dominguiz's abdomen. A tiny trickle of fresh blood appeared, marking one of the classic cuts of war surgery, a large paramedian incision. Such long incisions were not usual in ordinary surgical practice; they left large scars. In Spain their use became commonplace.

Cortés now completed the cut, which gave him easy access to the entire abdomen. Working with care, he explored the ruptured tissue. Teresa placed one instrument after another in the surgeon's hands. Slowly Cortés scissored, clamped, and sutured to stop the internal bleeding. He would make no attempt at reparative surgery until he had stopped all hemorrhaging.

At last Cortés completed his exploration. He told the team around him his diagnosis: He did not think the damage irreparable.

Teresa breathed her relief. Cortés looked at her, then examined the scalp wound. He always examined all injuries before deciding on the order of repair. Dominguiz's scalp had been cut open by shrapnel, exposing splintered bone. But there was no bleeding. That decided the surgeon. He would begin on the abdomen.

All afternoon Antonio Arazamagni had shuttled back and forth along the road from Marquina to Guernica, bringing wounded soldiers to the hospital. A mile outside Guernica, his car finally ran out of gas.

Resignedly, the young baker walked back to the hospital and explained to the mechanic in the ambulance pool that he had spent his own "fuel, time, and money in the service of the government." The mechanic was unmoved.

Antonio then walked to the garage where he had orginally obtained his supply. The garage man listened sympathetically. But he, too, was unable to help—until the baker fell back on a familiar ploy.

"An extra pastry in the morning," offered Antonio.

"Free?" asked the garage man.

Antonio nodded. By four-thirty he was back at his car with a gallon can and was pouring the gas into the tank.

When he looked inside the car, he winced. The seats were covered with bloodstains. Then he remembered what he had read in a motoring magazine: The best way to remove stains from car seats was to wash them off with gasoline.

The baker headed his Ford in the direction of the garage, musing that if he were to be successful again, he would have to offer the owner more than mere pastries.

By 5:00 P.M., the last lesion had been repaired, the last bleeding point controlled, the last stitch knotted to close the abdomen of Juan Dominguiz. The bullet wounds in his arm and leg had also been attended to. There remained only the head wound to deal with.

Dominguiz was repositioned on the table. Using an ordinary straight razor, Cortés shaved the scalp. The area was washed with an antiseptic solution. At regular intervals the anesthetist confirmed Dominguiz's pulse rate.

Teresa looked with compassion at the young officer. Although still very handsome, he was scarred for life. She knew that if he survived the further shock to his body, it would be months before he would be able to leave the hospital. And then, she could not help wondering, what sort of husband would he be for Carmen Batzar? The surgery that Captain Cortés was about to perform could produce terrible aftereffects: paralysis, a permanent speech defect, perhaps blindness.

Forcing herself to remain calm, Teresa gathered together the additional equipment Cortés might need: a brace, burr and perforator, surgical hammer, and cold chisel. She added bone-nibbling forceps, sets of retractors for peeling back the scalp from the bone, and long, finely pointed scissors for cutting the dura mater, the membrane covering the brain.

The surgeon injected a local anesthetic near the wound area; the skin bubbled up from the effect of the drug. The anesthetic would act to reduce hemorrhaging.

"Irrigation."

Teresa handed Cortés a syringe and he gently squirted the operation area clean. There was no fresh bleeding. Cortés cut around the wound. Regularly, the surgeon turned to a metal basin mounted on a stand and washed his gloved hands in antiseptic solution. He found it easier to work with his rubber gloves damp; they clung better to his hands and gave more sensitivity to his fingers.

Soon he had retracted a bone flap, which he then hinged back from the scalp. Teresa handed Cortés the pads she had soaked in a strong antiseptic solution. He covered the flap with the pads.

The surgical team looked at the dura mater. It had been ruptured.

Cortés asked for a tenotome. Teresa handed him the small scalpel with its finely honed blade. The surgeon nicked a corner of the membrane. He asked for scissors. With infinite care he slipped a point of the scissors into the cut and started to clip, fraction by fraction, a section of the membranous covering, exposing the brain. It was a healthy color.

"Irrigation."

Teresa handed him a syringe. Cortés gently washed the brain, at the same time using a rubber catheter to suck away the minute particles of bone lodged in the tissue. Twenty minutes passed before he was satisfied he had removed the last splinter. After a further twenty minutes, all the bleeding points were sealed off.

Cortés turned to the anesthetist, who nodded. Dominguiz was continuing to withstand the shock to his nervous system.

Cortés carefully replaced the dura mater over the brain.

"Stitch."

Teresa handed him a small needle. The surgeon sewed a tiny fragment of the membrane, tying the stitch with a neat knot. He called for a new needle. After each tie he inspected his handiwork, looking for any signs of stress. There were none. Fifteen minutes later, the last suture was in place.

"Forceps."

Teresa passed Cortés the long-handled instrument. With it he removed the pads covering the bone flap and lowered it back in place. Then he replaced the scalp.

Teresa gave Cortés the needle specially designed for sewing

scalp tissue and once again the surgeon began stitching. Finally, all that remained to show that Juan Dominguiz had undergone brain surgery was a thin reddish-pink line that curved around the side of his head. That, too, was soon hidden beneath a head dressing.

For Captain Cortés the operation was the last this Sunday. Alone, he went to his office to write up the day's case notes. While he was writing, Mother Augusta arrived with Carmen Batzar, and for the first time Cortés learned who his last patient had been. He assured them everything possible had been done. He added that the fate of Juan Dominguiz was now "in the hands of God and the nursing staff."

Dominguiz was moved to a recovery ward. Carmen was allowed to stay by his bed for a while; then Mother Augusta led her away.

In the operating room, Teresa was already working beside another surgeon who had come on duty at 6:00 P.M.

6:00 P.M.—Midnight

•14•

Von Richthofen completed the seventy-five-mile drive from Vitoria to Burgos airfield in the same number of minutes.

The Condor Legion's main bomber base was a camouflaged, orderly world of almost two thousand ground and air crew who serviced and flew the three squadrons of Junkers-52 bombers, the experimental squadron of new Heinkel-111s, and a miscellany of other aircraft.

From behind the main office block came the sound of airplane engines. The chief of staff had timed his arrival perfectly. The first Heinkel, its bombs slung under the wings, was just taking off for the attack on Bilbao. Even though he could not recognize the pilot, Von Richthofen knew who it was. Only First Lieutenant Rudolf von Moreau had the skill and the daring to take a fully laden twin-engine bomber into the air as if it were a single-engine fighter.

By the time the other pilots were in the air, Von Moreau had disappeared into cloud. Von Richthofen guessed the young Bavarian was circling impatiently, waiting for them to join him. Then, in a series of "chains"—three aircraft to a chain, each chain separated by half a mile of airspace—the squadron would head for Bilbao.

After the last Heinkel was gone from sight, Von Richthofen drove back to the office. Major Fuchs, the wing commander, was waiting for him at the main door, map case clutched under his arm, forage cap set squarely on his shock of black hair. Fuchs saluted,

117

climbed into the front passenger seat, and the two men headed for the center of Burgos.

As they drove, Fuchs briefed Von Richthofen on the meeting ahead. Fuchs was directly responsible for ordering the Legion's aircraft into the air and giving the squadron leaders their instructions. He was barely thirty; yet with his studied speech and careful mannerisms he contrived to look far older.

The meeting was to be a full gathering of senior Nationalist commanders in the north. Von Richthofen disliked these occasions with their undertones of jealousy, opportunism, and back-stabbing. At the last meeting, the Italian air commander, General Velani, had made ridiculous claims about the bombing skills of his pilots. In fact, the Italians were so inaccurate they had even bombed their own lines.

Von Richthofen had kept silent as Velani spoke, because he was anxious not to disrupt the already strained relationships among the various Nationalist commanders. The slow progress of the northern campaign had exacerbated that strain. But the chief of staff knew he could not remain quiet this evening if Velani indulged in more boasting.

Nor would Von Richthofen mince words about the way the Spanish were conducting the ground campaign. Three weeks earlier, there had been a "fearful row" when Commander in Chief Sperrle had castigated General Mola for the tardiness with which his Spanish troops followed up attacks by the Legion. Mola had replied that the German fliers were "not exactly suited for this sort of action."

Sperrle had erupted. He was a huge man—he stood six feet six in his boots and weighed over 250 pounds—and his angry voice had reverberated around Mola's headquarters. Unless things improved, he had said, he would take the Legion elsewhere in Spain. In a towering rage he had gone to Salamanca and told Commander in Chief Franco how little he thought of the Nationalist troops in the north and their leadership. Franco, used to dealing with temperamental Spanish subordinates, had successfully calmed Sperrle.

That had been early in April. Now, three weeks later, Von Richthofen did not believe matters had improved much. There was still "too little follow-up by the Spanish to the opportunities the Legion creates," he later wrote.

The narrow roads around Burgos Cathedral were jam-packed with hundreds of people enjoying an evening stroll. It took Von Richthofen far longer than he had intended to reach the three-storied Town Hall. The clock on the tower guarding the entrance showed almost six-thirty. Moments later, Von Richthofen and Fuchs were climbing the stairs to the second-floor conference room.

Waiting at the top of the stairs was Colonel Juan Vigón, a small, wizened man well into middle age. On his head he wore a black Basque beret with three burnished stars, his only badge of rank on a drab khaki uniform. Vigón took off his beret and smiled to reveal decaying, uneven teeth. With his scrawny neck, hands pocked with liver spots, and eyes magnified by powerful steel-rimmed spectacles, Vigón looked what he had once been: a private tutor to some of the children of Europe's lesser nobility.

Vigón was now chief of staff to General Mola, the Spanish commander in the north. He was one of the very few Spaniards whom Von Richthofen liked, trusted, and even admired. In one of his confidential reports to Berlin, Von Richthofen had described Vigón as "streets above the mass of his countrymen as regards sense of duty, willpower, decisiveness, and dedication."

As they greeted each other, Vigón and Von Richthofen solemnly shook hands—a custom the German insisted on, even though they now met several times a week. Then the Spaniard solicitously inquired about Von Richthofen's health and his drive from Vitoria. He virtually ignored Fuchs. The wing commander, trailing behind with the Spanish aides and escorting officers, regarded Vigón as an affected snob.

Some Spanish officers saw Vigón as a harsh disciplinarian who publicly rebuked senior commanders in that reedy voice they had come to hate. Periodically, he took personal command in battle —and the enlisted men responded immediately to the sight of this wrinkled gnome galloping along the front, urging them on. The Moors idolized Vigón. He was reported to have told them that as long as they fought well, they were entitled to the spoils of war.

Von Richthofen was the better military tactician, Vigón the

superior political thinker. Together, they formed a formidable team. But the bond that linked them was their common belief that the enemy should be pursued without letup, shown neither mercy nor remorse.

Midway along the blue-carpeted corridor, the officers turned in to the conference room. It was dominated by a long, highly polished oak table surrounded by carved, high-backed chairs; the furniture had been specially brought from one of King Alfonso's palaces. Heavy chandeliers lit the table even though the evening sun still shone into the room.

Von Richthofen took his usual place to the right of Vigón, who sat at the head of the table. Across from him, General Velani, the Italian air force commander, sat bolt upright in his chair, dressed in the most splendid uniform in the room. Rumor had it that Velani's servant spent an hour a day polishing his master's boots. Around the rest of the table were the officers who guided the Nationalist war machine in the north. With relief, Von Richthofen saw that General Mola's customary seat was vacant. Theirs was another of the personality conflicts that beset the Nationalist command.

Vigón explained to the meeting that Mola was in Salamanca to discuss the war situation with Franco. Then smoothly, like a teacher questioning pupils, he asked the Spanish field commanders to report on conditions on their fronts. Each officer gave a lengthy dissertation. When Von Richthofen's turn came, he said with emphasis, "The Reds have broken. There is a twenty-five-kilometer gap in their lines. I suggest we consider how best to exploit that situation."

Vigón called for maps. The gap Von Richthofen had referred to was just east of Marquina, the area the Legion had bombed earlier that day.

General Velani was the first to break the silence. He would like it written into the minutes of the meeting that "this very afternoon Italian aircraft attacked the region with great success."

Von Richthofen demanded to know whether the Italians were claiming total responsibility for the enemy rout.

Vigón interceded. He told the minute writer to note that "today our German allies launched a concentrated air attack in the Marquina area, which our Italian allies followed up to good effect."

Then, having shown his skill in diplomacy, Vigón, once more coldly professional, put questions to the Spanish officers about Nationalist and Republican troop movements.

Von Richthofen tried again. In fluent Spanish, a language he knew Velani still had difficulty with, he asked the commander of the Navarre Division exactly what was being done to exploit the air success around Marquina.

Flushing, the Spanish general began to recite arguments familiar to Von Richthofen: The terrain was difficult; there was no need for a "frenetic pursuit of the enemy when slow and gradual pressure would produce successful results"; in any case, it was "unreasonable" to expect "too much of attacking troops."

Von Richthofen pounced. "Nothing is unreasonable that can further destroy enemy morale, and quickly. It is already crumbling because of the air attack. It is essential that every effort be made on the ground to complete the collapse."

Looking directly at the Spanish brigade commanders, he continued, "The infantry must not rely on the air force and artillery to create favorable situations. They must pursue their own attacks with all energy and toughness, forcing their own openings. The infantry must have the intention to harass the enemy and to pursue him, making his life absolute hell."

An uncomfortable silence settled over the room. Vigón let it stretch, as if to emphasize the importance of what had been said. Then, blinking owlishly, Vigón looked at the Navarre brigade commanders. One after the other they agreed to pursue the enemy through the Marquina gap.

Satisfied, Vigón invited them all to study their maps once more. Then he said simply, "Gentlemen, I think it clear enough what next has to be discussed." Later, Von Richthofen would say that the situation "was so obvious that even a first-year student at a war academy would have spotted what had to be done."

Nevertheless, General Velani had a question: Were Guernica and its environs defended?

Vigón looked expectantly around the table. Nobody could provide the answer.

Von Richthofen said it did not matter what defenses there were.

The Condor Legion would still attack. It was, he added, essential that the retreat of the Republican troops be delayed, if not halted, at the funnel leading into Guernica.

Another silence ensued as all of them examined their maps again, studying where the roads from the east joined at the junction by the bridge.

"The question is, When to attack?" said Vigón.

One of the Spanish generals argued that the attack should begin immediately.

Von Richthofen disagreed. That would mean a night attack over hazardous and unfamiliar territory against a target difficult to identify in the darkness.

"My fliers would be willing to undertake such an operation," said Velani.

Von Richthofen argued fluently, listing other tactical objections against a night attack. "For all we know, the enemy could have crossed into Guernica already. In that case we need the roads leading into the town intact, so that our troops can puruse them on the ground. Equally, if the enemy has not yet entered Guernica, and we now destroy or obstruct their means of entry, they would have time to regroup and find some other way of falling back to Bilbao before our troops can catch them. I believe we should postpone any decision to attack until the morning. Then we will have the benefit of the latest air reconnaissance."

Vigón agreed.

Velani had one further question: Who would actually make the attack?

Vigón saw the pitfall. Although the Italian air force had not enhanced its reputation during the northern campaign, to deny them an active role in the war would lead to serious problems with Mussolini. Choosing his words carefully, Vigón said that the Germans would attack first, and "if necessary, the Italian air force can also join in."

Von Richthofen knew that would not be necessary. By the time his bombers had finished, the escape route for the Basques would be pounded to rubble.

Finally Vigón closed the gathering. Not once had he, or anybody else in the room, referred to the fact that the road intersection and bridge they planned to attack were close to one of the most historic towns in all Spain.

As the men left the conference, Fuchs said to Von Richthofen, "Such a target is never easy."

Von Richthofen nodded, remembering that on previous occasions the Legion had failed in its attempts to knock out bridges. Then he brightened. With quiet confidence he told Fuchs, "Use Von Moreau to lead the attack."

Seventy miles to the north and nearly 9,000 feet above Bilbao, First Lieutenant Rudolf von Moreau gazed in fascination at the spectacle below him. Industrial areas on either side of the River Nervión were covered with a steadily spreading screen of smoke. At irregular intervals, reddish patches glowed and flared, marking the spots where 550-pound bombs had fallen.

Flying across the city on his second run, Von Moreau banked his new Heinkel-111 bomber, No. 25-3, high over the great park of Doña Casilda de Iturriza. Behind him, to the east, the last Heinkel was coming in on its bombing run. Its bombardier was Von Moreau's closest colleague, Count Max Hoyos. Following the course of the Nervión, the Heinkel made its final approach to the docks.

The squadron leader lost sight of the plane as he took his own Heinkel at 180 mph across Bilbao. Over the railway station at Amezola, Von Moreau banked to the east, heading back for the narrower upper reaches of the Nervión. In another minute he had completed a full circle over the city.

Von Moreau's eyes scanned the skies for enemy fighters. Just a week earlier one of his Dornier-17 bombers had been shot down by the most famous Republican pilot on the northern front, twenty-one-year-old Felipe del Río. The loss had severely damaged the Legion's reputation and had even caused questions to be asked in Berlin.

Von Moreau could not know that Del Río himself had been shot down two days later over Bilbao by his own antiaircraft defenses.

Now, without Del Río, the Republican fliers, vastly outnumbered by the Condor Legion, their few planes inferior to the recently arrived Heinkels, refused to fly.

Von Moreau always flew on the basis that "any second we might be jumped." He craned his neck to look back through the cockpit window but saw no enemy aircraft. To the west he could see Hoyos's Heinkel climbing away from the docks to the safety of stratocumulus.

Satisfied that all his aircraft were now safely behind the shelter of cloud, Von Moreau pushed the steering column forward and his plane swooped down toward the river. At the end of every raid he carried out his "farewell look-see" of a target; it had become almost a trademark, a sign to those on the ground that it was the legendary Von Moreau who had bombed them.

He could just make out tiny figures on the decks of ships; some of the old coal-burners were sending up shafts of smoke that almost reached the low-flying Heinkel.

From Iturriza Park, reddish-yellow, winking lights also climbed to meet the aircraft. Von Moreau felt the controls shudder as the ack-ack shells began to explode around him. A near miss tilted his starboard wing downward. Instinctively he allowed the bomber to slip sideways through the sky, across the city, and out of range of the antiaircraft battery.

Over Bilbao's main plaza he banked, then, using the Gran Vía as a rough-and-ready navigation aid, he climbed swiftly toward the marshaling yards of the Estación del Norte. There he again reached cloud cover—wet, cold, and comforting to Von Moreau and his crew of three. They could see nothing. Nobody could see them.

A mile or so south of the city, the Heinkel emerged into the evening sun. Over several square miles of sky, Von Moreau could see his squadron orbiting around the map reference point he had earlier given each pilot.

Far below, out of range, he could distinguish Bilbao's "ring of iron." From 12,000 feet it looked like no more than a jagged scar curving across valleys and hillsides. Von Moreau knew that on some of the peaks were antiaircraft guns. But his bombers were too high for them.

Inside the "ring" was the industrial center of Galdacano, which was also the Basque military GHQ. The night before, a Junkers-52 squadron had attacked the dynamite factory there. The object of the raid was psychological. It was hoped that the noise of the exploding dynamite would terrify the people of Bilbao—which it did.

The raid was also in keeping with Mola's curious belief that Spain was overindustrialized; he had asked Von Richthofen to use the Legion to destroy "at least half of Bilbao's factories for the future good health of the Spanish nation."

Von Moreau had welcomed this opportunity for bombing practice.

Now, another mission almost over, he relaxed, studying the country below: high mountains and short valleys intersected by rivers; inaccessible, primitive, but rich in wild vegetation. It reminded him of home, the Black Forest of Bavaria.

Almost a year had passed since he had last seen the Schwarzwald. During that time Von Moreau had become even more famous on the Nationalist side than Del Río on the Republican.

Von Moreau had arrived in Spain by ship from Germany on August 7, 1936, only three weeks after the war began. It was he who had first commanded the Junkers-52 squadron that had ferried Franco's Moroccan troops to Spain. Although he was known in Germany for his record-breaking flights from Berlin to Tokyo and New York, his reputation in Spain was mainly founded in the dawn of August 21, 1936, when he had flown a Junkers-52 over enemy lines at Toledo to reach the besieged Alcázar fortress, where Franco's troops were on the point of being starved into surrender.

He had brought the bomber down to parapet level over the Alcázar. Fifty feet below, he could see the Republicans camped at the foot of the fortress, too stunned to shoot at him. Flying between the four towers of the Alcázar, he had dropped food containers into the inner courtyard, merely sixty yards square. It was a feat, said one of his colleagues, "the equivalent of sprinting a hundred meters and dropping a pebble onto a postage stamp somewhere along the track." And it was a feat that Von Moreau repeated.

Within weeks he had carved himself a permanent niche in the air annals of Spain. If any target required daring combined with precision bombing, he was chosen for the job. Legend had it that no objective, however small or well defended, was safe when Von Moreau was in the pilot's seat.

He did not deny the stories; he enjoyed the fame. By the end of 1936, at age twenty-four, Von Moreau was the most experienced bomber pilot in Spain. Early in 1937 Von Richthofen appointed him commander of the experimental bomber squadron, made up of Heinkel-111s, Dornier-17s, and four Junker-86s, which had just arrived from Germany.

Von Moreau's task as leader of this special squadron was "to perform test and trial operations of various kinds against various objectives." This meant he could attack a target in any manner he chose—he could bomb from high altitudes, dive-bomb, launch a low-level attack. In the air he was answerable to no one; on the ground only Von Richthofen could challenge his decision.

For the moment there was no more action. Von Moreau told his radio operator to transmit orders to the other aircraft to form up for the return flight.

At 7:50 P.M., the telephone linking Vitoria with the bomber base at Burgos rang in the operations room in the Frontón Hotel. Captain Gautlitz took the call, listened, and replaced the receiver. "They're on the way home," he said.

The news was greeted with broad smiles by many of the operations room staff. Now they were free to patronize the Legion's brothel, drink in one of Vitoria's dozens of bars, visit one of the town's cinemas, or simply sit around and gossip in the hotel.

Lieutenant Hans Asmus intended to do none of these things. In the past week he had been improving his Spanish with the help of a delectable local girl. They would sit together in a coffeehouse, and he would repeat after her, sentence by sentence, "the words of the most beautiful language I had ever heard."

Asmus was one of the few Germans still trying to learn Spanish. Most of the Legionnaires had come north expecting to be welcomed as liberators, as they were in southern Spain. Instead, here at Vitoria they frequently found themselves looked on as conquerors. The cause, Asmus believed, was the attitude of the local priests: "Many of them were militants. They painted totally wrong pictures of us."

Now, as he tidied up the files and maps, Asmus wondered how long it would be before some priest warned his girl she should not be seen with him in public. Her friendship had made his off-duty hours bearable, helping him to forget that the mail service to and from Germany was poor, that censorship was strictly enforced, that the food was often inedible, that lice thrived in his tick mattress even though he sprayed it daily.

As long as he could go on seeing his Spanish friend, Asmus was not unduly worried about going home. He was earning more in Spain than he could have hoped to earn had he stayed in Germany, and he was banking most of his salary. He was popular with his colleagues. There was only one thing he wanted: to return to flying duties. At the first opportune moment he intended to ask Von Richthofen to transfer him back to a squadron.

·15·

In Guernica the clock of Santa María struck 8:00 P.M. Father Iturran lowered his Bible and looked toward the presbytery window. From the direction of the main square he could hear the low notes of the *txistu*, a Basque flute, playing a melancholy melody.

The memories of the past few hours filled his mind. Leaving his assistant priest to attend to the church, Father Iturran had pondered all afternoon whether he was right to preach as he had. He remembered the shock and fear his words had produced. At first he had been satisfied with this reaction. Later, he wondered. Should he have ascertained conditions in Bilbao before urging a mass exodus there? Should he have checked with the bishop of Bilbao before he had spoken?

In the early evening there had been a knock on his door by the mayor, José Labauría. Father Iturran had invited him in. Labauría would come no farther than the whitewashed entrance hall. In his black suit, the mayor had delivered a protest. The sermon, he said, had done a disservice to the community.

Father Iturran had warmly told Labauría to "remember you are talking to your parish priest. Only my bishop can challenge my word. And I do not believe you are yet bishop of Bilbao." He had thrown open the presbytery door and motioned the mayor to leave.

Labauría's attitude convinced the priest he had, after all, been right to speak out that morning. He regarded the mayor as "a weak man, ready to do nothing at every opportunity."

After Labauría's departure, Father Iturran prayed and read his Bible. The scriptural certainty of the Old Testament gave him comfort until the clock, striking eight, broke his concentration.

Now Father Iturran recognized the distinctive way the *txistu* was being played. Only one person could play so well—Javier Gardoqui, a fourteen-year-old altar boy at Santa María Church.

Then, as he listened, came the sound of a second *txistu*, and a third, each flautist providing his own improvisation, yet uniting with the others to build up the theme. The flutes were joined by a *txalaparta*, a tomtom. Next came the crash of tambourines. Finally, loud and harsh, came the brass section, dominated by the deep lowing of a euphonium.

Guernica's town band was warming up for the regular Sunday night dance in the main plaza.

Putting aside the Bible, Father Iturran walked to the window. Across in the Plaza Las Escuelas he could see hundreds of people congregating under strings of colored electric bulbs festooned through trees.

He had failed. His sermon had gone unheeded.

He was about to turn away when a new sight stopped him. From his window he had an excellent view down the Calle Santa María. Coming toward him, just passing the *refugio* in the middle of the road, was a throng of soldiers.

The old priest watched them trudging up the hill. When they reached the presbytery he opened a window and called out to ask who they were and where they had come from.

One of the soldiers looked up at him and said, "We're from the front. Can we sleep in your church?"

Father Iturran was too astonished by the question to answer immediately. By the time he had replied that they could "rest and pray" in Santa María, the small group had disappeared from his view.

From the square the sound of music grew louder and gayer. It was, the priest would later write, "like being in Sodom. The war was on our very doorstep and people were still dancing."

For a moment longer he stood at the window, looking out. Then he made his decision: If he could not save the people, he could at least salvage the holy relics in his church. But he would need help to move them to safety.

Father Iturran left the presbytery. Outside, he unhitched his donkey. Hoisting up his cassock, he climbed on to the barebacked animal and spurred it forward with his heels. At a steady clip he jogged down Calle Santa María, squeezing past the air-raid shelter, and crossed the Rentería Bridge.

He took the track that led to the Convent of La Merced.

Although farm boy Juan Plaza had yawned at the beginning of Father Iturran's sermon, this evening he was convinced that, if anything, the priest had understated the danger. For the past two hours, sixteen-year-old Juan had been shuffling back and forth across the dusty square in front of the Convent of La Merced, eavesdropping on the hundreds of soldiers milling around. The snatches of conversation he had heard made Juan "tingle and tremble with fear." Nearly forty years later, he would remember the soldiers' words with anger: villages wiped out, women and children murdered; mass graves, pits, and trenches; the lines of bodies nobody bothered to bury; the chilling testimony to the systematic extermination of "political prisoners."

The Plaza family farmed a small holding two miles outside Guernica. Theirs was a hard, unremitting existence with little to break the monotony of tilling and sowing and reaping from one year to the next. On Sundays, the family walked to Mass at Santa María Church. On Mondays, Juan rode with his father to market to sell their produce. Nowadays, the income barely provided the basics of life.

That afternoon Juan had sat on his farmhouse gate and watched the ambulances careening down the road from Marquina. The diversion was so welcome it hardly occurred to him they carried wounded men. He had been surprised to see Antonio Arazamagni's car among the ambulances, the baker seated importantly behind the wheel. Juan had waved. Antonio had not returned the greeting.

Shortly after 5:00 P.M., a line of soldiers had crossed his father's fields, disturbing the farm's herd of four cows. By the chicken run, the soldiers had halted. One of them asked Juan whether he had seen any airplanes. Puzzled, the boy said he hadn't. The soldiers had moved onto the road and formed up in marching order. One of them had produced a bugle and begun to play the "Hymn of the Republic." As they trudged down the road, the soldiers had sung along with such sincerity that the anthem took on a meaning Juan had never before felt.

Impulsively, Juan had tagged along behind them. At six o'clock they had reached the square in front of the convent. As more soldiers arrived, many slightly wounded, some on makeshift crutches, all unshaven and dirty, a feeling of doom had gradually settled over the square.

Even to Juan Plaza, untutored in the ways of the military, "these soldiers smelled of defeat. I was ashamed of them."

Now, shortly after eight o'clock, the boy was edging out of the square. Suddenly a few yards from him, the main convent door was thrown open. Standing in the doorway was a young lieutenant, pistol on hip, cap at a rakish angle.

"*Silencio!*"

Twice more Juan heard the officer shout before an uneasy silence came over the troops.

Speaking slowly, emphasizing every word, the officer began. "I am Lieutenant Gandaría. This is Loyola Battalion headquarters. And you are supposed to be in the Army."

The contempt in his voice carried to all corners of the square.

"Smarten yourselves up. Stand to attention when an officer speaks to you."

Juan could see that many of the men around him were uneasily straightening.

Gandaría continued, "The retreat stops here! You are paid to fight. Every one of you. No more running. No more hiding. By God, each one of you is going to fight!"

Juan heard muttering from some of the soldiers.

He watched as the lieutenant removed his pistol from its holster. Tapping the butt against the palm of his hand, the officer warned he would shoot any man who gave the first hint of insubordination—or cowardice.

The murmuring stopped.

Gandaría ordered the soldiers to form into platoons. All those without rifles were to fall out before him, and they had "better have good reasons for not having guns," he added grimly.

With much shuffling, the troops sorted themselves out into units. Juan found himself standing alone.

Gandaría looked down at him. "You, boy. Do you know the field beside the cemetery?"

Juan nodded.

"Then take these platoons there." Gandaría indicated two squads of men.

Juan didn't hesitate. His sense of shame was replaced by a new pride. He would always remember his feeling that "with men like Lieutenant Gandaría we could still win."

Chanting the words of the "Hymn of the Republic," he led the soldiers out of the square. Behind him, in growing strength, men took up the refrain.

Father Iturran spurred his donkey toward the convent door, where Lieutenant Gandaría still shouted orders.

"My son," the priest said, "I wish to speak to you."

Gandaría gave no sign of having heard. He continued to issue orders. Raising his voice, Father Iturran added, "It is a matter of some urgency and importance that we must speak about."

The lieutenant paused and looked quickly at the old priest. Then he motioned for Father Iturran to follow him into the convent. In silence the two men walked down the central passageway to a small office, bare except for a desk and two chairs.

As soon as they were seated, Father Iturran spoke. "I need your help. I want soldiers and a truck or two."

Gandaría smiled. "Father," he asked, "are you intending to start your own war?"

The priest shook his head. In a quiet, matter-of-fact voice he explained his request. He concluded, "I cannot move the church to safety. But I can save its contents. Some of the relics are priceless."

Gandaría rose to his feet. "How thick are the walls of the church?" he asked.

Puzzled, Father Iturran replied he thought they were at least three feet thick.

Gandaría nodded. Then he spoke flatly. "Father, my only concern with your church is this: If we are attacked, I will have to use it as a defensive position. Those walls could withstand even heavy shells."

Father Iturran shot to his feet. Attempting to control his rage, the priest cried out, "It is my church you are talking about, my church—"

Gandaría continued from where he had been interrupted. If the town were attacked, the church, "by its very position," would be doomed. The Nationalists would undoubtedly shell it, as they had shelled other churches. Far more important than safeguarding religious relics was the necessity of preparing the Church of Santa María as a defensive post. As such, it was without equal in Guernica. Apart from the church's thick walls, its windows would command a field of fire that could halt an enemy advance for many hours, perhaps even days. In the interests of Guernica and of Basque freedom, the church should be readied now.

"Father," the young officer urged, "the Fascists are coming. Be sure of that. We must do everything to stop them."

Trembling, Father Iturran pointed out there were other strongly built buildings in the town.

Gandaría promised they would also be used. "I will take any building, big or small, that can be adapted to delay the enemy."

The priest stared unbelievingly at the officer. "My son, you are a Catholic, of course."

Gandaría shrugged. "In name only."

"But even so, you wish to destroy my church?"

"No, Father. To make good use of it to protect other churches in Bilbao and elsewhere from being destroyed." Gandaría leaned across the desk. "The enemy, Father, is now only a few miles from here. Your church has only a matter of days. It is better it is prepared—"

"Never!"

Gandaría and Father Iturran stared at each other. Then both looked toward the open door. From beyond, in the convent chapel, came the sound of singing. *Las Mercedarias* were ending their day with Matins.

"My son, you will be damned forever if you touch the church," said Father Iturran.

Slowly, the old priest walked from the office. In the corridor he paused, listening to the singing. He had far from given up his fight to save the Church of Santa María.

Every night at eight-thirty, one of the nuns in the Convent of Santa Clara unlocked the outside door of an antechapel so that it could be entered from the alley beyond the door. Then the nun lit a votive candle and retired back into the main cloisters.

Inside the chapel, close to the statue of Our Lady of Peace, she had left a silver tray. Down the years on that tray had been placed hundreds of messages asking for the special prayers of the Sisters of Penance.

Many of the requests were written on cheap lined paper; a few were penned on expensive embossed cards. Prayers were asked for the sick, the dying, for sinners and penitents, for men and women burdened with anxiety and sorrow. Spinsters asked for prayers to find a husband. Children prayed for an ailing mother. Recently, there had been many prayers to bring husbands, fathers, and brothers safely back from the war.

Every night, for an hour, the chapel was open to receive these messages. Later they would be divided among the nuns, who would read the requests and, in answer to them, pray during the coming days.

Tonight, minutes after the street door was unlocked, Carmen Batzar lifted the outside latch and stepped into the tiny chapel. From beyond, somewhere in the cloisters, she could hear Matins being sung. With a deep genuflexion, Carmen paused before Our Lady of Peace. Then she placed a folded note on the tray. Inside she had written: "Your prayers are asked for Juan, gravely wounded in the cause of God."

Carmen hurried from the chapel, anxious to return to her fiancé's bedside. She was too preoccupied to give more than a glance to the soldiers she passed, standing around the entrance to the convent. She was some way down the street before an instinct made her stop and turn around. The soldiers were no longer to be seen.

Briefly she wondered where they had gone. Then she walked on—never guessing that the troops had done something no man had dared for more than three hundred years.

They had gone into the nuns' cloisters.

In quickstep, Juan Plaza led his column of soldiers over the Rentería Bridge, across the railway line, and then wheeled left into the long, cobbled Calle Don Tello.

Seeing the many bars and cafés in the street, some of the soldiers broke ranks. There were angry complaints from those who continued to march. Refugees thronging the sidewalk joined in jeering at the men who left the column. Fists flew, but trouble was averted by the NCOs in the group. They rounded up as many of the defectors as they could and forced them back into line.

Even so, the column lost almost a third of its original complement.

Peering down from his apartment window on Calle de la Estación, José Rodríguez thought they looked like "a column of lunatics chanting like dervishes."

Rodríguez turned in disgust from the window. The soldiers were a reminder that time was running out, the war now "only a bullet shot away."

It was not bullets but the prospect of bombs that most disturbed Rodríguez. Since Rufino Unceta had first raised the possibility that the Germans might be unaware of the factory's loyalty and importance to the Nationalist cause, Rodríguez had spent many hours pondering how to protect it from an air attack. Each scheme he thought of had to be rejected because there was neither time nor equipment to implement it. He had been forced to return to his original plan of removing vital machine parts "and trusting in God that in the event of an air attack the factory would be missed."

Rodríguez peered down into the street. The marching column had now almost crossed the railway plaza; the tail enders were still "cavorting about." If only, thought Rodríguez, he could make the troops guarding the armaments complex show such a lack of discipline. It was going to be very difficult for him to smuggle the machine parts out of the factory under the watchful eyes of Lieutenant Gandaría.

The soldiers were dancing to the music they could hear coming from the Plaza Las Escuelas, some two hundred yards away. Encouraged by Juan, the soldiers filled the night with raucous singing.

As they passed the Unceta complex, Juan proudly explained, "This is where we make guns to kill Franco's Fascists." As the word was passed down the column, the singing died away and the men became uneasy.

Juan could not understand what made them so nervous.

The bells of Santa María were tolling nine o'clock when Rufino Unceta completed his customary evening stroll. He, too, had been preoccupied with thoughts of how to save his factory. The sight of the column of troops led by a boy puzzled him. The road they were taking led to the cemetery, on the southern outskirts of the town.

He hurried to catch up with them. In response to his question, one of the soldiers told him they were going to form a new front line.

"Where?"

The soldier nodded toward the hills west of the town, in the direction of Bilbao.

Rufino Unceta turned away. If the soldier was right, then the new Republican line would be somewhere behind Guernica. In that case, the Basque forces were probably going to abandon the town. With growing excitement Unceta realized the Nationalists might occupy the town without firing a shot.

Unceta decided to prolong his walk to see what further signs of activity he could find. Briskly, he strode up the hill toward the Parliament Building. Another group of soldiers was marching toward him. He watched as they, too, took the narrow road toward Guernica's cemetery.

The Parliament Building was in darkness; the tall iron gates in the high, railed fence surrounding the building and its gardens were locked.

Behind the gardens, at the rear of the Parliament Building, rose the Convent of Santa Clara. Ordinarily, at this time of night, its windows would also be in darkness. Tonight, lights burned in the upper rooms of the convent. And in those rooms Rufino Unceta saw something that sent his hopes crashing.

Framed in the windows were soldiers.

A few of them, acting as lookouts, had rifles; two were stationed in the belfry. No matter how far back the front line would extend behind the town, Rufino Unceta now knew one thing: The Convent of Santa Clara had become part of the latest Republican defenses.

Stunned, Unceta turned and walked back down the hill.

On her way to the dance in the main square, María Ortuza would never have looked up if one of the soldiers had not softly called down to her. The vision of a bearded man hanging out of a window of the Convent of Santa Clara was too much for María. With a shriek she ran down the road. She was still running when she reached the Plaza Las Escuelas, where the dance was in full swing. Calming herself, she looked for somebody in whom she could confide what she had just seen.

Isidro Arrién was taking his usual Sunday night stroll in the town, keeping an eye on the fare Guernica's other restaurants were offering.

Tonight, as usual, he had no need to fear the competition. The menu of the Julián Hotel was reduced to one course—a stew. The Taberna Vasca, the Arrién's main competitor, was also offering modest food and a dubious ersatz beer sent up from Bilbao.

Near the Taberna, new slogans had been pasted up on the walls:

DO NOT WASTE BREAD. IT HELPS THE ENEMY.

OUR CHILDREN NEED BREAD. DO NOT WASTE IT.

There were other indications of austerity. Few of the bars offered the Basques' traditional open sandwiches of sardines and pimientos. Coffee brewed from burned barley cost 50 céntimos a cup—almost a day's salary for some workmen. Wine, anisette, and vermouth were all watered. Tobacco was scarce; those who smoked the weekly ration of twenty cigarettes complained the butts tasted of cow dung. For Isidro, the most telling sign of all was the increasing number of homeless dogs, cast out by their owners to roam the streets, their ribs stark against the skin. He knew that some of the town's butchers passed off small dogs as rabbits and larger ones as lambs.

Tonight, as he headed back to his restaurant, Isidro estimated he would be able to continue only one more week before the deficiencies of his larder became obvious. Although he could prolong the situation by introducing cuts now, that would not be in keeping with his policy of offering the most varied menu in Vizcaya. It was better to go out in style, he had told his wife, than to "linger on, counting every chick-pea in every bowl of soup."

Isidro paused to listen to the band. It was playing, loudly but not very well, a medley of tunes that the bandleader had introduced as "a tribute to the foreign soldiers who have come to Spain to support the struggle." The titles sounded strange to Isidro: "Popeye the Sailor Man" and "The Music Goes Round and Round."

He turned away and found himself face-to-face with María Ortuza. He knew her slightly; they often nodded at each other in the early hours of market days when both were after bargains.

Now, she was flushed and breathless. He assumed she had been dancing. She spoke to him. But with the music and the noise of the large crowd, he could not quite understand what she was saying.

In such a situation, Isidro fell back on a trick he had learned early in the restaurant business. He nodded sympathetically and said he entirely agreed. Then he excused himself and walked away. But the more he thought about it, the surer he was that he had misunderstood María. He knew her as a sensible young woman, not at all the sort to tell wild tales about soldiers and nuns.

Juan Plaza led the soldiers into the field. Waiting there were some officers who had arrived by truck. They stood by its tailboard, watching the enlisted men doling out bundles of brushwood. A score of campfires were soon burning; water was boiled, coffee brewed, and hunks of bread dunked in the liquid.

Watching the men sprawled on the grass, with their stubbled faces and filthy clothes, Juan sensed they were close to total demoralization. Away from the bright lights of the town, they no longer sang or showed the bravado they had displayed on the march. The officers did nothing to restore morale; they huddled by the truck as if they, too, seemed to be waiting for leadership. Moving from one group to another, sixteen-year-old Juan thought, "If they had tails, they would be between their legs."

From time to time, men rose and disappeared in the direction of the cemetery. Juan followed one of them and saw him scramble over the cemetery wall and drop down onto a grave. A low cursing came from behind a headstone. Juan could make out the shapes of men lying among the tombs and mausoleums. When he called out to ask what they were doing there, a voice replied there was no better place to be in the event of an air raid.

Besides those in the cemetery, some two thousand soldiers would be billeted in and around the town by nine-thirty that Sunday night.

Three hundred of them were in the gardens and monastery of the Augustine Fathers. Close to a hundred occupied the dormitory of the Convent of Santa Clara, forcing the Sisters of Penance to camp out in their refectory. In addition to the two hundred troops in the Convent of La Merced, Gandaría squeezed in nearly six hundred more. Most of the remaining men camped out by the cemetery and on the slopes west of Guernica.

Gandaría's phone rang. It was Captain Cortés, from the hospital in the Carmelite Convent, requesting transport to move convalescing patients to the Residencia Calzada. Cortés wanted to transfer thirty cases and use their beds for the injured from Marquina.

"Why don't you use your ambulances?" Gandaría asked.

"Because I don't have any," Cortés replied. "Two have broken down and the third was sent to Bilbao half an hour ago at their request."

Gandaría told Cortés he would send a truck to ferry the patients across town.

Hardly had he replaced the telephone than there was a knock on his office door. An orderly said a young baker was seeking an appointment on an urgent matter. Wearily, Gandaría ordered that Antonio Arazamagni be shown in.

Antonio described his day, beginning with the cat episode, then his service as an ambulance driver, culminating in the struggle to get more gas to clean the blood off his car seats. That was why, he continued, he had come to see the lieutenant. He had used his small quota of fuel as part of the war effort. He hoped the lieutenant would agree he was entitled to full recompense for the money he had spent.

Rising, Gandaría gripped Antonio by the arm and silently led him from the office. Outside was the 1929 Ford. Gandaría took the baker over to the car, opened the door, and motioned Antonio to get in. "If you ever come here again looking for anything, I will have you locked up."

Then, for the second time this Sunday, Antonio was pressed into military service. Gandaría ordered him to drive to the Carmelite Convent and help move the convalescent patients to the Residencia Calzada.

·16·

By 10:00 P.M., the flow of patients into the operating room had eased. Teresa Ortuz walked to the *poupinelle* to collect a set of instruments for the next operation. She handed them to the relief nurse, then went off duty after working eighteen hours in the past twenty-four.

Tonight she would not be going home. Mother Augusta had arranged for a number of nurses to sleep in the nuns' wing, where extra beds had been prepared. For the first time Teresa was going to have a glimpse of what her life could be like as a nun.

Mother Augusta was waiting for her at the door leading to the wing. She explained that Teresa's rest would not be interrupted unless there was a crisis during the night. The Superior then led the way to a narrow, cell-like room, barren except for a bed, a cupboard, and a crucifix on the whitewashed wall. There was one small window.

For a moment Mother Augusta hovered in the doorway. Then she told Teresa that the Second Basque Surgical Unit had been diverted to Bilbao to deal with those injured in recent air raids. That meant Teresa's father would not be coming home. But, added Mother Augusta, he had telephoned earlier that evening to say he was well.

"He also told me, my child," continued the Superior, "that you wish to join an order."

"Yes, Reverend Mother."

"Then, when the time is right, we shall talk."

Left alone, Teresa sat on the bed, too tired to fully appreciate what the Superior had said. Soon she was asleep.

In the Bar Catalán, Juan Silliaco was experiencing his busiest night in weeks. He knew it would be several hours before he could close up and go to bed. Several dozen soldiers filled the bar, elbowing aside refugees and regulars alike. Their behavior and unkempt appearance made Silliaco angry.

He had heard rumors about men like these—the "weak elements," soldiers who had broken in the face of the enemy. It was because of them that he would have to send his son to safety in Bilbao the next morning.

"God help us," he suddenly shouted, "if this is what our army has come to."

Silliaco hammered on the bar counter and announced he would serve no more drinks to "comrades who should be in the field defending us."

One of the soldiers looked at the barman. "If you want to fight so badly, then you go."

"Not while you remain here," retorted Silliaco.

The soldier glared, then muttering, left, followed by his companions.

In other parts of the town, other soldiers were also receiving a cool welcome. Mayor Labauría found some of them loitering around the entrance to the Town Hall and told them to move on. The police stopped troops going into the public school and the Church of Santa María. A police patrol watched over the Parliament Building. By then, the Convent of Santa Clara was once more in darkness; there was nothing to show that troops were inside the building.

Soldiers soon gobbled up the Hotel Julián's stew at 50 céntimos a plate; they asked for more and eventually had to be ejected by the police. Along with other small groups of tired soldiers, they drifted toward the one place in town where they appeared to be welcome—the open-air dance.

Usually, the dancing ended around 10:00 P.M. Tonight, on instructions from the town's police chief, the band kept playing. The chief hoped the soldiers, many of them now fortified with wine, would wear themselves out, dancing the endless reels and polkas. In the meantime he made his way to discuss the troops' conduct with Lieutenant Gandaría. When he reached La Merced Convent he found Gandaría had gone to bed, leaving strict instructions he was not to be disturbed, "unless the commander in chief wants me."

In the presbytery of the Church of San Juan, Father Eusebio Arronategui realized that Father Iturran was repeating himself. The old priest was obviously lonely and eager to pour out his fears for the safety of the valuable objects in Santa María. He made it clear that he expected Father Eusebio not only to devise, but to supervise, a rescue operation.

The young priest remained noncommittal. But now Father Iturran was insisting that he join in a further attempt to persuade Lieutenant Gandaría to provide transport to remove the statues, paintings, ornaments, and holy relics to Bilbao.

Father Eusebio hesitated. He did not wish to hurt the old man, but he knew enough about Gandaría to guess that the lieutenant would feel he had more important uses for his trucks than moving the contents of a church. Yet he knew what an effort it was for Father Iturran to come to him for help after all the weeks of tension between them.

Father Eusebio let Father Iturran talk, while expressing no opinions himself. Encouraged, the older man spoke with passion about the attitude of the Vatican toward the war; the pope was being deliberately misled, he said.

The young priest remained noncommittal. But now Father Itur-covertly endorsed the Franco cause, just as he had more openly supported Mussolini from the first year of his pontificate in 1922. He knew, too, that the pope had a deep-seated dread of communism, and that this had undoubtedly influenced his position on the Spanish war.

Father Iturran reminded him that only a month before, in March, Pope Pius XI's latest encyclical, "With Burning Anxiety," had denounced Nazism.

Father Eusebio said that the pope should have extended his attack to cover the behavior of the Germans fighting for Franco.

"It is not only the Fascists who behave badly," Father Iturran replied. "Look what they want to do to my church. A machine-gun post . . ." The old priest's voice trailed away.

Father Eusebio explained that all they could do was search for some means of transport, though he had no idea where he could find a suitable vehicle; the look of hope on Father Iturran's face made him determined to try. As Father Eusebio poured him another cup of coffee, he promised the old man that tomorrow he would make some inquiries.

In the excitement of dancing, María Ortuza's fears diminished. The memory of the soldiers in the Convent of Santa Clara no longer troubled her.

Moving from one partner to another, the dark-haired young woman waltzed and reeled over the smooth concrete slabs of the plaza, drawing spontaneous applause from groups of admiring soldiers.

As the band struck up another waltz, she found herself in the arms of a handsome, solemn-eyed trooper. He was a poor dancer, and María found herself having to lead him. In the end she abandoned the struggle. Staring down at her, the soldier growled, "You'll have to do better for the Moors." The soldier pointed toward the eastern hills. "They're out there. So are the Germans and Italians. Thousands of them. You'll soon have a choice of dancing partners." He thrust María aside and walked away.

Looking for a friendly face, María saw Antonio Arazamagni in the crowd and told him what the soldier had said.

Antonio was tired, but when he saw that María was frightened he tried to soothe her.

She told him about the troops in the Convent of Santa Clara. Antonio shook his head in disbelief. María took his hand and offered to show him. Together they walked along the curved narrow lane behind the Parliament Building. When they reached the convent, it was in total darkness.

"You see," chided Antonio, "nothing."

"Listen," María whispered.

Through one of the open windows above, Antonio heard a man's voice asking for a cigarette. Stunned, he led María away from the convent. When they reached the broad Calle Allende Salazar he told her, "You should go to bed and forget what you have seen."

He escorted her to the door of the Arriendiara house, then, shaking his head, turned homeward.

Juan Plaza arrived home shortly before eleven o'clock. The farmhouse was in darkness; his parents and younger brothers were asleep.

Moving carefully about the darkened kitchen, Juan located his father's prized possession—a wireless set. For weeks now, the dial had been set to receive Radio Bilbao's news bulletins. Mealtimes had been regulated so that the family could listen to the newscasts.

Tonight Juan was eager to know if the radio would mention the new troop deployments around Guernica. He switched on the set, lowered the volume, and strained to hear as the announcer reported heavy air attacks on Bilbao.

Suddenly, through the static, came a new voice, speaking in a dialect Juan could not easily understand. Raising the volume slightly, Juan could make out the words. It was Radio Salamanca, the Nationalist station, warning that Franco was about to deliver "a mighty blow against which resistance is useless." The voice urged, "Basques! Surrender now, and your lives will be spared. Resist, and you will surely die."

From upstairs, Juan's father called down in a sleepy voice to switch off the radio.

Isidro Arrién, hearing the broadcast, told his wife the threat was meant for Bilbao. The Nationalists would not "waste their ammunition attacking Guernica," he said. "They'll just walk in and take us when the time comes."

Perhaps, he mused, Nationalist occupation would be good for his business. Free from the uncertainty of recent weeks, with supply lines stabilized, life might return to normal; the restaurant could maintain its reputation for fine dishes.

Father Eusebio, politely gesturing Father Iturran to be silent, caught only the end of Radio Salamanca's threat. The old priest stared transfixed at the radio until Father Eusebio switched it off and tried to cheer up his companion by dismissing the broadcast as "mere propaganda."

Father Iturran shook his head.

"We'll move everything we can from your church in the next few days," Father Eusebio promised.

The old priest pulled himself to his feet, and with a downcast "Good night," left the presbytery.

Father Eusebio was tempted to "go after him, to comfort and reassure him. But I did not, for sometimes a man and his thoughts must be left alone."

In the Carmelite Convent, those of the hospital's night staff who were standing by the radio during a coffee break exchanged looks. For them the radio's warning could mean more casualties.

Seated alone in a corner of the common room that nurses, doctors, and nuns shared, Carmen Batzar heard them talk of shortages of equipment and lack of bed space. She knew the men and women around her were right to maintain a professional distance from their patients; she could not. Putting down her coffee cup, she hurried back to her bedside vigil. Her fiancé was still unconscious. But now, as she gently massaged his hand, she felt his fingers tighten on hers.

·17·

Shortly after 11:00 P.M., Von Richthofen arrived from Burgos at Vitoria airfield. Overhead, the wind was chasing banks of clouds across the moon. To the north stretched a solid mass of cloud that was advancing on the clear patches of starred sky.

Von Richthofen hoped the front would drift clear of northern Spain by morning and spill its rain over France. If the wind dropped, the rain clouds might hang over the Vizcayan mountains, grounding the Legion once again.

When he reached his suite in the Frontón Hotel, he sat at his desk and wrote in his war diary: "Only the weather can actually defeat the Legion."

Every night before retiring, Von Richthofen spent a few minutes with his journal. In a bold scrawl, on cheap, lined notepaper, he recorded his orders, vented his anger, expressed his hopes, described his future plans, and brutally criticized the Spanish commanders and Sperrle.

In his writings he complained that Nationalist generals "do not get up until eight o'clock, so the war cannot start properly until then, at least if they are to be consulted." Von Richthofen had protested to Vigón about their tardiness, and eventually Franco would order that his commanders "be fully awake, briefed, and ready for action at the same time as the Germans."

Von Richthofen's diary and his official reports give a clear picture of the contempt he had for almost all the Spanish leaders, apart from Vigón. Nor was he better disposed toward their troops, who "are slow and tardy in pursuit, enabling the enemy to regroup constantly and to overcome its panic."

Von Richthofen often wrote of the need to destroy enemy morale: "Fear, which cannot be stimulated in peaceful training of troops, is very important, because it affects morale. Morale is more important in winning battles than weapons. Continuously repeated, concentrated air attacks have the most effect on the morale of the enemy."

Von Richthofen carefully folded the pages of his diary and placed them in an envelope addressed to his wife. That envelope was then placed in another, addressed to Max Winkler, Berlin W8, Post Schliessfach 81—the special mail drop through which all correspondence to and from the Legion was processed. In Berlin, the chief of staff's words would be read by a censor and then forwarded to Baroness von Richthofen. She would carefully smooth the pages and insert them in yellow cloth-bound files already bulging with the day-to-day thoughts of her husband.

Two floors below in the hotel lounge, Captain Franz von Lutzow, the fair-haired commander of the HE-51 fighter squadron, expertly clasping an accordion, sang in a rich Rhineland accent to the group of pilots swaying around him:

> "Along the Hamburg–Bremen line
> A lovesick maiden crept.
> And when the train from Flensburg came
> She laid her down and wept.
> The driver saw her lying there
> And braked with trembling hand.
> The loco failed to stop in time—
> Her head rolled in the sand."

The others roared out the chorus:

> "Who begrudges the miser his money
> Or the sultan of Zanzibar his crown?
> There isn't a finer sensation
> Than mounting the best tart in town!"

A heartfelt cheer rang out. Then the young officers and technicians in the lounge belted out another song. Although their jollity was almost a nightly ritual, the excuse for this Sunday night was twofold: They were continuing their celebration of Hitler's forty-eighth birthday, which had occurred five days before on April 20, and they were welcoming a new fighter pilot.

The song-filled evening was one of the first entries in the diary twenty-three-year-old Hans Joachim Wandel planned to keep of his time in Spain. For a young man who had left Germany only two days earlier, the Condor Legion's camaraderie must have been exciting.

Around him on a dozen lips was the refrain *"Trink aus! Trink aus!"*

The hotel lounge was newly redecorated in a style somewhere

between fin de siècle and a German travel bureau. Posters showing
Berlin, Munich, and the Black Forest were tacked to the walls. The
ceiling was festooned with Spanish bric-a-brac: castanets, a
bullfighter's sword, and several pairs of garters filched from tarts in
the Legion's brothel. The floor was covered with fringed rugs and the
wall lights dimmed with red shades. Heavy curtains covered the
windows. Stuffed armchairs stood in groups around the room. In the
corner was a bar, tended by a Spaniard.

There were no women in the room—the local girls had resisted all
the efforts of the Legionnaires to entice them into the hotel. The
patrons of the lounge fell back on shoptalk and colorful descriptions
of visits to the approved brothel.

At a dozen tables the conversation concerned the technicalities
of flying and bombing. The conversation drifted to the subject of
damage during low-level attacks. Many knew what it was like to
return with bullet-riddled wings, an aileron shot away, a tail plane
jammed; it was amazing that some of the planes had stayed airborne. Most of the pilots could look back on many months of sorties
that had subjected them to extreme nervous tension and emotional
strain, situations where they had been saved only by the merest
quirk.

But the pilots made light of the dangers. Sangfroid was part of
their carefully cultivated code, and Von Richthofen made it clear
that any flier who showed signs of distress would be sent home.

Tonight, as usual, a number of them masked their feelings by
swigging local brandy or the weak Spanish beer, and joined in one
bawdy chorus after another.

> "A thousand miles from Hamburg
> A lonely flying lad
> Lies dreaming of the Reeperbahn
> And all the girls he's had. . . ."

Across the room Operations Officer Gautlitz was surrounded by
a knot of fliers anxious to pump him about the following day's
targets. He responded in his usual laconic way—troops, roads, a
bridge; to the fliers it sounded like more of the same. A discussion

started on the best way to strafe troops. Wandel listened, wide-eyed, as the men around him talked of hedgehopping over the fields to machine-gun the enemy. Somebody asked where tomorrow's attacks would be concentrated.

Gautlitz replied, "Probably near a place called Guernica."

"Never heard of it," shouted a pilot.

"Just another Spanish dump," said another.

Half a mile from the hotel, twenty tired Spanish girls could be had for a price. They were the medically inspected and approved whores of the official Legion brothel.

The Legion's administrative officer had commandeered a villa on the road to Vitoria airfield and turned it into the most elegant brothel in the town, so that "the lads can copulate in comfort."

Lieutenant Hans Asmus found such reasoning "typical of the way things were done." He himself had no desire to visit the brothel with its blue bedrooms for officers and lilac-green cubicles for the other ranks. He preferred to keep company with his nice Spanish girl. Tonight, while he was brushing up on his Spanish, a number of his fellow officers were lining up to pay 100 pesetas for fifteen minutes on a bed with a girl. To meet demand, the whores refused to spend longer with any man.

The price, a Legionnaire later recalled, was "all inclusive, two big towels, soap, and an aluminum box containing two contraceptives."

The girls worked a twelve-hour day, with an hour's rest after six hours' duty. They spent one shift in the officers' bedrooms, the next in the cubicles. Ten percent of their earnings went to the "house." It was said that in a month here a girl could earn more than she would make in a year in a brothel catering to Spaniards.

Tonight, the line for their services was unusually long. It always was after a day of combat.

Inside the villa was a waiting room where all ranks sat, eyeing each other and the doors leading off on either side: officers to the left, NCOs to the right. While the men waited they could buy Spanish champagne, and if they wanted, look at erotic photographs.

When a man's turn came he paid his money to the old galleon who functioned as madam. Arabic by birth, she affected what she believed was the classical Spanish look: lank kiss curls gummed to her temples and an outsize comb nested in her hair. She wore bedroom slippers and a dress that encased rolls of fat. From time to time she coughed, emitting a sound similar to an aircraft with an engine fault. Her knowledge of German was limited to a choice range of expletives. It was widely believed that she reserved her own special services for the German corporal who was in charge of the bordello. Tonight, as always, this short, potbellied soldier stood beside her, watching the steady procession of customers to and from the rooms. With midnight approaching, there was no letup in the line of men.

The Legion's brothel in Burgos was also experiencing a steady demand. Some men, frustrated by the long line at the approved whorehouse, broke the strict Legion rule and patronized Spanish brothels where a girl was available for the equivalent then of five U.S. cents. The chance of contracting venereal disease was high; discovery of infection meant being drummed out of the Legion and sent home. A number of airmen had experienced this fate. But others continued to visit the off-limits bordellos.

For Squadron Leader Hans Henning, *Freiherr* von Beust, the idea of visiting any brothel was quite unthinkable. The twenty-four-year-old scion of one of Germany's oldest families had made a firm vow since coming to Spain "not to tangle with the local girls."

Tonight, as usual, Von Beust was passing the evening in his hotel sipping wine with Wing Commander Fuchs and First Lieutenant von Moreau. Their conversation turned to the recent loss of three Legion fliers. The trio had gone out for an afternoon drive on April 5. Near Durango their car had wandered across the Basque lines. One of the pilots had resisted capture and was shot. The other two were now prisoners in Bilbao. The incident had caused Von Richthofen to ban all Legion personnel from driving in the countryside.

Von Moreau believed the captured men would be exchanged for

Russian pilots held by the Nationalists; such exchanges had occurred before. Even so, he thought the whole incident stupid. "We take enough risks in the air without sticking out our necks on the ground."

Then talk turned to the enemy defenses. All agreed it was "foolish talk" for anyone to claim Bilbao's defenses were easy to pierce. Only last Sunday there had been the loss of the Dornier-17 shot down over the city.

"We've got to stop them from strengthening their 'ring of iron,' " said Von Moreau.

Then Von Beust brought up the problem of accurate bombing in the JU-52. The problem was not new, but it was peculiar to the model of JU-52 used in Spain. When that bomber approached a target, the navigator, who flew in the right-hand cockpit seat, had to climb back through the fuselage to a point in the floor where "the pot" was, a metal-plated cupola containing a machine gun and the bombsight. Before bombing, the pot had to be lowered by a hand winch, so that it was suspended beneath the fuselage like a huge egg between the wheels. After locking the pot in position, the navigator climbed down a short iron ladder and became the bombardier. He had to squat, facing forward on the cupola's thin metal floor, and his head was above the level of the metal sides, protected only by a glass windbreak.

On the bombing run, the bombardier peered through the primitive bombsight to line up a target. Gripping the ladder with his knees for support, he guided the pilot toward the bombing point by pushing buttons that flashed red, green, or white lights in the cockpit; red was for left rudder, green indicated a need to veer right, "hold steady" was signaled by the white light.

"It's a wonder we hit anything at all," complained Von Beust.

Nevertheless he, like the other bomber pilots, had shown considerable accuracy during bombing missions.

Once, after dropping his bombs, Von Beust was told the pot had jammed and could not be retracted. His navigator was seriously wounded and trapped inside it. With the bomber badly damaged by Republican fighter planes, Von Beust had nursed his JU-52 homeward, the pot reducing his airspeed and dragging him toward the mountain peaks. Finally, he knew he would have to land on the nearest available flat ground.

Ahead, he saw a suitable strip. What followed would be etched into his memory. "I decided to try to land very, very slowly in the hope the pot, with my navigator inside, would be pushed up into the plane by the ground. I had no idea whether I was landing in Nationalist or Republican territory. As it turned out, I hit the deck just five hundred meters inside our lines and the pot was pushed up successfully. Unfortunately, the navigator died soon afterward from his wounds."

The feat made Von Beust a hero to his fellow fliers; it was another escapade in what Von Moreau described as "our great Spanish adventure."

A few blocks from where the Germans sat and gossiped, Colonel Juan Vigón was in his office signing copies of the latest Daily Intelligence Summary—an assessment of enemy intentions in the coming twenty-four hours. This one, the Spanish chief of staff believed, should give little cause for complaint. While the prose might be purple in places, the facts were accurate enough. A great hole had been punched in the enemy line and its troops were now in "a state of rout toward Guernica."

"Reliable sources" established that the enemy had lost a great deal of equipment, was short of food and low in morale. The summary spoke of "impending catastrophe" for the Republicans.

Vigón initialed the summary and handed it to an aide for distribution. One copy would be delivered to Vitoria for Von Richthofen to peruse in the morning.

Now Vigón could no longer delay dealing with the problems of the Moroccan troops commanded by General Juan Yagüe. The Moors had been brought north, and their very presence helped create panic among the enemy. But during a recent lull in the fighting they had been taken out of the line. Reduced to mere guard duties, the Moors had grown restive. There had been reports of thefts and assaults, and a story that some Moorish soldiers had

Right: Lieutenant Colonel Wolfram, *Freiherr* von Richthofen, chief of staff of the Condor Legion, who gave orders to bomb "without regard for the civilian population." In World War II he would rise to the rank of field marshal, join Hitler's personal staff, and receive credit for perfecting the aerial blitzkrieg technique he practiced in Spain. *(Photo: Jutta, Baroness von Richthofen)*

Below: Von Richthofen, a soldier's view. This photograph was taken on Monte Oiz the afternoon Guernica was attacked. *(Photo: Hans Asmus)*

Above left: Colonel Juan Vigón, commander of the Nationalist Army of the North. A former schoolteacher, he was the only Spanish officer to win respect from the exacting Von Richthofen. *(Photo: Hans Asmus)*

Above right: General Alfredo Kindélan, commander in chief of the Nationalist air force. *(Photo: Hans Asmus)*

Left: Captain E. von Krafft, leader of the No. 3 Squadron of JU-52 bombers in the Guernica attack, during off-duty hours in Burgos. *(Photo: E. von Krafft)*

JU-52 BOMBER

Top: The underside with its pot lowered. From this exposed position the bombardier guided the pilot to the target. *(Photo: E. von Krafft)*

Center: A section of the control panel of a bomber used in the attack on Guernica. *(Photo: Hans Asmus)*

Bottom: A close-up of the nose, showing No. 3 Squadron's emblem: a red bomb with white wings in a black circle. *(Photo: E. von Krafft)*

Above left: Captain Klaus Gautlitz, chief operations officer, the man who ringed the target. *(Photo: Hans Asmus)*

Above right: Lieutenant Hans Asmus, assistant operations officer. *(Photo: Hans Asmus)*

Below left: First Lieutenant Hans Henning, *Freiherr* von Beust, leader of No. 2 Squadron. *(Photo: Freiherr von Beust)*

Below right: Lieutenant Hans Wandel, fighter pilot. *(Photo: Authors' Collection)*

Above left: A Heinkel-111 of von Moreau's experimental squadron receives its bomb load at Burgos. *(Photo: Hans Asmus)*

Above right: First Lieutenant Rudolf von Moreau (with map) briefs his squadron for the raid on Guernica. *(Photo: Hans Asmus)*

Below: The Heinkel-111. *(Photo: E. von Krafft)*

Above: This photograph was taken as JU-52 bombers of No.3 Squadron returned from bombing Guernica. *(Photo: E. von Krafft)*

Below left: In May 1939, members of the Condor Legion assembled in Berlin for a victory parade. Bedecked with flowers and their Spanish medals, they passed in review before Hitler, Sperrle, and Von Richthofen. Field Marshal Göring commended the men for their achievements in Spain. *(Photo: Gerhard Berger)*

Below right: A smiling Francisco Franco visits the Condor Legion headquarters in Vitoria after the attack on Guernica. *(Photo: Hans Asmus)*

carried off a number of women to their camp, who had not been seen again.

Ordinarily such incidents would not have troubled Vigón unduly; he had authorized the Moors "to live off the land" as part payment for their services. But in the last few days there had been clashes between off-duty Nationalist troops and the mercenaries from Morocco. Serious trouble had been averted by confining the Moors to their camps. But again Spanish commanders had complained, and Vigón knew he must act swiftly.

Unlike the Spanish troops, the Germans were friendly toward the Moors. The Condor Legion admired their fighting ability, sometimes sought their company, and at times insisted on taking them into smart restaurants, forcing other patrons to leave. Von Richthofen had once affectionately referred to "our dusky friends," as feared on the ground "as we are in the air."

Vigón knew he had to be careful. If the Moroccan commander, General Yagüe, felt his men were being slighted, he would likely enlist German support—and cause yet another rumpus at High Command level. Vigón was under orders to maintain a policy of "peaceful coexistence" among the various Nationalist factions; at this critical stage of the war Franco did not want to alienate his allies.

It was close to midnight before Vigón hit upon the solution to his problem, one that would undoubtedly satisfy Von Richthofen's continued demand that ground troops be used immediately to follow up air attacks. It would also give the Moroccans a further chance to vent their blood lust.

Vigón would send the Moors back into the front line—to the sector in front of Guernica.

MONDAY
April 26, 1937

Midnight—6:00 A.M.

·18·

In the small hours of this Monday morning, a soldier patrolling near La Merced Convent challenged a shadowy movement. There was no response. The soldier fired, and other soldiers ran to the scene. Together they advanced on the intruder—they had killed a stray dog. His was the first death in Guernica that day.

The soldiers' nervousness stemmed in part from the intermittent shelling in the mountains; flickering summer-lightning flashes followed by dull thuds, and once, the sound of a heavy machine gun. The patrol's fears were heightened by the small groups of soldiers who continued to enter the town throughout the night. After hours of blind plodding across rough fields, these stragglers displayed the fatigue of retreat.

Occasionally an ambulance drove over the Rentería Bridge to the Carmelite Convent, where the night staff coped with the wounded and the newly dead.

Carmen Batzar twice jerked awake while dozing at the bedside of Juan Dominguiz. Both times she was disturbed by orderlies carrying out a corpse and bringing in a new, critically wounded man.

All around her, she whispered to the night sister, were "the faces of men dying and not knowing it."

The nun monitored Juan's pulse rate, frowned, and hurried away. Moments later she returned with a doctor. He rechecked

Juan's pulse and listened to his breathing, then turned to the nun and said there were signs of postoperative shock.

In the next hour the doctor came several times. On each occasion he told the night sister there was no change.

Carmen sat staring imploringly at Juan's face, "willing him with my prayers to live."

Around 4:00 A.M. Mother Augusta appeared with Captain Cortés, who carried a saline drip. Swiftly he linked Juan to the drip tube. Then he listened to the lieutenant's breathing.

Cortés looked at Mother Augusta and shrugged, a gesture the Superior interpreted as "more eloquent than words. God and the young man's willpower would decide if he would live or die."

Mother Augusta and Cortés left Juan's bedside. At 5:00 A.M., they returned. Cortés listened through a stethoscope to Juan's breathing, then turned to Carmen. "He's pulling up. Go and get some sleep."

Mother Augusta led Carmen to the wing where the nuns slept, showed her to a cell-like bedroom near the one where Teresa Ortuz was sleeping, and promised to call her if there was any change in Juan's condition.

Antonio Arazamagni, determined that nobody would steal any more of his precious flour, spent an uncomfortable night stretched out on sacks in the shed behind the bakehouse with two of his cats for company. Shortly after 5:00 A.M., aching in every muscle, Antonio stumbled from the shed.

In a tiny cobbled courtyard he sluiced sleep from his eyes under a cold tap, stretched, and studied the sky. One glance told him it promised to be a fine day. Over the mountains a spreading pool of light mingled with the flood of ocher rising from beyond the horizon. The rain clouds had disappeared; only a handful of soft cirrus remained to catch the reflection of the rising sun. It was a classical Vizcayan dawn.

Antonio humped a sack of flour into the bakehouse. He might be late delivering this morning, but nobody would complain about the quality of his loaves. After racking the last tray in place, Antonio relaxed.

Whistling cheerfully, he stepped out of the bakery into narrow Goyencalle. His good humor vanished the moment he caught sight of his car. Soldiers were stretched out on the seats; rifles, blanket rolls, knapsacks, and burlap bags were stacked against the wheels and on the hood; rifles and cartridge belts stood against the body.

Antonio gave a shout and rushed to the car. The soldiers might have thought they were being overwhelmed by a small army as, fists flailing, Antonio pushed them and their equipment clear of his Ford. Startled neighbors emerged onto Goyencalle and offered Antonio vocal support. The soldiers fled.

At 5:30 A.M., Mother Augusta woke Teresa Ortuz. For a moment the nurse lay on her cot, listening to the rustling sounds of nuns rising from their straw-filled mattresses. Then from somewhere a voice intoned, "Praised be the Lord." In the tiny cubicles on either side, Teresa heard the soft bump of bodies dropping to their knees on the bare wooden floor. There was a moment of silence. Then began the recitation of the Hail Marys.

Teresa followed the words of their prayers, knowing that if her special prayer were answered, this was the way she, too, would awaken every morning. She knelt and again asked God to grant her wish.

Around her the nuns offered up their Aves, saluting the Virgin in clear, glad voices. Then, with starchy rustles from their habits and the clink of keys attached to their leather belts, they left their cells to have breakfast.

Teresa was not hungry. She walked down the corridor and back into the hospital.

In the operating room Captain Cortés was scrubbing up, his first case of the day already on the table.

Across town, in the Convent of La Merced, Lieutenant Gandaría was reading the overnight situation reports. Despite the intermittent shelling, the Nationalist troops had made no serious move under cover of darkness; in places they had even been pushed back by the Basques. This was not unusual. During the day Mola's troops could move forward more easily, protected overhead by the Condor Legion. At night, without that umbrella, they often lost half of the ground they had gained. Gandaría knew the final result was that the Republicans would continue to lose ground.

His mood became blacker as he read the overnight report from within Guernica. There had been several incidents between townspeople and soldiers.

Gandaría had always believed it essential for the garrison to maintain a good relationship with the civilian population. Although he felt no sympathy for the people of Guernica, he made sure soldiers under his command behaved correctly toward them. In the space of a few hours, the behavior of the retreating soldiers had damaged that relationship.

Angrily, he began to draft a report to his commanding officer, requesting swift punishment for all transgressions. If punishment were not meted out, he said, civilian morale would slip, "and so present me with further problems."

Having completed his report, he walked outside. Below him in the courtyard, companies of men were forming up to salute the Basque flag.

Then Gandaría watched as the men marched to the field kitchen in a meadow beyond the convent. This was an obvious danger point, easily seen by aircraft. Gandaría looked upward. There were no planes.

The lieutenant turned away and looked back into the town. From the roof of the Carmelite Convent he spotted a reflected glint. He raised his field glasses and brought into focus a reassuring sight. Two nuns were sitting on the roof, back to back, each scanning the sky for enemy aircraft. Beside them was the hand bell that would be rung to warn of air attack.

He knew that after a time the large binoculars would make their arms ache. Yet the two nuns must endlessly repeat the same procedure; holding the heavy glasses to their eyes, each swung her binoculars very slowly through an arc of 180 degrees. After a brief pause, they duplicated the movement in the opposite direction.

This morning, apart from a lone soldier on La Merced's roof, the two nuns were the only lookouts specifically charged with watching the sky.

Gandaría turned his glasses away from the Carmelite Convent and swept the hillside behind the town, to the west. On a brow, high above Guernica, the church of the hamlet of Luno stood out in bold relief. Below the church, in the bushes and trees of the hillside, were many soldiers. But in spite of his searching, Gandaría could see very few signs of them; for all he could tell, they might have disappeared. Once he had viewed with sympathy men who cracked and ran away. Now Gandaría had one answer for any deserter: a bullet in the back of the head.

Lower down the western slopes of the town, the roof of the Parliament Building came into focus; long ago Gandaría had earmarked the building as an ideal machine-gun position. With more machine guns in the Church of Santa María nearby, the combined firepower from their elevated position would decimate any advancing force.

Behind the Parliament Building, Gandaría could see the top of the bell tower of the Convent of Santa Clara. As it was a closed order whose nuns never ventured outside, it was one building he had promised to try to spare.

Gandaría lowered his glasses, having failed to notice that the convent's sanctity had already been pierced.

María Ortuza was so intent on watching the soldier in the convent's belfry that she forgot the time. From her attic bedroom she could see him clearly as he examined the countryside through binoculars, sweeping over some thirty square miles of fields and villages.

The sight of that soldier rekindled in her mind the events of the previous night. But now, in the daylight safety of her bedroom, her fears were replaced by anger that the convent had been occupied. Cupping her hands around her lips, María shouted to the soldier "some rather unladylike words."

Startled, he swung his glasses to María. She shook her fist and closed the window, suddenly aware she was still in her nightgown.

Then she also realized that for the first time in two years she was in danger of being late for work. Dressing quickly in black smock and white bonnet, she crept down four flights of polished stairs to the basement kitchen.

An undermaid had already laid out her mistress's breakfast tray. María hurried to a broom closet and opened the door. From inside came a nervous clucking. Swiftly she removed an egg from under each of the two hens roosting in the cupboard. María kept them there to protect them from thieves.

This morning when María entered her mistress's bedroom to deliver breakfast, she found the señora standing in her nightdress at a window, peering through a telescope.

She turned to María and said, "The Moors are out there." The old woman thrust the telescope at her housekeeper: "Look for yourself."

María took the eyepiece and scanned the countryside. She could see nothing. She lowered the telescope and said soothingly, "Do not be alarmed. There is no one there."

She guessed that a combination of high-strung nerves and the sounds of shelling in the hills was probably the reason for her mistress's strange behavior.

6:00 A.M.—Noon

•19•

At 6:00 A.M., Von Richthofen awoke, walked to the window. The sky was clear overhead, but to the north, toward the Bay of Biscay, clouds were rolling up. It would be touch and go.

He hurried through his calisthenics, shaved, showered, dressed, dropped the letter to his wife in the mailbag outside the operations room, and drove to Vitoria airfield.

There, his mood of impatience communicated itself to his staff, who, as usual, had meticulously prepared maps and reports.

He scanned the Spanish intelligence summary. Nationalist troops were converging on Marquina; Monte Oiz had been taken; Durango was at last about to capitulate.

Von Richthofen turned to a logbook stenciled: SECRET. AIRCRAFT AVAILABILITY. Inside was clipped a copy of a telegram Lieutenant Asmus had sent to General Alfredo Kindélan, the Spanish air commander, on April 12. It stated that, apart from Condor Legion aircraft operating in the south of Spain, in Burgos there were "twenty-three JU-52 plus two under repair, three HE-111 plus one under repair, two DO-17 plus one under repair, three JU-86, twelve HE-70." Based at Vitoria airport, the telegram continued, were "twenty HE-51 plus two under repair, six ME (BF)-109 plus three under repair, and four HS-123."

Since that telegram had been sent, Von Richthofen knew, they had lost only the Dornier-17 shot down over Bilbao on April 18;

enough time had elapsed for the planes then "under repair" to have been made operational, making a total of some eighty aircraft now available.

The three squadrons of trimotor Junkers-52s, the mainstay of the Condor Legion, could carry a bomb load of one and a half tons per plane; Von Moreau's experimental squadron with the faster two-engine HE-111s could drop about the same weight of bombs per aircraft; the Heinkel and Messerschmitt fighter planes could splatter the target with light bombs, hand grenades, and machine-gun fire.

Von Richthofen ordered Wing Commander Fuchs in Burgos to send up an HE-70 with the Legion's most experienced reconnaissance expert, Lieutenant Balthazar, to survey the area between Marquina and Guernica. Von Richthofen wanted "every inch photographed," wanted to know where the enemy guns and ammunition were positioned, wanted a special watch kept for telltale tracks into the forests, indicating heavy vehicles sheltering there; above all, every road and track was to be surveyed for troop movements. Balthazar was to avoid flying directly over Guernica, so that "the enemy would not know of our intentions."

Von Richthofen looked again at a map of the area and issued further orders. A second reconnaissance aircraft, an HE-45 from Vitoria, was ordered up to duplicate Balthazar's flight. The Legion's two weather planes, the cumbersome W-34s, were sent off to fly a high, wide track over Vizcaya and out to sea to establish the weather pattern.

Until their aircraft returned with information, there was nothing more Von Richthofen and his staff officers could do. Rather than remain idle in the presence of the chief of staff, and risk rebuke, his officers left the office.

Alone, Von Richthofen sat and brooded over the maps and reports. For weeks he had waited for just such a situation: the enemy retreating into a bottleneck that he could cork with a fusillade of bombs. Here was an opportunity to deal a devastating blow in one concentrated attack and produce instant, sensational results.

On the far side of Vitoria airfield, Lieutenant Hans Joachim Wandel settled himself in the open cockpit of the HE-51. The early-morning sun had beat upon the gray-painted canvas fuselage and wings, and now the seat and controls were pleasantly warm to the touch. The smell of high-octane fuel was in the air.

When he left the party in the Frontón Hotel, it had been after 4:00 A.M. Too excited to sleep, his mind spinning with stories of the Legion's exploits, Wandel had dressed in his new khaki uniform with the Spanish stars in its epaulettes, and come to the airfield.

He was surprised to find Von Lutzow, his squadron commander, already supervising the mechanics servicing the fighter planes. Von Lutzow paused to explain, "Here we work and play equally hard."

Wandel, a trained architect, was concerned about his limited flying and technical experience. Von Lutzow had assigned him his HE-51 with the words: "Treat her like a women, with love and care, and she won't let you down." Now he gave Wandel permission to carry out a familiarization flight in which he could also test his machine gun.

The HE-51 was slow, barely reaching 200 mph in a dive; it was lightly armed, carrying only two fixed machine guns synchronized to fire through the propeller; compared with contemporary Russian and Italian fighter planes, it did not maneuver very well, and it had an inferior rate of climb. Because it was outclassed in aerial combat, the Legion was reluctant to risk it against enemy fighters. Instead —and in any case there was now very little opposition from enemy aircraft—the HE-51 was used almost exclusively to strafe and to bomb from low level.

Sitting in the cockpit, flying helmet hiding his fair hair, goggles on his forehead, Wandel was the personification of National Socialist propaganda. His face had the same jutting determination the new Nazi state portrayed on its postage stamps to project its idealized image around the world.

Across the airfield a long figure walked purposefully toward him. Uneasy, Wandel waited until Von Richthofen had reached the plane. The two mechanics saluted. Without a word Von Richthofen walked around the HE-51 and inspected each control surface to be sure it was free-moving.

Wandel would remember feeling "like a schoolboy who hadn't done his homework properly." He knew he should have checked the control surfaces before strapping himself in. He guessed that Von Richthofen had noticed his oversight—and had delivered this silent reprimand.

Without speaking, the chief of staff walked away.

One of the mechanics stood by the propeller. Wandel slipped his shoes on the rudder bar pedals and then moved the control column back, forth, and sideways to make sure the controls were free of obstruction. He scanned the instruments and checked his safety straps. From below, a mechanic called out, "Watch the water-cooler flap indicator." It was a familiar warning; pilots tended to ignore the gauge, risking engine failure in the thin mountain air.

"*Frei!*" yelled the mechanic by the propeller, giving it a turn.

"*Frei!*" acknowledged Wandel, pushing the starter switch.

The wooden propeller blade jerked around, a flash of smoke came from the exhaust, the blade completed a second turn, caught, and spun smoothly. Finally there was a satisfying roar.

In front of Wandel the instrument panel, with its gauges and needles, came alive: oil pressure, fuel pressure, engine temperature, fuel content, tachometer, coolant temperature, and direction finder. He checked the magnetos, satisfied himself the rev drop was within limits. He throttled back to check the slow running, and then gave the signal for "chocks away." The two mechanics jerked the chock ropes and indicated to Wandel he was clear to taxi.

He lowered his goggles, pushed the throttle wider, watching the rev counter flick around. Even through his flying helmet the noise was deafening. Wandel took a final look around the cockpit, released the brakes, and the fighter rolled across the grass.

Ahead, he could see the takeoff strip marked out with flags; for night flying, the flags were replaced by flares. Wandel braked for a moment, running the engine to maximum revs. When he could feel the brakes would no longer hold, he released them and sped across the grass.

In a few minutes the airfield was below and behind him. Ahead rose the towering granite mountain range north of Vitoria.

He glanced down at the map spread on his knees. Then he gently banked the fighter to the east, away from the mountains and the front line. At little more than rooftop height he roared over Elburgo, glimpsing startled faces peering up. He now felt the excitement other pilots spoke of when they had buzzed a town. It would be another "first" for the diary he carried in his breast pocket.

North of Elburgo, he found what he was seeking: a river. He swooped across the water, released the safety catch over the firing button, and fired the twin machine guns into the water. The sour smell of cordite fumes whipped back into his face. As he pressed the firing button again, he felt the whole plane shudder. Twice more he shot up the river, watching tiny columns of water spout and subside. He experienced another emotion he had been told to expect. One pilot had described it to Wandel as "a feeling of unstoppable power." Wandel would add: "total excitement and satisfaction."

Wandel practiced the textbook drill of a marauding fighter pilot. He dipped first one wing, then the other, so he could look down and ensure no enemy fighter was attacking him from below. Then he looked behind, to make sure there was no one on his tail. He roared up the riverbed, pretending it was a road and that he was strafing a fleeing enemy.

At a bend in the river he pulled back on the control column and the Heinkel began to climb, its propwash disturbing the water's surface. Although his machine was slow, he was forced back in his seat.

High over some villages west of Vitoria, he leveled out. At this height, close to 6,000 feet, he could see the distant mountain ranges around Durango. He knew that was where the enemy was, a few flying minutes away. He moved the control column forward, and using the rudder bar, dived toward Vitoria. He watched the airspeed build up and thought, "It's better than being a bird."

Happy, he returned to the airfield. There was, he told the mechanics, no doubt about it: An early-morning flight was the best cure he knew for a hangover.

The normally placid operations officer was this morning showing signs of tension. Captain Gautlitz had surprised everyone by arriving unusually early with the Spanish liaison officer to the Legion, Count del Cadagua, a splendid figure decked out in the uniform of an officer in the Spanish Navy.

Lieutenant Asmus watched the two men study the situation maps and overnight reports. Once more, Asmus wondered what, in practical terms, the count's exact function was; the advice he offered was always listened to politely, but there the matter usually rested.

This morning, Cadagua, a Basque nobleman born in Bilbao, did not need to proffer suggestions. The day's principal target was clear—the bottleneck at Guernica. The count might have used this occasion to draw the German's attention to the sacred position Guernica held for the Basques, but he did not.

Lieutenant Raunce had already posted the target as an operational order. Gautlitz ordered it taken down, reminding him that junior aides did not post targets until they had been confirmed.

Gautlitz then questioned the elderly meteorological officer about weather conditions. The weatherman shuffled his papers, spoke technical jargon. Gautlitz demanded, "Will we or will we not be able to fly?"

The unhappy met officer replied it was impossible to know until the weather planes reported.

Disgusted, Gautlitz busied himself once more with his maps and reports.

•20•

Early that morning, Mayor José Labauría made an unpleasant discovery. His civic authority was now vested in the bespectacled troubleshooter President José de Aguirre had ordered into Guernica, Francisco Lazcano.

Lazcano knew that by temperament and background, Labauría was ill-suited to lead the town. But he also realized that to ignore the mayor would be a tactical mistake. He decided to give Labauría at least nominal responsibility for his future actions. To this end he presented himself as a presidential adviser, offering suggestions that the mayor should endorse.

He wished, he said, that the situation did not call for the drastic measures he knew the mayor would approve. But the facts allowed for no alternative.

Seated stiffly at his desk, Labauría listened as Lazcano explained that in the eyes of the Basque government, Guernica was now a linchpin in the Basque military strategy.

Accordingly, Lazcano was authorized by the president to discuss with the mayor hitherto secret plans. The first called for the town to be turned into a defensive fortress. Every street, he explained, every house would be strongly defended. There would be no surrender. Every hour gained would be an hour more for Bilbao to prepare. So long as Bilbao was held, there was the chance of a negotiated peace with the Nationalists.

Indeed, unknown to the Basques, the secretary of state at the Vatican, Cardinal Pacelli, had already sent messages to Republican government headquarters in the south, suggesting possible peace terms.

"How long do we have?" Labauría asked.

Lazcano said calmly, "Two days, three at the most. By Friday, the Nationalists will be here. And we must be ready for them."

Stunned, the mayor listened as Lazcano delivered his second thunderbolt. A plan must be devised to evacuate everyone in the town except soldiers before Friday.

Lazcano ordered the mayor to instruct the police chief to send his men out to all the roads leading into Guernica to stop people from coming into the town. Even though it was market day, any vehicles now in the town center must be removed to allow unrestricted movement.

Antonio Arazamagni calculated he had just enough fuel to complete his bread rounds. Beginning tomorrow, he would have to deliver the loaves on foot.

Dropping a loaf into the presbytery of Santa María Church, he asked Father Iturran whether he might borrow his donkey for future deliveries. The priest agreed. He was far more concerned with saving his church relics.

Cheered by the promise, Antonio rattled over the bumpy streets. Near the market, in front of the Arrién Restaurant, he was surprised to see fourteen-year-old Javier Gardoqui, the expert *txistu* player and altar boy at Santa María Church, toting a fishing rod. Javier explained that as it was a fine day, he was going to miss class and go fishing.

Antonio grinned. "Bring me a fish—otherwise I'll tell your mother."

On Calle Don Tello, Antonio parked his car outside No. 29, a tall, narrow-fronted apartment house. The widow Lucita Bilbao's daughter, Victoria, was celebrating her fifteenth birthday, and Antonio had baked her a cake. He climbed the four flights to the garret where mother and daughter lived and worked twelve hours a day, six days a week, as seamstresses. Antonio waved aside payment. It was, he said, his treat.

The widow Bilbao thanked him profusely and Victoria smiled. "Mama," she said, "we'll keep it for teatime."

Parking his car at the mouth of Barrencalle, by the Church of San Juan, Antonio delivered his last loaves. Waiting on her doorstep was Jacinta Gómez, a twenty-seven-year-old housewife and mother of three. The children ran toward him, and Antonio handed them each a sweet from the pocketful he always carried.

Jacinta gave him a cup of coffee, and while he drank, they exchanged small talk. Why was he so late? Antonio explained that he had spent the night sleeping on flour sacks in a shed, and then asked Jacinta whether she had news of her husband, who had gone off to the war a month before. Jacinta shook her head.

"He will return soon," said Antonio. "The whole front is pulling back."

By the day's end, Antonio would lose close to a hundred customers. Almost twice as many would be injured. And every second house Antonio had passed on his rounds would be a pile of rubble.

———

Lieutenant Gandaría was breakfasting in his office when Mother María came in. It was the first time Gandaría could recall seeing the Mother Superior outside her quarters. As always, he felt uneasy in her presence.

Mother María requested a truck to evacuate her nuns and their belongings to Bilbao this evening. Gandaría explained that all transport was already committed to military service.

In that distant voice he would always remember, Mother María announced that without suitable transport, she "regretted" *las Mercedarias* would be unable to leave. It was quite impossible, she added, for them to travel by public transport, as they planned to take their large chapel cross with them.

The officer and nun were still engaged when Father Eusebio arrived. His presence in the convent was not unusual; among his duties was that of chaplain to the nuns. Once a week he came to La Merced to hear their confessions and to advise them on spiritual matters.

Through these professional visits he had also come to know and respect Lieutenant Gandaría. Father Eusebio regarded him as "a capable soldier, not religious but Christian-principled."

Gandaría looked upon the priest as "an excellent spiritual leader. He would have made a good officer." Father Eusebio was one of the few townspeople that Gandaría liked. Once he had told Father Eusebio, "Anything you ever want, you can call on me."

This morning, Gandaría was about to be reminded of that pledge.

Father Eusebio explained his promise to Father Iturran to obtain transport and remove the holy relics from the Church of Santa María.

Gandaría protested he had already refused Mother María's request for a truck, and in any case this was not the time to be worrying about "stone statues."

Mother María suggested that he raise their requests with his commanding officer, but Gandaría rejected the idea. He knew the no-nonsense commander of the Loyola Battalion would turn down the request.

Choosing his words carefully, Father Eusebio said he believed a couple of trucks were a small price to pay for the right to turn the Church of Santa María into a fortress.

A shocked sound came from Mother María.

Gandaría knew very well what Father Eusebio was suggesting: He would tacitly support the move to convert Santa María into a military stronghold in return for transport to move its religious relics to safety.

"One truck. That is all I ask," said Father Eusebio. "The Reverend Mother and her nuns can share it as well."

"And Father Iturran?" asked Gandaría.

"I will explain matters to him," promised Father Eusebio.

Gandaría capitulated.

Mother María leaned across the desk and traced the sign of the cross on his forehead. Wishing him good day, she and Father Eusebio left.

Gandaría did not know where he would obtain a truck, but he need not have worried. He would never have to keep his promise.

Seated beside his father in their donkey cart, sixteen-year-old Juan Plaza bumped toward Guernica. In the back of the cart were a crate of chickens and a few sacks of garden produce. Juan expected each chicken would fetch some 50 pesetas, almost ten times the price it would have brought six months earlier. He hoped the leeks and carrots would also go for high prices.

Momentarily, the Plazas would be wealthy from their trip to market. But Juan knew that all the money would be needed to buy such equally price-inflated essentials as soap, sugar, and flour. He and his father would return home with barely enough change for the family to exist another week.

Along the road they stopped to pick up a neighbor who had sold his donkey to a butcher. Today he had been out since daybreak, trapping sea gulls on the River Mundaca. He had caught several, plucked them, and proposed to sell them at market.

They were nearly within sight of the Rentería Bridge when

they were stopped by a policeman. He told them the mayor had ordered everyone to avoid the town.

Juan Plaza would remember his father's reaction: "He said to the policeman, 'Tell the mayor that if he will buy what I have to sell at my price, and sell me in return what I need, I will turn back.' Then he prodded the donkey and we trotted on. The policeman must have been too surprised to say anything. In no time we were around the corner and out of his view."

It was barely 7:30 A.M., and the police patrolling the roads into Guernica were not yet properly organized. Even later in the morning, for every trader they turned back, many more slipped into town across the unguarded, open fields.

Approaching the Rentería Bridge, the Plazas passed the Convent of La Merced. On a normal morning there would have been only a few soldiers in sight. This morning Juan could see "the building was bursting at the seams. Soldiers were hanging out of the windows, leaning up against the walls, sitting on the ground."

His father urged the donkey over the bridge and they crossed into the town. On most Monday mornings, Calle San Juan was lined with stalls offering snacks to traders who had often journeyed a considerable distance. Now Juan saw there were only a handful, the others having been driven out of business by the food shortages.

Without bothering to stop, they continued down the street, turning off into Artecalle, the road in the center of town leading to the market. For as long as Juan could remember, an old man had stood at the corner of Artecalle, selling fruit ices. This morning he was there as usual—with an empty tray. The boy guessed that force of habit had brought him there.

Juan Silliaco packed his son's suitcase slowly to delay the inevitable. Pedro watched his father solemnly. Now that the hour of farewell was close, both found it hard to speak. Silliaco was to remember he wanted to "hold him, tell him how much I would miss him. But I was scared he would break down, and if he did, I wouldn't be able to let him go. And he had to go on that bus. I thought it was his last chance of escaping before the Moors came."

It was Pedro who found a way to cope with the last difficult moments together. He asked his father to take him to the fire station so he could say good-bye to the two dray horses that pulled the town's fire truck.

Carrying the suitcase, Silliaco walked with his son up Calle de la Estación toward the fire station, next to the Bank of Vizcaya.

A brisk breeze was blowing. Silliaco looked at the sky. The sun was breaking through the clouds. It could be a fine day.

He noticed the traffic was unusually light for a Monday morning, with only a handful of wooden-wheeled carts creaking toward the market. At the fire station he found the stable boy in a state of excitement. The lad told him of the soldiers camped out in the town cemetery, in the convents of Santa Clara and La Merced, and in the monastery of the Augustine Fathers.

Then the boy blurted out an even more sensational story. During the night enemy saboteurs were said to have infiltrated the town and poisoned the River Mundaca. Silliaco asked from whom he had heard the story. The boy said some refugees had told him, and they had heard it from a policeman. He added in triumph, "It must be true. That's why all the refugees are leaving."

Under normal circumstances, Juan Silliaco would have dismissed the yarn. But after the uncertainty of the past weeks, even the levelheaded Silliaco felt he had a duty to inform others that the Mundaca had been poisoned; only later would he stop to consider that the river was already heavily polluted and whether poison had been added to it or not would make little difference.

Hurrying from the fire station, he alerted a number of parents putting their children on the bus to Bilbao. In no time the story grew and spawned other rumors. One that gained swift credence was that the saboteurs were still in the town, sheltered by refugees. Tension between townspeople and refugees, already high, increased.

Juan Silliaco waved good-bye to his son as the bus left for Bilbao, then wandered through the market. It was here that rumors were most rampant. Some, like the one about the police closing off the roads from the town in order to trap enemy spies, certainly seemed plausible; even the tale of the Nationalist warships anchored off Bilbao had a basis in fact. But the story that the railway line from Bilbao had been cut was disproved when a train appeared.

For an hour María Ortuza combed the stalls, shopping for basic commodities. After some spirited haggling, she bought chick-peas, vegetables, and a bottle of cooking oil. For each purchase she insisted on receipts to show her mistress.

Near the fish market, María was surprised to meet one of her dancing partners from the night before. Rafael Herrán, manager of the candy factory near the Rentería Bridge, was hunting for the ingredients to titillate the most discerning taste buds in Guernica, those belonging to members of the town's oldest cooking club.

There were four of these all-male clubs in Guernica. The members were all excellent cooks, and every week one of them prepared lunch for his fellow members.

Tomorrow was Rafael Herrán's turn. He explained to María that in spite of the shortages he must still "put on a show." Fish, he said, would be the centerpiece of his meal.

María went with him to the fish market. There, after much debate, he bought some shellfish and dried cod. With the air of a mystic imparting some ancient secret, he explained to María how he would simmer the cod and serve it with a rich garlic-flavored sauce garnished with the clams.

María wrinkled her nose. Garlic, she said, would destroy the delicate taste of the clams; any first-year cook could have told him that.

On the north side of the market square stood the Taberna Vasca, the oldest restaurant in Guernica. Six days a week the middle management from the Unceta factory and tellers from the town's banks brought their families here for a leisurely lunch or dinner. Afterward the tables would be cleared for the complicated Basque card games that would go on for hours.

Monday lunch trade was different. From noon until around 3:00 P.M., sheep and cattle dealers from the market took possession of the restaurant, using the occasion to eat, drink, and make deals.

The owners of the restaurant, the Guezureya family, enjoyed these sessions. They heard news from the surrounding countryside, and sometimes Pedro Guezureya would learn of a farmer with a pig or a sack of beans to sell. Then Pedro would set off in a donkey cart with his eldest sons, Juan, age eighteen, and Cipriano, fourteen, to buy what he could.

A few days ago they had been especially lucky and had purchased a sow and her litter. The litter had been killed for *fabada*, the restaurant's famous bean stew with chunks of pork.

This morning Cipriano had been sent to the market to buy carrots for the stew. Tall for his age, he was not afraid to stand his ground and barter with the vendors. Hefting the sack of carrots on his shoulder, Cipriano returned to the restaurant.

Earlier in the morning his father had been horrified to discover soldiers asleep on the Taberna's doorstep, and now Cipriano was glad to see that they were gone. But when he went inside, he saw they had simply moved to the kitchen door and were watching his parents preparing caldrons of *fabada*.

His brother Juan told the soldiers it would be several hours before the stew was ready, and then they, like everyone else, would be welcome to a helping—at 50 céntimos a plate.

The soldiers drifted away.

Shortly before 8:00 A.M., Antonio Arazamagni paused in polishing his car to watch two men approaching up Goyencalle. He recognized the mayor. The man with him was a stranger, dressed in smart city clothes.

Glancing at the 1929 Ford, the mayor's companion told Antonio he wanted every car off the streets and parked on the tree-lined Paseo de los Tilos by evening.

Antonio grinned after them. Before his car moved, it needed one vital ingredient: gas.

The bells of Santa María had not finished tolling eight o'clock when one of the two nuns on the roof of the Carmelite Convent shouted she could see airplanes in the direction of Marquina. Her companion clanged the hand bell.

Below, an orderly ran into the convent, shouting, *"Avión! Avión!"*

Mother Augusta went outside. The nuns on the roof called down that the planes had disappeared into the clouds. Mother Augusta hurried to the operating room.

Captain Cortés paused to listen to the Superior's report, then turned back to his work. "If we stop for every plane, we'll never get anything done," he said.

Mother Augusta continued to carry out the procedure for an aircraft alert: She telephoned the Convent of La Merced.

Lieutenant Gandaría told her the airplane had already been reported to him, and had now apparently left the area; he would not be sounding a general alarm. "The planes were probably only surveying the results of what they did to Marquina yesterday," he said. Then he asked her to compliment her nuns for their sharp watchkeeping.

·21·

At 8:00 A.M., at the Condor Legion's base at Burgos, teams of mechanics, electricians, fitters, and riggers climbed in and out of cockpits and probed under engine cowlings.

Tall and thin-faced, First Lieutenant Karl von Knauer was the leader of No. 1 Squadron. Under his command were nine trimotor JU-52s, each capable of carrying a bomb load of 3,300 pounds over 930 miles at a cruising speed of 185 mph. The Junkers had a four-man crew, and its armament consisted of three light machine guns.

After the previous day's attack on Marquina, the pot of Von Knauer's bomber had begun to lower itself as he was landing. By the time he had taxied the plane to a stop, the pot was dangling dangerously between his wheels. Mechanics had removed it, checked its mechanism, and traced the trouble to some faulty linkage that now had been replaced. This morning, under the watchful eyes of Von Knauer, the mechanics demonstrated that the pot was once more operating properly.

As an indication of his squadron's special status, Von Moreau had parked the experimental HE-111s away from the cumbersome-looking JU-52s, closer to the canvas-covered bomb dumps. In this position his squadron could be loaded and away before the others.

The range of bombs in the Burgos dumps included the 110-, 550-, and 1,100-pound high-explosive bombs, each fitted with braced tail fins that produced an unnerving whistle as they plummeted earthward. The bomb casings were made of high-grade steel rather than cast iron, giving them superior powers of penetration. They could be used with or without delayed-action fuses. Only the Stukas carried the 1,100-pounders, but even the lightest explosive bomb could destroy a typical two-story Spanish house.

Kept a little apart from the high-explosive bombs were the 22-pound splinter bombs, designed for use against enemy troops and populations. These were not popular in the Legion, because of their tendency to explode while being loaded or after the aircraft was airborne.

In a separate dump were the incendiary bombs. The Germans had pioneered the use of these weapons in World War I, and had secretly improved on them since. The ones available to the Legion weighed either 9 or 2½ pounds. Those stored at Burgos and Vitoria were probably among the most advanced of their kind in the world. Being light, they could be carried by fighters as well as bombers. Some pilots made up their own devices, wiring together four of the smaller incendiary bombs to cans of petrol.

Viewed from the air, exploding incendiaries gave off pretty pink flashes that were visible for miles. They were also clearly visible from the ground, and so were sometimes dropped at the end of a bombing attack against enemy troops to show the Nationalist soldiers it was safe for them to move forward.

Until now, the Legion had had little experience of the effectiveness of incendiaries on towns. They had not been used against Durango. Indeed, like the splinter bombs, the incendiaries were likely to burst into flames inside the aircraft.

It was a possibility that made even Von Moreau worry. His HE-111s were too new and too valuable to be risked in such a way. Although their playload was the same as the Junkers'—3,300 pounds—they could deliver it at almost 200 mph, and were more maneuverable.

Von Moreau had personally groomed each of his Heinkel crewmen to weld his squadron into a tight-knit unit. The men had their private jokes, their favorite off-duty bars and restaurants; at times a number of them together would visit the approved brothel. They had their own flight offices where they stored their gear, played cards, and read. They largely ignored the other squadron crews, and were ignored by them.

Von Moreau had made his squadron's markings as distinctive as possible. Many of his pilots had painted on each side of their plane's fuselage, within the large black dot separating the plane's recognition letters, a Condor vulture carrying a bomb in its claws. The upper halves of the Heinkels were camouflaged in a sandstone color; underneath, they were pale gray. The wing tips were white, as were the rudders, on each of which was painted the St. Andrew's Cross that distinguished all Nationalist aircraft.

Von Moreau's squadron had returned unscathed the previous evening after bombing Bilbao, and the maintenance checks this Monday morning were mostly routine. His own Heinkel, 25-3, had already been checked and refueled. All it now lacked was its consignment of bombs.

The important decision on the type of bombs to be carried was almost always reserved for Von Richthofen.

First Lieutenant Hans Henning, *Freiherr* von Beust, commander of the Legion's second JU-52 bomber squadron, wondered how he could persuade the hotel to give him a more comfortable room. The subject of accommodations was one he often discussed with Von Knauer and the leader of No. 3 Squadron, Captain Ehrhart von Dellmensingen Krafft.

In Seville, while transporting the Moors from North Africa to Spain, Von Beust had lived in comfort in the Hotel Cristina. Then, in February, No. 2 Squadron's previous commander had crashed after a night raid on Madrid. Von Beust had taken over and was already making quite a name for himself as a squadron leader. But despite his title, his rank, and his reputation, his hotel room in Burgos seemed a penitent's cell. The rooms of the more senior Von Krafft and Von Knauer were little better.

The hotel's dining room offered beans, potato mash, and meat that smelled suspiciously sweet. Connoisseurs said it was high-quality horseflesh. After almost a month of this fare Von Beust had taken to dining at the officers' mess on the airfield. There at least the coffee was good.

This morning, after several cups, he waited for orders.

Wing Commander Fuchs felt as though all the minutiae of running the Condor Legion crossed his desk. Every day the paperwork piled up: orders from Sperrle's adjutant, Major Heinz Trettner, transferring staff back to Germany—indeed, Fuchs himself, along with Von Moreau and Von Krafft, was about to return to Germany—routine directives from Berlin to be circulated, data on fuel consumption and bomb expenditure.

At 8:30 A.M., the direct-line telephone from Vitoria airfield jangled in his office at Burgos. The reconnaissance and weather flights had landed at Vitoria.

Four aircraft taxied to a halt in front of Von Richthofen's office. Their crews hurried inside, watched by the fighter pilots. Old hands thought the number of aircraft used unusual.

Captain Gautlitz and the meteorological officer went into the rooms adjoining Von Richthofen's office, where the weather forecasts were prepared and aerial photographs developed and printed.

Then at about nine-thirty, Von Richthofen summoned Von Lutzow, commander of the HE-51 fighter squadron, and First Lieutenant Herwig Knuppel, leader of the Messerschmitt-109s, to his already crowded office. Spread out on his desk were sets of still-wet aerial photographs.

The met officer reported that weather conditions in the Guernica area, although not at the moment unfavorable, should nevertheless improve during the day, and by late afternoon conditions would be as follows: estimated three-tenths cloud cover scattered between about 2,000 and 20,000 feet; a probable 8- to 10-knot wind, veering south to southwest; visibility good, but with the possibility of some ground haze, especially near the coast.

Those weather conditions would be ideal for bombing. Even the expected scattered cloud and haze could be beneficial, helping the aircraft to reach the target undetected.

When the met officer had finished, the men in Von Richthofen's office grouped around the photographs. Guernica was not visible on them, but Lieutenant Asmus would remember that they "showed enemy traffic in the vicinity of Guernica, on the roads leading into the town."

Von Richthofen instructed the men in the room to stand by for an attack that would begin probably in midafternoon. When the men filed out of his office, Von Richthofen tried to telephone Colonel Juan Vigón, General Mola's chief of staff, but learned the colonel had left for the front. Gathering up the photographs, Von Richthofen thrust them in his map case, left the office, and drove to meet his Spanish counterpart.

For the heavy attack Von Richthofen planned, Vigón's approval was desirable, though not essential.

·22·

At ten o'clock, a dozen officers entered the map-lined office in the Convent of La Merced that had once been the Superior's parlor. Except for a crucifix, all traces of Mother María's occupancy had been removed. From an inner office emerged Captain Juan de Beiztegi, commanding officer of the Loyola Battalion. A squat, blue-jowled man in his early forties, Beiztegi was a popular commander. He made up what he lacked in battle experience with determination and energy.

As usual, Beiztegi opened his daily strategy and planning conference with the traditional Basque greeting, *Gora Euzkadi Eskatuta* ("Long live free Euzkadi").

Gandaría noticed that Beiztegi looked determined after his weekend visit to Basque GHQ at Galdacano. Standing behind the only piece of furniture in the room, a desk, Beiztegi riffled through a small pile of reports, frowned at some of them, and finally thrust the papers aside.

He would, he said, waste no time reviewing past events. He turned to a wall map and, in silence, slowly traced a line from the Biscay coast at Lequeitio down to Marquina and farther south, skirting Durango.

Then he said one word—"Mola"—indicating all the territory east of the line was held by the Nationalists.

"No-man's-land"—the palms of his hands covered an area of map west of the line he had traced.

"Our new front"—with care he traced another line, running from Bermeo, at the mouth of the Mundaco estuary, through

Guernica, down to Amorebieta, and then curving back toward Bilbao.

Speaking rapidly, Beiztegi said this new front had been approved by President Aguirre. Guernica was to be a focal point for a new stand.

Turning from the map, Beiztegi told the officers how Aguirre had electrified the Basque General Staff with his words. "He made it clear that the time for running is over. We must now stand and fight. The president promised he would provide us soon with planes, they are coming from France. But we must hold our positions. The enemy may be superior in numbers. But they must find your will to resist more than equal to the situation."

Listening to his commanding officer, Gandaría felt relieved. Aguirre's oratory had "at last woken up GHQ."

Beiztegi read aloud the latest intelligence report on enemy intentions. Mola's troops were reported regrouping near Marquina. Moorish troops had been spotted among them. On present expectations, he concluded, the Nationalists would not reach Guernica until about Friday.

Beiztegi put the paper back on his desk. By Friday, he said, the town would have been evacuated by Lazcano. Unhampered by civilians, the Army would then turn Guernica into "our Alcázar, which we shall defend to the last brick."

Pausing to pick up another paper, he continued, "Lieutenant Gandaría has already prepared a list of suitable buildings. We are fortunate to have his specialist knowledge in these matters."

Beiztegi read out Gandaría's report requesting disciplinary measures against troops who had misbehaved since arriving in Guernica. "There will be no punishment for what has happened. But I have ordered that henceforward all troops are banned from the town center unless they are specifically required there. Any soldier who breaks this order is to be severely punished."

An officer asked what was to be done about the soldiers now in the Convent of Santa Clara.

Beiztegi looked at Gandaría. The lieutenant said he had issued no instructions for the convent to be occupied. The other officer admitted he had given the original order, and Beiztegi rebuked him. But, he added, the soldiers could remain: "The convent is a good defensive position. And I have received no complaint from the nuns."

After giving more detailed military directives, Beiztegi ordered the officers to return at 6:00 P.M. to report progress. Gandaría was asked to remain behind to discuss plans for defending Guernica.

Consulting a map of the town, he and Beiztegi agreed it should be divided into a number of overlapping enclaves. Each enclave was to have its key buildings sandbagged, ready to be defended by platoons. What they lacked in heavy artillery would, hoped Beiztegi, be made up for by the defensive positions themselves: a determined machine gunner, burrowed behind sandbag-protected walls, would be very difficult to dislodge.

Gandaría believed the enclave containing the Church of Santa María, the Parliament Building, the house of the count of Montefuerte, and the Convent of Santa Clara could withstand for days the most intensive artillery bombardment. Unceta's mansion would make an admirable position from which to defend the southern approach to Guernica. Both the Arrién Restaurant and the Taberna Vasca would give an uninterrupted arc of fire across the marketplace.

The two men then considered the Church of San Juan. Situated directly in the face of the Rentería Bridge, its stone walls were a formidable barrier to all but the heaviest fieldpieces. Ultimately, predicted Gandaría, the church would be reduced by continuous shelling, but a machine gun nesting in its crypt, protected by adequate sandbagging, could hold out for priceless hours.

"What about the priest?" asked Beiztegi.

Gandaría assured him there would be no problems with Father Eusebio.

"And the old man of Santa María?"

"He will go with his holy relics."

Beiztegi turned back to the town plan.

Gandaría circled the Rentería Bridge. It was the only link between the Convent of La Merced, in which the two officers now stood, and the town. If they were forced to retreat over the bridge into Guernica, the bridge would be dynamited afterward.

Similarly, on Calle San Juan, certain buildings were earmarked for demolition. Mola's troops would find themselves delayed by the destruction and caught in a crossfire once they entered the town.

Altogether it was a textbook example of how to fight an urban rearguard action. Gandaría now turned to the question of removing the equipment from the Unceta complex. Would the freight trains and Soviet technicians arrive the following day to dismantle the machinery and ship it to Bilbao?

Beiztegi did not know, but he told Gandaría he had returned from GHQ with one order that should please him. The General Staff were concerned about the possibility of sabotage at the Unceta plant and had authorized an increase in the number of soldiers guarding it. Gandaría was to take a platoon to the factory, "and put a man on every machine. Anyone suspected of sabotage is to be shot at once."

Armed with this order, Gandaría led a column of troops out of the convent and across the Rentería Bridge.

Just beyond the bridge was the rail track that ran from Bermeo in the north, through Guernica, and on to Bilbao. It would have been quicker for Gandaría to take his men directly down the track to the factory, but he chose the more roundabout way through the town. After the previous night's incidents, he wanted to demonstrate to the townspeople the presence of disciplined soldiers.

Inside the Unceta factory, Gandaría posted soldiers by every workbench. Each trooper was told to report anything suspicious and to inform the workmen under his surveillance that any attempted act of sabotage would be punished by shooting.

Gandaría then went to the first-floor executive offices, where José Rodríguez was waiting for him. When Gandaría asked to see the latest production figures, Rodríguez reluctantly handed them over. They showed the factory's stockpile, some nine hundred newly manufactured weapons. Explaining they would all be taken away that morning, Gandaría signed for them.

Rufino Unceta came into the room and demanded to know when they would receive payment for the guns.

Gandaría would remember feeling "the old boy had guts. He

knew the situation was critical, that with one wrong move he might be killed. But he was not going to be cowed."

The lieutenant grinned at Unceta. "You will be paid as you have always been, without delay."

News that more soldiers had gone to the Unceta factory fanned further rumors in Guernica. So, too, did the sight of NCOs rounding up the remaining troops in the town center and marching them away. Some boys arrived in the market with the tale that certain troops camped out in the cemetery had forced locks on the larger mausoleums and were sheltering inside with the coffins.

Juan Plaza repeated this bizarre story to Julio Bareno, manager of the Bank of Vizcaya. The farm boy would recall how Bareno, on hearing the tale, stood before the Plazas' market stall "white-faced, gritting his teeth."

Bareno returned to his bank, wondering if now was the time to implement the remaining part of a plan he had devised.

Julio Bareno did not at first strike strangers as a man capable of any farsighted action. The portly fifty-two-year-old had an engaging smile, polished shoes, sharply creased trousers, and soft, well-scrubbed hands.

Behind this cultivated facade was a fierce commercial drive coupled with a deep-rooted belief in the Basque cause. During the six months he had been manager in Guernica, he was always the first to arrive and the last to leave his office. Even on Sundays he was at his desk, checking the accounts and planning new ways to increase business. In the evenings he attended political meetings where he enthusiastically gave the clenched-fist salute and took home tracts expounding the need to defend Basque independence. He denied he was a Communist sympathizer, preferring to call himself a humanist.

Any reservations Bareno's bank directors in Bilbao may have had about his political beliefs were offset by the fact that while the other two banks in Guernica were now experiencing poor times, the Bank of Vizcaya had prospered. Julio Bareno had even persuaded many of the refugees to open bank accounts. On Saturdays he traveled to the hamlets around Guernica, drumming up business, and when the opportunity arose, pushing the Republican cause.

Ever since Mola's campaign had begun, Bareno had kept little cash in the branch, never more than 10,000 pesetas. Twice a week he personally carried the bulk of the branch's deposits to the bank's head office in Bilbao. That was the part of his plan he had already implemented.

The other half was to close the bank, leaving locked in the safe all the cash he could not carry—mostly coins—and to take to Bilbao the ledgers showing each customer's debits and credits.

Several times in the past days Bareno had been tempted to implement this part of his plan. Each time he had hesitated. Even though the bank's directors had now told him he must "assess developments on a day-to-day basis," he knew they would regard with disfavor any manager who closed his branch at the first sound of gunfire.

Bareno also had to consider the attitude of his most important customer, Rufino Unceta. It was Unceta who had persuaded the bank to open its branch in Guernica in the first place. Through the years Unceta had advised successive managers on important matters, and Bareno had benefited from his guidance. He was tempted to seek it again, but recently his relationship with the arms merchant had cooled. Bareno wondered if it was because of his outspoken pro-Basque views. If it was, too bad; he would not temper his opinions even for Rufino Unceta.

In any case, Bareno thought, the additional soldiers he had just seen marching to the arms factory suggested that Unceta now had his own problems. The bank manager decided not to consult Unceta before making his decision.

At 11:00 A.M., Father Iturran was trying to decide what to save from the Church of Santa María. His mind was in turmoil.

Father Eusebio had warned him that space on the truck would be limited; in return for that space, Father Iturran must accept the fact that Santa María would become a military post. Dazed, the old parish priest had gone to his church.

There, gradually he calmed himself. He walked around the church, which still retained the beauty he had felt when he first arrived in Guernica.

Its mixture of architectural styles, Basque-Baroque and Gothic; its soaring nave supported by ten pillars; its chapels and marble-walled crypt; its famous portico; the magnificence of its main altar—all were visible reminders of the building's history, which Father Iturran knew by heart. Designed in 1418 by Sancho de Empara, the church had taken three hundred years to build. Twice during construction it had been laid waste: first when the count of Salinas had looted and burned the church in the fifteenth century; then, in 1521, when fire had destroyed it along with all of Goyencalle. In 1795, Santa María had been pillaged of its silver by the Spanish government to help finance the war against France.

The church had last been given a facelift in 1926–27. All signs of that were now faded except for the main altar, where the gold leaf glittered in the light of the candles.

In the pulpit was the massive leather-covered Bible from which he had read the Scriptures for the past twenty-three years. Father Iturran fondled the pages. He would take the Bible, part of a small but valuable library of books, most in the Basque language, that had been donated to the church through the centuries. The others, housed in the presbytery, would have to remain behind.

He paused before the main altar. He would take the sacred altar cloths, blessed long ago by a bishop, but because of their weight he would be forced to leave behind the massive altar candleholders. For the same reason, the ancient christening font must remain. The gold-plated incensory, which he had swung metronomelike at the beginning of every Mass, would go with him.

In the Chapel of Our Lady of Begonia were clear reminders of the war: candles lit for those who had died or been wounded on the battlefield, or had been captured by the Nationalists. Father Iturran encouraged the lighting of these candles, believing it a conscious act of acceptance of what had happened. Only when such acceptance came could he provide meaningful comfort. He lingered at the chapel with its small, exquisite, stained-glass windows. The statue of Our Lady, he knew, was too big to take. He turned away.

Nearby was a life-size Christ encased in a glass box. By pressing a button, one could light a score of tiny bulbs, angled to emphasize the blood on the statue's lifelike body, the suffering on its face, and the stigmata on its hands. The statue must also remain.

He reached the rear of the church, acutely aware of how much there was to save, yet how little time or space he had.

Father Iturran was still deep in thought when he heard the heavy wooden main door creak open. He was about to go forward to greet the visitor when he saw who it was.

Lieutenant Gandaría closed the door behind him and walked into the church.

Father Iturran, in the shadows, watched the young officer as he walked down the nave. Gandaría paused at each of the supporting columns, looking up to the roof. Then he walked on.

The priest guessed Gandaría was calculating how well the columns would withstand artillery attack. The thought made him clutch at a new hope: If Gandaría could be convinced the pillars would collapse under shelling, he might abandon his plan.

Gandaría was crossing before the high altar when Father Iturran "emerged like a phantom, pointing at the pillars and saying they would all fall down."

The lieutenant was discomfited by the appearance of the priest. He explained the pillars could probably withstand all but a direct hit. Even if they were eventually toppled and the roof caved in, the church could still be used as a strong defensive position. He indicated the yard-thick stone walls.

"You are quite determined to go ahead, then?"

"Father, I have no alternative."

"You will be damned for what you do."

Gandaría rounded on the priest. Had the Holy Church condemned the Nationalists for desecrating places of worship? Until the Vatican condemned their actions, he added, Father Iturran would be well advised to remain silent.

Lieutenant Juan Dominguiz regained consciousness. His tongue felt swollen and dry. His throbbing head seemed to be encased in a massive white dome. He lifted a hand to try to touch it, and realized that his arm was also bandaged. His other hand was unencumbered. He moved it under the sheet and felt the bandage strapped across his stomach. He tried to move his legs and discovered that one of them was also enveloped in bandages. He closed his eyes. The smell of ether caught in his throat. Then he became aware that something hard and cool was being forced against his parched lips. From afar a voice spoke. He opened his eyes. An elderly nun was bent over his bed.

Mother Augusta coaxed him to sip from the cup of water. She continued to speak, telling him what she told every awakening post-operative patient—that his fuzziness would soon clear, that the fear he now experienced was a normal reaction. So, too, was the pain; it was the first step in the long process of recovery. As he became more aware, she warned him, he would feel increased pain, and though he would receive medicine to ease it, he should look upon the pain as part of the knitting together of his damaged body.

As he drank, she saw the awareness return to his eyes. Mother Augusta took his unbandaged hand in hers and told him to squeeze her fingers. His grip was surprisingly strong. She smiled at him, as she always did when satisfied with a patient.

Later, Dominguiz would remember, "She went away to attend to some new cases who had just been brought in. One man started to scream. A terrible sound. Then he struggled for breath. The doctor stood there, able to do nothing. She held the man's hand until he died. Then she pulled the white sheet over his face."

Dominguiz turned his eyes away from the scene, and as he did so, the memories of yesterday returned, bringing tears to his eyes.

That was how his fiancée found him. And later, in her diary, Carmen Batzar would write how he asked her what had happened to his platoon. She listened as he told her of their retreat through the mountains, of his joy to be coming home, and how suddenly the planes had appeared and he could remember no more.

Carmen did not tell him that she had seen him arrive at the hospital or of the fight to save his life; she would keep that for her diary. Now she was simply content to let him talk, to listen as he told her that once he was out of the hospital they would marry, and he would invite all his men to their wedding.

He did not know that most of those who had not been killed in the air attack were now only a few yards away.

The few survivors of Lieutenant Dominguiz's platoon were among the three hundred troops who had occupied the grounds and monastery of the Augustine Fathers.

Some of the soldiers squatted beneath the trees, still too exhausted to move. Many had dumped their equipment over the floors of the monastery. In the courtyard, plank tables were laid with tin plates and spoons. A field kitchen had been set up to heat caldrons of potatoes and stew. The cooks lounged around, playing cards or reading well-thumbed magazines.

Behind the monastery, on the gentle lower slopes of Monte Cosnoaga, soldiers dug foxholes, firing pits, and communication trenches. They worked silently and with no great enthusiasm.

Faustino Pastor, a tough, battle-experienced, twenty-year-old machine gunner in the Saseta Battalion, looked at the men around him. Some of them had joined up with him, come through the same perfunctory training, and spent the same months tensed for Mola's onslaught against the Basque provinces.

Now they were preparing to resist again. They filled and lugged sandbags to the firing pit they had dug. By 11:00 A.M. their machine gun was mounted and boxes of ammunition were neatly stacked behind a protective battlement.

Pastor settled down to clean the cheap camera he had carried with him during all the fighting. Below, away to the right, was the Carmelite Convent. As Pastor watched, stretcher-bearers left the main buildings, carrying sheeted bodies to a smaller building.

·23·

Sometime after 11:00 A.M. that Monday, Von Richthofen and Vigón met alone in, according to Von Richthofen's diary, "a field near Monte Mouchetagui."

The two men studied the reconnaissance photographs and discussed the military situation. Then, without reference to higher authority, a Spaniard from Madrid and a German from Silesia settled the fate of the Basques' spiritual home.

•24•

As the morning drew to a close, Isidro Arrién was a worried man. Mayor Labauría, in an unprecedented move, had canceled his table for lunch at the Arrién Restaurant. A number of market traders had folded their stalls and hightailed it out of town. That, too, had never happened before.

Isidro sent one of his sons to scout. The boy returned with news that the Taberna Vasca Restaurant also had cancellations, that more refugees were leaving town, that troops around the cemetery were digging in.

From the doorway of his restaurant, Isidro observed a figure perched on the roof of Santa María, clearly a lookout. And in the marketplace, the mayor was walking with a stranger to whom he was showing unaccustomed deference.

Puzzled and rather worried, Isidro went back to the kitchen to supervise the lunch preparations.

Francisco Lazcano finished his tour of the town with a realization of how vulnerable it was. There was no civic plan to cope with an attack. It was he who had taken the elementary precaution of placing a lookout on Santa María's roof. The town's air-raid shelters did not impress him. There was no time, nor point, in improving the shelters in view of his intention to evacuate the town.

He chose the coming Wednesday to accomplish this task. Midweek, the town would be at its lowest commercial ebb. But what he had seen of Guernicans made Lazcano think they were going to be difficult to budge. There was about them a fatalism that depressed him. In the old quarter, hundreds of families lived cheek by jowl, knowing that their homes were fire risks and that the town's horse-drawn fire truck would be incapable of controlling a serious blaze. Further, the municipal water supply was poor; the pipes were close to the surface and could easily be ruptured by shells. But that was a problem for the military. By the time the town was shelled, he and the civilian population must be clear of Guernica.

How, he wondered, did he tell a family to pack all they could carry into a few suitcases and leave their homes—perhaps forever? Would he order them? Try to reason, cajole, and plead?

His walkabout made one thing clear. Panic must be avoided if the narrow exit roads were to be kept open. By the time he reached the mayor's office he had decided that the best way to avoid panic on Wednesday would be to flood the town with troops. Their presence, he hoped, would reassure people they were leaving their homes in safe custody—and the soldiers could act as a deterrent to anybody who still insisted on staying behind.

Juan Plaza loaded the donkey cart with the few supplies his father had been able to purchase from the sale of their chickens and produce. Juan had never before seen his father so agitated: "It was not like him to leave so early. He would not even stop on the way home for a drink. He kept saying everybody was mad and he just wanted to go home and forget everything."

Others had the same idea. Before midday there was an un-precedented line of carts and wagons crossing the Rentería Bridge and heading out into the countryside. Traffic was heavy on the roads leading north to Bermeo and south to Bilbao.

The most probable estimate is that between one and two thousand people escaped from Guernica that morning. Even so, there remained in the town a civilian population greatly in excess of Guernica's normal seven thousand, due to the refugees who had not yet left, and the many hundreds who had come in for the market.

Housekeeper María Ortuza, pausing in her preparation of lunch, went to Goyencalle to buy extra bread from baker Antonio

Arazamagni. She found the narrow cobbled street "as busy as ever," but Antonio's bakehouse was shut. She tried a nearby cake shop. It had sold out hours before. María remembered having "quite a struggle pushing through the hundreds of people milling in the street."

Calle Don Tello, by the railway station, was also crowded. But Juan Silliaco had never known his Bar Catalán to be so empty: "I had the feeling that people did not want to be inside, but out in the open, so that they could see what was going on."

Opposite his bar stood the Julián, the only hotel in the town. Its three floors contained twenty-two bedrooms and two bathrooms. What it lacked in comfort, the Julián tried to compensate for with "devoted friendliness," as a sign over each bed proclaimed. A family business, the hotel was unpretentious, its kitchen homely, its plumbing chancy.

In peacetime its clientele had been almost exclusively drawn from the arms dealers who came to do business with Rufino Unceta. The war had put an immediate end to Unceta's foreign dealings. Recently, those refugees with a little money to spend had stayed in the hotel. But this morning the last one had checked out, leaving the Julián without a guest.

José Rodríguez hurried past the hotel. He knew he would have fired any employee who walked out as he had done. Yet, if challenged, he doubted he could have excused his abrupt departure.

All his working life he had abided by the principle: "If you can't see it, don't believe it." But moments ago he had been at his office window, watching the train leave with its consignment of arms for Bilbao, and had looked at the sky: The clouds were disappearing, it was going to be a nice afternoon.

"It was all so peaceful. Suddenly, I had an overriding feeling that the attack would come this very day. Everything was right. The weather, the town filled with troops, the market. It was perfect."

His first thought was to rush home and persuade his wife to return with him to the factory, ready to shelter in the concrete bunker at the rear of the works.

When he reached home his wife soothed his fears, promising she would come to the factory during the afternoon. He begged her to come with him immediately after lunch, but she would not be persuaded.

Rodríguez sensed his wife believed that all the weeks of strain, of coping with Gandaría, of being under constant threat, had finally taken their toll. And, he admitted to himself, it was perfectly possible that he had allowed his imagination to take over. He began to feel "a little foolish."

Rufino Unceta listened carefully to what he hoped was artillery fire in the hills to the south of town. The railway line from Guernica to Bilbao ran through those hills. A well-placed Nationalist salvo might hit the two boxcars carrying the arms from his factory—or better still, close the line, so stopping the evacuation of his factory in the morning.

He turned to his son, Augusto, and said, "A few more days are all I need."

Fourteen-year-old Augusto, who had spent the morning at the factory "to get the feel of the business," wondered what it would be like under Nationalist occupation.

In the Church of San Juan, Father Eusebio was checking over a plate camera when he heard the artillery rumble. He went to his presbytery window. In the street he could see people looking toward the east.

Father Eusebio went back to the camera. A parishioner had lent it to him, together with a set of plates, asking him to photograph the church. Until now the weather had not been favorable. But this afternoon looked as if it would be ideal for taking pictures.

The two nuns on the roof of the Carmelite Convent swung their binoculars toward the hills at the sound of the gunfire, then resumed their methodical scanning of the sky.

Lieutenant Gandaría was probably the first man in Guernica to know that the artillery fire came from Basque gunners to the southeast of Guernica, ranging in on Nationalist troops. Telephone calls to forward observation posts revealed this information, and the news cheered him greatly. He was also pleased with the way the communications setup was working between La Merced and other parts of the front.

Captain Juan de Beiztegi paused at the sound of the gunfire and then continued his telephone conversation with Francisco Lazcano. Beiztegi promised to provide five hundred troops for Wednesday's planned evacuation of the town.

A few yards from Beiztegi's office, Mother María, the Superior of *las Mercedarias,* gathered together her flock for Sext, their noonday devotions. She told them that in their prayers they must ask for God's help and guidance for the journey they would soon take. She warned them of the possible perils ahead. If they were captured, they were to offer no resistance. Their status as nuns was no guarantee that they would not be violated. But if they were assaulted, she could promise they would be absolved from any sin. Father Eusebio had assured her of this.

Outside the pelota *frontón,* a small crowd watched as an official put up a notice stating the stadium was closed until further notice, "by order of the mayor."

Across town, on Calle Ocho de Enero, the manager of El Liceo cinema, owned by the Count of Arana, was refusing to agree to a Town Hall request that he should not open that afternoon. He told the official only the count could sanction such action, and anyway, in this time of trouble, the late-afternoon matinee would provide welcome relief.

All morning, baker Antonio Arazamagni had searched through the town, looking for the garage owner. He eventually found him in a bar outside the market. Antonio bought the man a drink and tried to persuade him to part with more gasoline.

The man shrugged his shoulders. Antonio bought him another

drink. Still the man shrugged. Antonio was about to buy a third round when the man took him by the arm and led him from the bar. In silence they walked to the garage. The man handed Antonio the gas hose and turned on the switch. Not a drop emerged from the hose.

"There isn't any fuel, and it may be weeks before I get more."

Antonio wanted to search for his relatives and girl friend; he hoped they had escaped the air attack on Marquina. Then it occurred to him that by now they could be in Guernica. Walking through the town, Antonio realized the civic authorities were unusually busy. The amusement stalls in one corner of the market had been told to close; a notice said that the mobile cinema had been canceled, along with the evening dancing in the Plaza Las Escuelas.

On Calle Santa María, Antonio saw municipal workmen placing more sandbags around the shelter in the middle of the street. Nearby, he found the entrance to the Town Hall basement open. Beside the door was a large notice: REFUGIO. The door of the fire station was also open. The horses were in their traces. It reassured Antonio to see that in some ways the town was "preparing itself for action."

In the railway station plaza, the mood of the remaining refugees was somber. People were ridding themselves of belongings they could not easily carry. Furniture and cooking utensils were piling up everywhere, along with litter of all kinds. The square more than ever resembled a junkyard.

Doubtful of ever finding the people he was looking for, Antonio left the plaza and ambled along Calle Don Tello.

Near the Bar Catalán he noticed a flour sack in the gutter. He picked it up and recognized by the stencil mark that it was the one that had been stolen from his bakehouse. Antonio threw it back in the road and walked on.

Carmen Batzar was ordered away from Juan Dominguiz's bedside so that her fiancé could sleep. Mother Augusta told her, "You both have a lifetime of talking ahead of you. Let him rest now."

The Superior refused Carmen's offer to return to duty. The

hospital, she said, was being evacuated of all but the seriously ill. For the moment Juan Dominguiz would remain in Guernica. Eventually, she said, he, too, would be moved to one of the Bilbao hospitals to complete his recovery.

Mother Augusta did not add that the decision to empty as many beds as possible had been made because Captain Cortés feared renewed fighting must bring an influx of further casualties.

As Carmen left the convent, more wounded were being loaded into ambulances. Almost twenty-four hours had passed since she had come to the hospital.

She reached home to find her mother out. Seated before her writing table, surrounded by her exercise books, Carmen recorded the events of the day.

Noon—6:00 P.M.

·25·

Shortly after noon, Von Richthofen arrived in the Frontón Hotel, Vitoria.

From the moment Von Richthofen returned to the operations room, and for the next six hours, he was always within the earshot or eyesight of Hans Asmus. Today, Asmus, an acknowledged admirer of Von Richthofen, clearly recalls what the chief of staff said and did during those hours.

Von Richthofen marched into the operations room and announced, "The attack is on."

Asmus remembers "the feeling of excitement that radiated from Von Richthofen. He tried hard to conceal it, because he was not the sort to show any emotion. But he had been given a real opportunity to deal the enemy a telling blow. And it was natural that he should show some reaction."

The response among the Legion personnel was, in Asmus's word, "electric." Von Richthofen moved to the plotting table, accompanied by Gautlitz, Raunce, and Asmus. The others in the room watched as Von Richthofen double-checked the weather reports, reconnaissance photographs, and intelligence summary.

Finally, he turned to the Aircraft Availability Logbook and issued orders.

Asmus recalls, "Von Richthofen jabbed at a large-scale Target Selection Indicator map and said, 'The bridge and roads leading to it must be closed.' On the map, Guernica was about three hundred meters west of the bridge. But this was war, and nobody stopped to say, 'Wait a minute, there is a town near that bridge.' Quite simply, the question of the proximity of Guernica did not come into our calculations."

The Rentería Bridge, Asmus would later claim, was chosen "as the prime interdictory target, and the roads leading to the bridge as subsidiary targets."

He would remember Von Richthofen saying, "Anything that moves on those roads or that bridge can be assumed to be unfriendly and should be attacked."

The chief of staff reinforced this order by pointing to the aerial photographs: They clearly showed troops moving down the roads from Marquina.

Nobody asked what should be done if troops had already crossed the bridge into Guernica. "The matter did not arise because we had no idea then that there were troops in the town," said Asmus. "However, it was standard practice that wherever troops were seen they were attacked. That is what war is about."

Von Richthofen now began to discuss the type and number of aircraft to be used on the raid.

He ordered all three Junkers-52 squadrons to attack "in a concerted, one-run stagger": twenty-three heavy bombers to hit the target in wave after wave.

In addition, the four Heinkels of Von Moreau's experimental bomber squadron were to act as "pathfinders"; Von Moreau himself was first to fly a solo sortie over the target area, testing out local antiaircraft defenses.

Six Messerschmitt BF-109s were to provide fighter protection for Von Moreau's bombing force; later they would strafe the target themselves. A squadron of ten HE-51s were to fly low-level attacks over the target area, bombing and machine-gunning.

Asmus would recall that Von Richthofen said the bombs were to be "the usual mix, including incendiaries—ideal for creating panic among a retreating enemy. One incendiary could set a truck on fire, the best way to block a road."

Von Richthofen wanted the second fighter squadron, using six

HE-51s, to fly a diversionary sortie ahead of the main task force, attacking the area immediately to the north of Monte Oiz, which had just fallen into Nationalist hands.

When the operational orders were written by Raunce in the DOR, Von Richthofen announced he was "going up to the front to try to see the attack going in."

He detailed Asmus to accompany him. Although the twenty-three-year-old was surprised to find himself "pulled out of ops for the afternoon," he relished the prospect of "seeing some real action again."

Von Richthofen decided that Gautlitz could conduct the briefing of the fighter pilots at Vitoria airfield. He was also to relay the attack orders to Major Fuchs at Burgos, so that the wing commander could brief the bomber squadron leaders.

The chief of staff looked steadily at Gautlitz. In a measured voice, he posed the question he always asked at the end of a discussion: "Is everything absolutely clear?".

Gautlitz said it was. He would, Asmus knew, "faithfully deliver the orders, not changing them by a single word."

Asmus and Von Richthofen drove to the front amid the fluffy clouds, warm breeze, blossoming trees, and birdsong of a mellow Vizcayan afternoon. Asmus would recollect Von Richthofen's saying, "We could not have hoped for better weather for this operation."

Soon after Von Richthofen's departure, Captain Gautlitz relayed his orders to Major Fuchs in Burgos. The two men then held a highly technical discussion concerning assembly areas for bombers and fighters, turning points, friendly ground-troop markings, bombing heights, time over target, bomb loads, predicted wind-speed over target, final approach direction, return routes to base.

When all these points had been agreed upon, Gautlitz assembled his own briefing team: the navigating officer, the intelligence officer, and the met officer. They arrived at the airfield about 1:30 P.M., and made their way to the briefing room, a stark hut furnished only with chairs and wall maps.

The room was already filled with fighter pilots dressed in flying jackets, breeches, and calf boots. Clutching his new flying helmet, Lieutenant Wandel felt slightly self-conscious. He had been one of the first into the briefing hut and was seated near the front.

Using a large-scale Target Selection Indicator map, Gautlitz identified the two main target areas: the "primary" one at Guernica; the "diversionary" target around Múnditibar, north of Monte Oiz.

Gautlitz dealt first with the diversionary attack at Múnditibar. He ordered six HE-51s from Fighter Squadron No. 2 to attack the area, adding, "Almost certainly there will be many retreating troops there." These fighters were to take off at 3:45 P.M., and would play no direct part in the attack on Guernica.

The pilots jotted down their instructions.

He moved on to the "primary target" and repeated the attack instructions he had been given by Von Richthofen.

First Lieutenant Herwig Knuppel's Messerschmitt squadron of six fighters was to provide a protective umbrella for Von Moreau's Heinkels. They would fly above the bombers, escort them to the target and back to Nationalist-held territory. Afterward, the Messerschmitts would return and attack the primary target area.

Captain Franz von Lutzow's ten HE-51s of No. 1 Squadron were to carry out a series of low-level attacks over the primary target area, machine-gunning and dropping light bombs.

The navigating officer took over. Using a map on which he had already traced the route to and from the target, he took the pilots stage by stage along the outward run. He indicated the assembly area over Villarreal and said he expected all aircraft to reach the area at the right height and on time—a reference to the recent poor timekeeping of some pilots.

He pointed to the first turning point, the village of Garay. It was here that Knuppel's Messerschmitts would rendezvous with Von Moreau's Heinkels.

He addressed himself to Von Lutzow's pilots. By the time they reached Garay, they must be flying in pairs close together, ready to go into the attack.

From Garay all aircraft heading for the primary target would bear slightly to the northwest. The next landmark, he indicated, would be the peak of Monte San Miguel; the mountain was one of the dominant features in the area around Guernica. Their course would take them just east of the mountain. After they had passed it, the River Mundaca would be on their port wing. They were to continue northward toward the Bay of Biscay, circle over the fishing port of Elanchove, near Bermeo, and then return southward, following the Mundaca estuary toward Guernica. "Follow the river, and you can't go wrong," concluded the navigating officer.

The intelligence officer spoke next. Little, if any, enemy fighter opposition was likely, and there had been no time for the enemy to prepare antiaircraft defenses. "In any event," he continued, "by the time you attack, the whole area will have been hit by the bombers."

The met officer was brief. The pilots should expect scattered clouds, a light wind, some ground haze. The initial attack would be downwind. "After that, it is up to you, but the weather this afternoon should cause no difficulties."

Captain Gautlitz had the last word: "Time is all-important. You must get to the rendezvous area on time, make your turning points on time, and get to the target on time, so that there is no danger of your being there when the bombers are overhead. I don't want a repetition of Durango."

At Durango, some of the HE-51s had been low over the town when the Junkers had begun their run—and the fighters had nearly been hit by their bombs.

"And stick to your route. It has been designed to achieve maximum surprise," continued Gautlitz. "Over the target there will be plenty of room to maneuver. The valley is about five kilometers wide. Use it sensibly. And watch your fuel. With full tanks you should have up to forty minutes over the target. Use that time to full effect. Get in close and low. Pick your objective and stick to it. You just waste ammunition if you chop and change all the time."

Along with some of the other newly arrived pilots, Wandel took notes rapidly.

"But don't take unnecessary risks. If you're downed, there is nothing we can do for you. So stay up."

For the first time, Wandel felt a bit nervous.

The experienced bomber squadron leaders seated in Major Fuchs's office at Burgos airfield took few notes. Von Moreau was ordered to take off at 3:45 P.M. and lead his squadron to the assembly area five miles north of Burgos. He would then leave on his own for Guernica; his squadron would proceed without him to Garay, where Knuppel's fighter escort would rendezvous with them. Von Moreau would complete his inspection of the target area, bomb it, and return to Garay to collect his squadron with their escort. The Messerschmitts would fly some 2,000 feet above the Heinkels, ready to pounce on any enemy aircraft, and after the bombing, would accompany them back over the Nationalist lines.

The main Junkers bomber force would take off at one-minute intervals after 5:15 P.M. and circle the rendezvous area. On the run northward each squadron would maintain a one-mile gap, so that by the time the last of Von Knauer's bombers were clearing the target, First Lieutenant von Beust's leading No. 2 Squadron would be lining up for their bombing run. Following a mile behind the last plane would be the third squadron, led by Captain von Krafft.

The squadrons would, as usual, bomb in "chains" of three aircraft flying in V formations from a height of some 6,000 feet. They would approach the bridge sideways. The standard method of attack would have been to bomb the bridge along its length in single file. But the desire for surprise, and the hills in the Guernica area, precluded such an approach.

Apparently none of the squadron leaders queried the bombing height. From 6,000 feet, on past experience, the Junkers bombardiers would be likely to have a high percentage of misses against such a small target. Despite the facts that no enemy aircraft were expected in the area and that antiaircraft fire would probably be nonexistent, no one suggested it would almost certainly be safe to reduce height to give the bombardiers a more reasonable chance of hitting the target.

And nobody voiced any concern over the danger to civilians that must have been apparent, even at this stage, to the airmen.

But years later, Captain von Krafft would recall that he had objected "with utter determination to the use of incendiary bombs."

He argued that from such a height the lightweight canisters would "fall like autumn leaves, out of control." Although he was the ranking squadron leader, his objection, he said, was brushed aside. "Fuchs would not allow any argument on the matter—it was an order. He was under considerable pressure from Von Richthofen, who wanted the mission to go ahead, and quickly."

Von Krafft testily concluded, "So we are to assume there are wooden bridges at Guernica." Fuchs ignored his comment and reminded crews about the correct procedures for jettisoning bombs.

The wing commander hoped the matter would not arise. But if bad weather suddenly developed, or enemy fighter planes did disrupt the attack, then all bombs must be dropped "in the general target area."

Von Beust would remember Fuchs's ending the meeting with the words "This mission is very important."

The squadron leaders left Fuchs's office to brief their crews.

Scores of Spanish workmen at Burgos airfield hauled the sledgelike bomb trains out of the dumps to the waiting aircraft. Under the supervision of German ground staff, they winched the bombs into their racks. As usual, Von Moreau's squadron was the first to be loaded.

Next, the bomb trains moved to Von Knauer's squadron of JU-52s. Each plane received a mixture of high-explosive and anti-personnel bombs—and at least 110 incendiary bombs. All told, the three Junkers squadrons alone would carry well over 2,500 incendiaries.

Von Knauer had never before carried incendiary bombs against such a target. It hardly seemed possible to him that the slim metal cases filled with thermite, a mixture of aluminum and iron oxide, would, when ignited, reach 5,000 degrees Fahrenheit.

Von Beust's No. 2 Squadron was similarly loaded. The incendiaries were together in one suspension frame in the forward bay of each bomber's hold; the big bombs were placed behind them in four separate racks. Over the target, the bombardier would release the incendiaries first; the other bombs would drop in sequence.

As usual, the German ground crews made sure the Spanish laborers removed any mud from the bomb casings and fins. A lump of mud could affect a bomb's balance as it plunged to the ground.

Finally the loading teams reached No. 3 Squadron, seven JU-52s dispersed in a rough arc. The Spaniards worked carefully. Still fresh in their minds was the recent incident when a badly fitted 550-pounder had fallen and crushed a loader.

Today there were no mishaps. The last bomb was in place, the last aircraft fuel tank filled.

At Burgos and Vitoria airfields, a combined force of forty-three bombers and fighters was ready. Among them they would carry 100,000 pounds of high-explosive, shrapnel, and incendiary bombs—in order, it would later be claimed, only to knock out a stone bridge just 75 feet long and 30 feet wide.

Such a heavy expenditure of explosives was a departure from the usual careful husbandry of Von Richthofen. In effect, he was prepared to use about 400 pounds of explosives for every square yard of bridge he wanted to destroy. And he was about to send the largest force until then ever assembled for an air attack in Spain to destroy a bridge so small it was supported only by two slim pillars.

Certainly, the bridge was near an important road junction. But destroying it would not trap the enemy to be rounded up by the Nationalist ground forces. A little upstream, the Mundaca was easy to ford; even if the Republican forces had to leave behind their trucks and ammunition carts, they could wade across the river, which in places was no more than ankle-deep. Von Richthofen, of course, may not have known that or even considered it.

But given that he was intent on hitting *only* the bridge, he had at his disposal a weapon far more suited to the task than the cumbersome Junkers. Each of his Stuka dive bombers was capable of carrying a single bomb weighing 1,000 pounds. Equipped with the latest bombsight, able to nose-dive onto a target, any of the four Stukas available that day would have had a high chance of taking out the bridge with one direct hit. Even a near miss with such a bomb would have set up a powerful shockwave that, if it did not cause the bridge to collapse, would doubtless have made it unsafe for traffic.

According to Lieutenant Hans Asmus, Von Richthofen never considered using the Stukas. He chose instead to rely mainly on the Junkers-52 bombers, with their antiquated bombsights and—because of the drag caused when their pots were lowered—notorious instability during the final run in to a target.

Wind has always been the nemesis of bombardiers; a sudden freak wind can upset even the most sophisticated calculations. However, those winds generally occur well above 6,000 feet.

The bombardiers soon to be over Guernica were certainly not justified, at least as far as their heavy bombs were concerned, in saying later, "The wind blew our bombs off target."

And the "mix" of bombs they were to drop was, to say the least, unusual for an attack intended primarily against stonework. The antipersonnel bombs would have little effect, and the one thing incendiaries could not do was burn down an all-stone bridge.

But "splinter" and "fire" bombs could be expected to create havoc in a town that Von Richthofen knew was no more than 300 meters away.

The question remains: Did Von Richthofen really intend his flying armada to rain most of their 100,000 pounds of bombs only on the bridge, or was it no concern of his whether they were scattered over a large area and killed defenseless civilians, so long as the retreating troops were delayed and disrupted?

If that question troubled Von Richthofen as he now drove north toward the front line "to see the action," he did not share it with Lieutenant Asmus.

And all Asmus would remember of that journey was "sitting tight in my seat as Von Richthofen drove his Mercedes as if it were a fighter plane."

·26·

At 2:00 P.M., Teresa Ortuz scrubbed up with Captain Cortés and the anesthetist for a midthigh operation on a soldier whose leg had gone gangrenous. This was the first amputation she had assisted with, and she was astonished what a simple job it was.

Antonio Arazamagni would remember the weather that afternoon as "created especially to make you forget everything except the joy of being alive." But the beguiling sun and breezes did not distract him from his task.

"I was still hoping to find my relatives and friends from Marquina," he later recalled. "The bottom of Calle Santa María was the poorer end of the street, and I thought that maybe without much money they had gone there to find a room. There weren't many people around when I got there, and I was about to give up looking when I heard this noise—it sounded like dozens of cats—coming from one of the lodging houses. I looked through the window. Inside, the room was filled with caged cats.

"I knew what this place was—a cat-processing factory. The poor cats were being kept alive to be killed when the market price went even higher for meat."

At first Antonio was tempted to go to the police. But remembering his unsatisfactory visit to report the theft of a sack of flour, he doubted that the police would bother to try to save a roomful of cats.

He went back to the bakehouse, selected a heavy pastry knife and a wrench from the toolbox in his car, and returned to the lodging house. Making sure he was seen by no one, he opened the door and slipped inside.

Antonio moved down a dark hallway. The stench was almost overpowering. At the end of the corridor a door was ajar Moving on tiptoe, he peered into the room beyond. A man was asleep on a bed. Antonio carefully closed the door, retraced his steps up the corridor to another door, opened it, and found himself among the imprisoned cats.

One by one he opened the cages. Hissing and spitting, the animals fled out of the house and into the street. In minutes, Antonio later calculated, he must have freed fifty cats.

Francisco Lazcano was enmeshed in his first meeting with Captain Juan de Beiztegi and Lieutenant Gandaría. Militarily, the situation was even worse than Lazcano had expected. Beiztegi said that the town's defenses were "short of everything except courage."

Lazcano promised to intervene personally with President Aguirre to see if some arms could be prized away from the redoubt around Bilbao.

Gandaría said bluntly, "To fortify Bilbao at the expense of all else is militarily and politically bad tactics."

Lazcano asked Gandaría what, in his view, would be good tactics.

Gandaría told him, "Guernica must become a new fortress, barring the way to Bilbao."

Lazcano was impressed. He felt that a mind like Gandaría's would be useful at GHQ.

Juan Silliaco noticed that some new slogans, typical Basque barroom humor, were going the rounds: "If wine interferes with your job, quit your job," and, "A night of good drinking is worth a year's thinking." The one he liked was, "If you are drinking to forget, please pay before you begin."

Too few people were drinking today. Bored with manning a virtually empty bar, Silliaco left an assistant in charge and went to the fire station. He was surprised to find its doors open and the horses in their traces. The stable boy explained the orders had come from Town Hall.

"Close the doors," growled Silliaco. "And unharness the horses. This isn't a circus."

From his office in the Town Hall, Mayor Labauría could see boys scampering around the marketplace. He probably envied their freedom; increasingly, his life was no longer his own. The smiling, polite Francisco Lazcano had gradually encroached on every aspect of his work. Now, at an hour when Labauría usually catnapped after a leisurely lunch, Lazcano was in his office, insisting they must finalize the evacuation plans.

Resignedly, Labauría turned his attention to the problem.

In the Unceta arms factory, José Rodríguez took his first step to stop Lieutenant Gandaría's plan to move the works to Bilbao.

Quietly and unobtrusively, he ordered trusted foremen to slow down production. First one machine, and then others, developed mysterious faults. The armed soldiers patrolling the factory floor watched uneasily as the diminutive Rodríguez displayed convincing rage about the breakdowns he had engineered.

Around midafternoon, Carmen Batzar returned to the Carmelite Convent with her newly updated diaries. She wanted Juan to read them.

When she reached his bedside he was asleep. After sitting with him for a time, she placed the diaries beside the bed and left.

For the banker Julio Bareno, business was slow all morning. He heard some of the new rumors as he stood in the bank doorway, thumbs in jacket lapels, looking into the sunlit street.

The goings-on at the fire station next door had bothered him: Harnessing up the horses and opening the doors could mean only that "fire was expected, and the only fire that could be anticipated was from enemy attack."

The gunfire in the hills seemed closer, more intense. A customer added to his fears by saying "it was a positive fact that Nationalist troops had entered Marquina."

They had not, but Bareno had no way of knowing this. His apprehension increased when he tried to telephone the bank's headquarters in Bilbao. The line was dead. He assumed it had been cut by enemy action; in fact, a fault in the bank's switchboard had made it inoperative. Engineers repaired the fault by 2:00 P.M., but by then Bareno had given up trying to reach Bilbao.

He decided to act on his own.

After the staff had gone home for their early-afternoon break, he locked the bank's door and began to bag up all the silver and notes, which he then placed in a massive steel safe at the rear of the building.

Among the written guarantees the safe carried was one stating it could resist heat up to 4,000 degrees Fahrenheit. Its manufacturers had not anticipated man's ability to produce slim canisters capable of causing temperatures well above that.

When the staff returned for the afternoon's work, he told them to "go home, collect your families, and leave town. This is no longer a safe place to be." Alarmed, the staff did as they were told.

Alone once more, Bareno gathered together the bank's ledgers and stuffed them into an old-fashioned mail pouch. Then, for the last time, he locked the bank doors behind him. He collected his wife from their apartment above the bank and walked out into the street. Sharing the weight of the heavy mail pouch between them, they headed out of town.

In his presbytery, Father Eusebio continued his careful inspection of the borrowed plate camera. Like most amateurs, he was not sure of angles and perspectives. Periodically he thrust his head under the tentlike black canopy to peer through the viewfinder.

María Ortuza was also preoccupied with photographs that afternoon—those in a woman's magazine she had saved for just such spare moments. Señora Arriendiara was visiting the Count of Arana, and she had told María she would not be home for dinner.

María knew she could safely steal an hour or two to lose herself in the glossy world of fashionable ladies posing in expensive surroundings. She had often entertained a secret dream—to recline in a splendid bed, sipping champagne like the most elegant models in the magazine.

•27•

Von Moreau strapped himself in and watched his navigator settle in the adjoining seat. Behind them, the radioman began to warm up his Morse code set. The fourth member of the crew was strapped in the open machine-gun turret above. For the rest of the raid he would be out of contact with the three men bunched up in the front of Heinkel bomber 25-3.

As regulations prescribed, Von Moreau asked the radio operator if his set was functioning properly. The radioman said it was. Von Moreau then checked his code list containing the Morse signals that could be transmitted to other aircraft or back to base: KA meant "proceed with mission as planned," KB meant "mission completed."

Von Moreau waited patiently for the signal to press the starter button.

Sometime after 3:00 P.M., Von Richthofen and Asmus reached the foot of Monte Oiz, just captured by Mola's troops. Its wooded slopes rose nearly 4,000 feet above sea level, and a Spanish officer said that from the summit the two men might be able to see the target area.

Von Richthofen led Asmus at a brisk pace up the mountainside.

At three-forty, one of the ground crew standing by Von Moreau's Heinkel removed the rudder lock on the rail and made a final inspection of the control surfaces. He then moved to the front of the aircraft, and positioning himself some distance before the Perspex nose, moved his hands up and down rapidly.

Von Moreau nodded and pressed the starter button. The port engine whined and its propeller spun into life; moments later, the starboard motor was also running. Watching the fuel and oil pressure, he tightened his hold on the control column as 22,046 pounds of aircraft, fuel, and bombs shuddered from the vibration of the engines. He pushed the throttles wider, watching the rev counters climb. Then, when he felt the tail wheel starting to rise, he throttled back.

He glanced at the navigator beside him, monitoring the instrument panel; the man affirmed, *"Alles in Ordnung."*

He looked in his rearview mirror; the radio operator nodded.

Von Moreau checked the time on the instrument panel clock and looked out over the nose of the aircraft. Two ground crewmen were waving him forward. He glanced again at the clock. Then he eased open the throttles and 25-3 began to move over the grass.

It was exactly 3:45 P.M..

The Heinkel taxied slowly away from the dispersal area to the southern end of the airfield.

By the time Von Moreau's aircraft had reached the runway, the rest of his squadron was beginning to follow. He pushed open the throttles, and 25-3 accelerated. Correcting for the incessant crosswinds at Burgos airfield, he gently juggled the port and starboard engine throttles and felt the exhilarating pressure of almost 2,000 horsepower hurtling the aircraft at over 100 miles an hour into the air.

Beside him the navigator called out each stage as it was completed. There was a thumping beneath their feet as the undercarriage retracted into its nacelle.

"Wheels up," said the navigator.

"Wheels up," acknowledged Von Moreau.

There was another, less noticeable, bump as the wing flaps slipped back into position.

Von Moreau altered the position of the throttles, reducing the aircraft's angle and rate of climb, and at the same time eased the control column forward.

Cruising at some 180 miles an hour, the Heinkel bomber continued toward the rendezvous point, gaining altitude all the time.

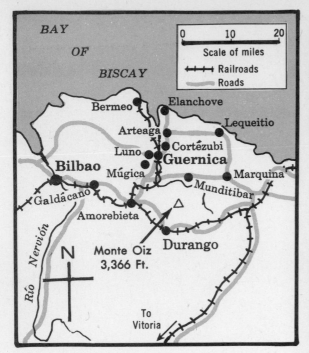

Guernica and vicinity

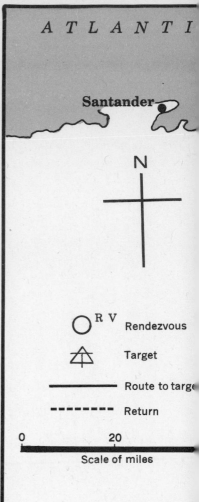

The attackers' route: from Condor Legion airbases at Burgos and Vitoria to Guernica and back

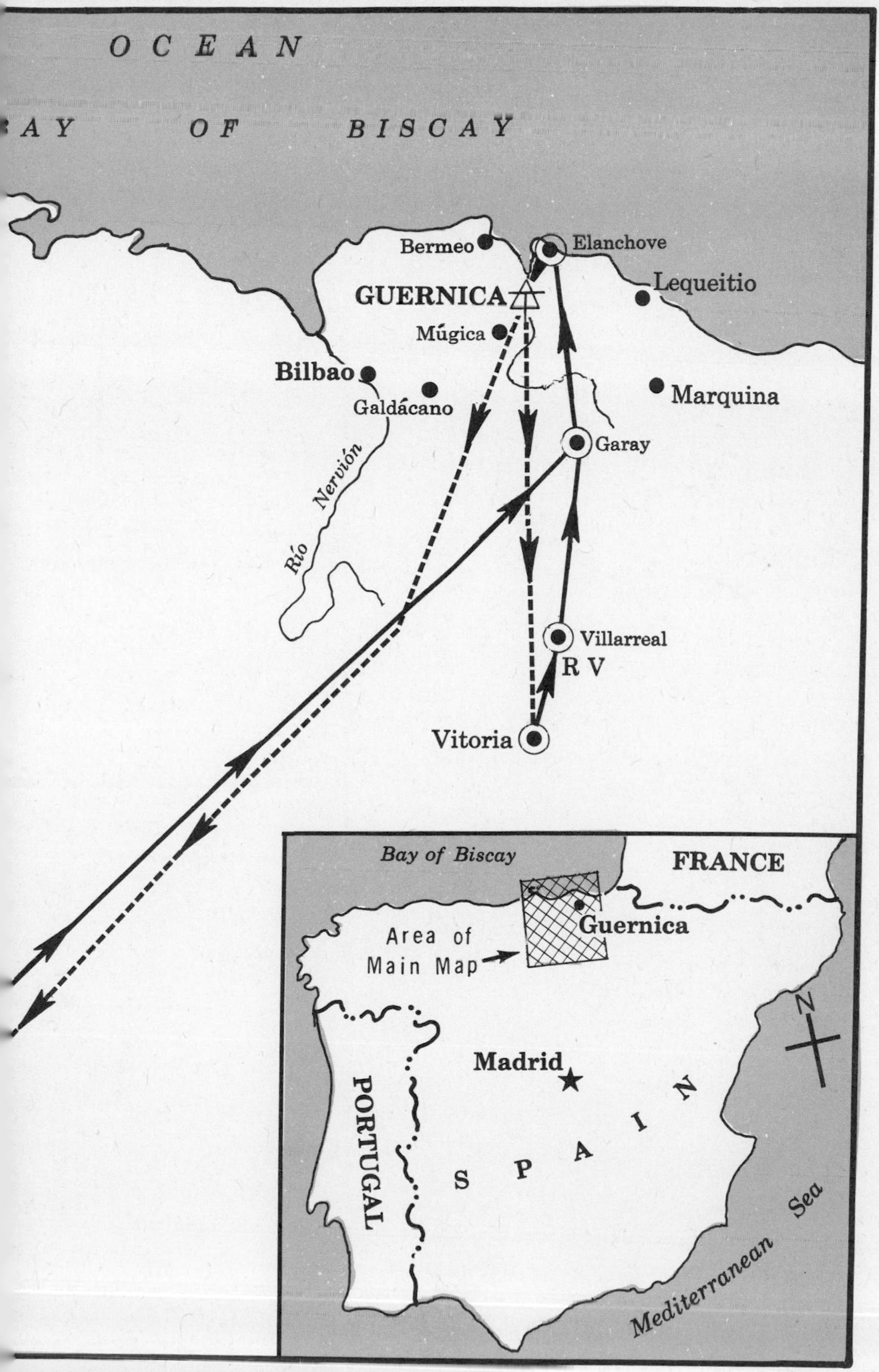

OCEAN

BAY OF BISCAY

Bermeo • ◎ Elanchove
GUERNICA ⩍ • Lequeitio
Múgica •
Bilbao • • Marquina
Galdácano •
Río Nervión
◎ Garay

• Villarreal
R V
Vitoria ◎

Bay of Biscay   FRANCE

Area of
Main Map →   Guernica

PORTUGAL

Madrid ★

S P A I N

N

Mediterranean Sea

Jaber

For every 500 feet it climbed, the temperature dropped one and a half degrees.

At 5,000 feet Von Moreau leveled out and circled the rendezvous point five miles to the north of the airfield. His gunner had an unsurpassed view of the other Heinkels coming up to meet them. He could also feel every course change Von Moreau executed. The gunner braced himself as he saw the wing flaps suddenly appear; moments later he experienced a bone-jarring jolt as the aircraft bounced upward.

Von Moreau used this technique to gain height rapidly. By lowering flaps 15 degrees, he caused the Heinkel to hit a wall of air that sent it shooting upward in 100-foot "bounces." Von Moreau called this "my aerial ladder."

At 6,000 feet he completed one circle over the aircraft beginning to orbit below. Then he trimmed the controls, corrected course for the changed wind direction, and headed northward. Behind him, the rest of the experimental squadron would form up, and in exactly thirty minutes' time, rendezvous with the Messerschmitts over Garay.

As Von Moreau's flight north began, the navigator made some calculations on his plotting pad. He checked his map. Then he confirmed they were on schedule, thirty-five minutes from TOT—their planned time over target.

In the operations room at the Frontón Hotel, Captain Gautlitz chaired the daily meeting of the Target Selection Committee, advising on the Legion's objectives for tomorrow.

In the absence of Von Richthofen, Gautlitz played it safe. He earmarked Bilbao for a series of raids next day.

There was only one drawback. The met officer announced another spell of unsettled weather for the next twenty-four hours.

Over the village of Garay, Von Moreau throttled back, banking the aircraft in a wide quarter-circle.

The navigator, now lying full-length in the bombardier's position in the Heinkel's nose, could see people looking up from the village. Consulting his watch to check whether they had arrived early or late over Garay, he was able to calculate whether the windspeed had varied from that predicted by the met officer.

Von Moreau's navigator was one of the most experienced bombardiers in the Condor Legion. He had an enviable record of bull's-eyes, and his coolness in action made him an ideal flying partner for the squadron leader. Together the two men had a well-deserved reputation for hitting targets accurately and consistently—a rare achievement in a war where bombing inaccuracy was standard.

In the exposed upper turret, the machine-gunner's main role was to defend the Heinkel against enemy aircraft attacking from above and behind. No attacks had occurred for weeks. Flying, for Von Moreau's gunner, had become extremely boring.

In the cockpit the sun was pleasantly warm. Behind Von Moreau, the radioman left his seat and crowded forward to look at the landscape ahead. Until they reached the target area, or unexpectedly encountered opposition, there was not much for him to do.

Von Moreau brought the Heinkel lower to get a better view of the broad, gently sloping valleys. There were forests of pine trees and white streams of water tumbling down sharp rock faces. Occasionally he saw farmers plowing with teams of oxen or tending pocket-size meadows.

Ahead rose the bulk of Monte San Miguel; on the summit was a small church, the cross on its roof glinting in the sun. The Heinkel passed to the right of the mountain and continued northward toward the sea. Away on the port side was the meandering River Mundaca; in front were the village of Elanchove and the Bay of Biscay.

Over Elanchove, Von Moreau banked in a steep turn, then leveled out, heading south toward Guernica.

Not long after, the bombardier twisted his head and shouted, "One minute to TOT." Then he turned back to his bombsight. They were above Arteaga.

Von Moreau throttled back. His airspeed dropped to 160 mph. This would be a "dummy run," an opportunity for his bombardier to practice lining up the target and for the rest of the crew to scan the area for antiaircraft emplacements.

Von Moreau dipped his starboard wing to get a better look at the Mundaca; here it was quite narrow.

In the upper turret, the gunner could see a castle close to the river. Once it had belonged to Isabel II. Today it was deserted, its huge gardens overrun with oaks and cypress trees, its four towers covered with creepers.

Now a small range of foothills lay below. There was a village in one of them. Von Moreau glanced at his map and identified Cortezubi. The Heinkel sped over the hamlet.

"Target in sight," shouted the bombardier.

Von Moreau and his crew sat silently at their stations. Immediately ahead lay Guernica. Only the machine-gunner in the upper turret, facing backward, could not yet see the town.

The two lookouts on the roof of the Carmelite Convent spotted Von Moreau's Heinkel approaching up the valley. They rang their hand bell and shouted, *"Avión! Avión!"* Mother Augusta telephoned La Merced Convent, but before anyone answered, she heard the bells of Santa María Church ringing their warning. She replaced the receiver and hurried to the operating room.

Captain Cortés told her he would continue performing surgery. Teresa laid out instruments for the next case.

In other parts of the hospital the ringing of the lookouts' bell initiated automatic emergency actions. Two nuns went out to the Bermeo road, ready to turn away all traffic in order to avoid drawing attention to the building. Inside the convent, nurses and nuns went to the upper-floor wards and began to take all the patients to the ground floor. Other nurses gathered together emergency medical supplies.

In the center of Guernica, most people were momentarily puzzled by the sound of the church bells. By the time they realized the pealing signaled an air-raid warning, 25-3 was almost overhead. A few ran to their nearest *refugios,* or to Santa María Church.

Outside La Merced, Lieutenant Gandaría trained his glasses on the Heinkel. He turned and shouted to Captain de Beiztegi, "It's a Fascist!"

The two officers ran into the convent, seeking, Gandaría later said, "any suitable gun to shoot at the plane."

Across town, in the Astra-Unceta complex, Luis Unceta rang the factory fire-alarm bell—the prearranged signal for the 120 workers to hurry to the bunker at the rear of the plant. The soldiers guarding the equipment did nothing to stop them.

Augusto, Luis's youngest brother, ran out of the factory gate to collect his mother, brother, and two younger sisters. Alerted by the bells of Santa María, they had already left their mansion for the bunker, as had the domestic staff. Augusto urged them along more quickly. The fourteen-year-old thought he was acting "quite calm and grown-up in the circumstances"— until his mother reminded him that an Unceta did not shout in public like some street urchin.

In Rodríguez's office, Rufino Unceta stood still as he watched the Heinkel approaching. Only his eyes followed the aircraft's course as it passed overhead, climbing steeply.

Unceta turned to Luis and quietly asked him to switch off the factory alarm bell, "because everyone must know by now that there are aircraft about."

Then, Rodríguez would recall, "with great dignity, Señor Unceta walked through his factory to ensure all the workers had gone to the bunker. He ignored the soldiers patrolling the factory floor. His only concern was for the safety of his workers."

Unceta's coolness helped dispel the general manager's "sickening feeling that my premonition was coming true." Even so, Rodríguez refused to leave until he saw his wife coming through the factory gate.

Behind her, he saw other people running into the railway station plaza. Rodríguez thought "how ill-advised they were to congregate there, when they should have been seeking shelter."

He and his wife hurried to the bunker.

By the time 25-3 passed over the southernmost part of Guernica, it had gained considerable height. While Von Moreau's eyes and hands were occupied with flying the bomber, part of his mind was weighing whether the troops he had glimpsed on the western slopes of the town indicated the area was, after all, fortified. Anxious not to be an easy target for any antiaircraft fire, he climbed steeply. But there was no flak.

Von Moreau's bombardier, spread-eagled in the nose, had little difficulty looking down on the River Mundaca and spotting the Rentería Bridge.

From near the bridge Juan Plaza saw the plane "climbing like a rocket. Then it leveled out and headed for Múgica [a small village two miles southwest of Guernica]. It did a sudden turn and disappeared behind the hills to the west of the town."

Juan, on his way from the farm to deliver homebaked bread to his grandmother, who lived near the Rentería Bridge, presumed the pilot was lost.

Faustino Pastor, crouching in his machine-gun pit on the slope behind the monastery of the Augustine Fathers, identified the aircraft as a Heinkel. His machine gun could not be inclined upward at a steep enough angle. It was impossible for him to fire at the bomber.

When the plane turned toward Múgica, other soldiers rose to their feet with relieved cheers. But Pastor was not so sure the danger was over. He dismantled the gun from its tripod so that, if necessary, next time he would have a freer arc of fire.

The ringing of the bells failed to disturb María Ortuza's reading. Curled upon her mistress's sofa, she was so enthralled by the love story in her magazine that she failed to hear the renewed shouts from the street outside: *"Avión! Avión!"*

Von Moreau returned for his second flight over the town, this time a textbook bombing run at about 4,000 feet. He was lower than the planned bombing height, but quite safe now that he had confirmed the absence of flak guns. The troops did not bother him; the danger of being brought down by rifle or machine-gun fire was minimal.

"Bombs ready," reported the bombardier.

As they approached the bridge and the town, he called out fractional course changes, which Von Moreau executed. Slowed to about 150 mph, the Heinkel bomber approached Guernica. Nothing disturbed the crew's concentration.

"Bombs gone."

As the bombs dropped away, the Heinkel, freed of their weight, rose. Von Moreau opened the throttle and banked away to port, above the Unceta factory and bunker and across the broad floor of the valley.

Von Moreau and his bombardier, despite their proved reputation for accuracy, had dropped their bombs hundreds of yards from the Rentería Bridge, in fact near the railway station plaza in the center of Guernica.

•28•

Juan Plaza guessed the Heinkel was directly above the Rentería Bridge when it dropped the bombs. They curved down, falling faster each second of their descent.

Half a mile separated Juan from the point of impact, "but the noise made my hair stand on end."

He watched as a curtain of dust swirled upward. Then came a sound that made Juan tremble. "It was a wild shrieking of terrified people."

He ran toward the town.

One 550-pound high-explosive bomb sliced away the front of the Julián Hotel across from the railway station, leaving four floors suddenly exposed after the rubble settled.

Another bomb fell behind the railway station, collapsing part of the rear of the building.

Other bombs fell in the station plaza itself, among people waiting for the next train to Bilbao, and those who had rushed to the square, believing it to be the nearest safe open space, following Von Moreau's first flight over the town.

Nobody would ever know how many were in the plaza when the bombs fell; probably between three and four hundred persons. Those on the edge of the crowd, having spotted Von Moreau's second run, had just enough time to run into adjoining streets before his bombs hit. Those in the center of the plaza had no chance.

Juan Silliaco was walking up Calle de la Estación, about a hundred yards from the square, on his way to the fire station because "that plane was up to no good," when the blast from the bombs knocked him off his feet.

From where he lay, he saw the first people die in Guernica: "A group of women and children. They were lifted high into the air, maybe twenty feet or so, and they started to break up. Legs, arms, heads, and bits and pieces flying everywhere."

Unaware of his own injuries—Silliaco's arms and legs were cut by splinters—he staggered into the dust to try to help.

He stumbled over something. It was the lower half of a woman. By the time he had passed a dozen corpses he no longer gave them a second glance, concentrating his efforts only on dragging the wounded clear of the debris.

Around him others, among them the volunteer firemen, began rescue work.

The injured screamed. The shocked, the bereaved, and the terrified screamed. The loudest sounds came from a group of women tearing at the pile of rubble in front of the Julián Hotel. When the hotel's facade fell in, a group of small children had been playing nearby.

Silliaco called the firemen. At the mound, he shouted for silence. Then he lay down on the rubble and listened. He rose to his feet and shook his head. Nobody, he believed, could be alive under the impacted rubble.

Antonio Arazamagni did not remember how he arrived in the plaza. He found himself kneeling beside the body of Javier Gardoqui, the altar boy at Santa María who had played truant to go fishing. The boy had been partly undressed by a freak side effect of the blast. But a puzzled Antonio could find no serious external injuries. The baker knew nothing of how the human lung can be ruptured by a pressure of 100 pounds a square inch, and how Javier's had collapsed under a force at least ten times greater.

Antonio recognized all three of the small corpses he helped drag from a crater near the railway station. He identified twelve-year-old Florence Madariaga by the pigtail attached to what remained of her scalp. Juliana Oleaga he recognized by her dress; it was the same one she had been wearing when he had met her earlier that morning. She had been decapitated. Fourteen-year-old Clara Almedia had suffered the same fate.

"Leave them," said Silliaco. "There's someone alive in the station."

Antonio joined the firemen picking their way inside.

Near the booking office they found the clerk, half buried beneath wooden beams and plasterwork. Antonio would never forget how, when they freed him, he gave a sudden convulsive shudder—and died.

They carried him outside and laid him at one end of a growing line of bodies.

Faustino Pastor was with the first group of soldiers to reach the plaza. By the time they arrived there, about fifteen minutes after Von Moreau had dropped his bombs, the immediate emergency was over. Miraculously, fire had not broken out, and the pall of dust was settling. Most of the dead had been located. The wounded were being tended on the spot by some of the town's doctors; those more seriously injured were taken to the Carmelite Convent.

The general feeling, Pastor would recall, was that "terrible though the aftermath was, no further attack need be expected."

The young soldier had seen enough of war to know that such

optimism was ill-founded. He hurried back to his machine-gun post.

Isidro Arrién did not stop to wonder whether more bombs might be coming. Those that had already fallen rattled the pots and pans in his kitchen. He ordered his wife and daughters to the Unceta bunker, his sons to the air-raid shelter in the basement of the public school.

When the bombs fell, his few late-lunch customers scattered. Isidro saw one man leave clutching his plate of food and wineglass. He polished off the meal in the open air—and disappeared without paying. Isidro never saw him again, and never forgave him.

The restaurateur told his sons he would join them in the public-school shelter after he had damped down the kitchen's coal ranges; he was worried about the possibility of fire. But he also knew that if he doused the fires, the flans, pastries, and stews cooking for the evening menu would be ruined.

Uncertain what to do, he walked to the door of his restaurant. Shouts were still coming from the direction of the railway plaza. At first he thought to help, then decided, realistically, that an overweight man of sixty years could render little assistance in a situation that would require physical fitness.

Isidro went back to his kitchen, stoked up the stoves, and poured himself a large glass of wine.

María Ortuza's peaceful afternoon was shattered by the blast from the station plaza. Her first reaction, she would recall, was that "old Unceta's factory has blown up at last."

Only when she became aware of the clanging of Santa María's bells did she realize the town had been attacked. Still not worried, she went out into the street. While some people were hurrying to the church, many more seemed uncertain what to do.

María would later recall, "We had become used to hearing gunfire and explosions, even if only from a distance. And we didn't want to appear to be panicking. There had only been one plane, and now there were no more in the sky. Apart from the dust down by the plaza, there was nothing to be seen from where I stood. Before long the church bells stopped ringing."

She considered walking down to the town center to see what had happened. But in the end the pull of her magazine proved stronger. She went back inside the house.

Francisco Lazcano, in the mayor's office, tried to establish the damage, contact the president's office in Bilbao, reach Captain de Beiztegi in the Convent of La Merced, and at the same time issue instructions to various civic officials.

He turned again to the telephone, his anger mounting. There was no response to his shouted *"Por favor, por favor . . ."*

Unknown to Lazcano, one of the bombs had severed the town's main telephone link with Bilbao, which ran underneath the railway plaza. He was also unaware that the bombs had severely damaged the lines carrying the town's internal telephone system. The line out of the Town Hall was among those now inoperative.

Lazcano left the mayor's office to call upon Captain de Beiztegi, garrison commander in La Merced.

Free of its bomb load of over 3,000 pounds, and helped by a tailwind, Von Moreau's aircraft made good time back to its rendezvous point with the other Heinkels and their escort of six Messerschmitt BF-109s.

He reached Garay, some ten miles to the south of Guernica, at about 4:40 P.M. People in the small town would remember airplanes "going around and around and doing nothing."

Von Moreau ordered his radio operator to transmit the coded signal that the mission was to proceed as planned.

Squadron Leader Knuppel's Messerschmitts spread themselves in protective pairs some 2,000 feet above Von Moreau's Heinkels.

Sergeant Henne formed up on one side of Von Moreau, Sergeant Zober on the other. Sergeant Meier brought up the rear of the formation.

At about four-forty-five, they headed north, reaching the mouth of the Mundaca estuary without incident.

As they encircled Elanchove, Von Moreau led the other Heinkels down to around 3,000 feet. The maneuver took three miles of airspace. The planes set off on the route Von Moreau had covered only twenty minutes earlier.

Ahead, the thin pall of dust hanging over the railway plaza was visible to the crews.

Above Arteaga, Von Moreau turned to his radioman and pointed upward. The operator transmitted in Morse: "Breaking away." Simultaneously Von Moreau began to climb to port, up toward the watchful pair of Messerschmitts guarding that flank.

Meier's Heinkel moved forward to take over the squadron leader's position, a few yards ahead of Henne and Zober. The bombardiers were in position in the nose of each aircraft. All was in readiness for the run in.

The scene in the Taberna Vasca was chaotic. When the first explosions had occurred, the sheep drovers eating there had raced to the door, tripping over tables and chairs. The floor was splattered with bowls of stew.

The only person now left in the restaurant was the owner's eldest son, Juan Guezureya. His parents had rushed the rest of their children to the nearest sanctuary, the Church of Santa María, just a few yards across Goyencalle.

Juan stayed behind to damp down the kitchen fires. He was about to leave the restaurant when his mother returned, shouting, "Where's Cipriano? We've lost him."

Juan sent his mother back to the church with the promise he would search for his younger brother. He began on Calle Allende Salazar, knowing the wide, tree-lined street was a favorite playground of the town's children.

As he ran into the street the bells of Santa María clanged again. From the upper windows of the Convent of Santa Clara, soldiers were aiming rifles. They were shooting at the three bombers that, Juan guessed, were still almost two miles away. As he watched, the aircraft swooped lower. He did not wait to see any more. He jumped over the nearest garden wall.

Juan did not know that only a few yards away, Cipriano and fourteen other boys had crawled into the entrance to one of the huge concrete viaduct pipes placed at various points along Calle Allende Salazar to carry away the seasonal floodwaters. The pipe the boys hid in was dry. To the youngsters its outer circumference of six-inch-thick concrete must have appeared a strong protective shield. They did not know that bombs are at their most destructive when exploded in, or near, an enclosed space.

Juan Silliaco knew that the three bombers coming down the River Mundaca toward the town were low enough "to be able to drop their bombs accurately wherever they liked." The fireman also felt they were flying too wide apart to be concentrating on one individual target.

"They're going to smash the whole town!" he shouted. Turning to the other fire brigade volunteers, he ordered them to follow him to the fire station.

The men ran from the plaza.

Faustino Pastor had barely propped up his machine gun on the firing parapet when the bombers appeared. They were low enough for him to see the silhouettes of the pilots. He fired at the planes but missed. The Heinkels passed above him at about 170 mph.

Pastor grabbed his camera and focused on the town. To him would fall the sad distinction of being the first to photograph the bombing of Guernica. During the coming hours he would go on to produce a rare record of a town under air attack—in between firing his machine gun.

"Bombs gone," reported the navigator in the nose of Heinkel 25-4. Sergeant Meier pulled on the control column and the aircraft climbed away over the town, banking to port. The other two bombers followed suit.

Eleven seconds after releasing the bombs from a height of about 2,000 feet—a time lapse that carried each aircraft 1,000 yards beyond the bomb-dropping point—their combined load of high-explosive, antipersonnel, and incendiary bombs fell on an area from the candy factory near the Rentería Bridge to the vicinity of the Arrién Restaurant.

A cluster of incendiaries landed among the fifty girls tending vats and molds in the candy factory. The bombs exploded with white flashes, then flared and burned fiercely, scattering red-and-white fragments of Thermit.

Factory manager Rafael Herrán emerged from his office in time to see a cascade of sparks envelop one of the girls, setting her overalls and hair alight. She collapsed in a fiery ball. Other women were screaming and running for the doors. A sheet of flame came from the far end of the building where the incendiaries had ignited caldrons of sugar solution.

Coughing and spluttering through the smoke, Herrán joined the stampede from the factory.

At the door he remembered the fish he had bought for tomorrow's meeting of his cooking club. He ran back to his office and picked it up. He risked his life, he would say afterward, "because I continued to believe everything would go on as normal. I couldn't accept what was happening."

Antonio Arazamagni, at the junction of the railway station plaza and Calle Don Tello when two bombs fell in the street, saw an old woman, seated outside her front door, calmly peel her potatoes until she had finished, then rise to her feet and walk back inside the house as if nothing had happened.

Fifty yards away, at No. 29, a bomb fell through the roof and tumbled three floors of plaster and lathe into the street. Among the eight people killed were the widow Lucita Bilbao and her daughter Victoria, who was celebrating her fifteenth birthday. In one of those freak happenings that people would remember long after, the cake Antonio had baked for Victoria ended up intact on top of the pile of rubble under which Victoria and her mother were buried.

The second bomb fell on No. 62 Calle Don Tello, a grocer's shop. The staff and customers, seven persons, were killed outright.

A policeman directed Antonio to the Plazuela del Mercado, at the foot of Calle Santa María. Several bombs, including a 550-pounder and some incendiaries, had fallen there. The incendiaries failed to detonate; the shiny canisters, bearing the name of their German manufacturer, were recovered and would later be one of the exhibits the Basque government would offer as "proof to the world of the German involvement in the terror attack." Not everyone would believe the story.

The 550-pounder had plowed through an office block, bringing down the roof and part of the building's facade, spewing desks and filing cabinets into the square. The worst damage occurred in a cake shop at street level. Among the debris, spattered with cream and pastry, were the bodies of the two young shop assistants.

They were the only immediately identifiable dead Antonio saw. He estimated there were up to forty people injured. It seemed to him a miracle the death toll was not higher.

In the marketplace, stalls were set on fire; people and animals were killed and injured. An incendiary landed in a bull pen, spraying two bullocks with burning Thermit. Maddened with pain, they broke out of the stall and charged through the market before falling into a bomb crater.

Smoke killed caged birds, blackened produce and household goods. In minutes the most famous market in Vizcaya was destroyed as flames spread through the canvas-roofed stalls.

Juan Silliaco and his volunteers were about fifty yards from the fire station when, before Silliaco's eyes, "it disappeared in smoke."

A bomb had curved over the adjoining roof of the Bank of Vizcaya to bring down the building. So complete was the destruction that it would be three days before the stable boy's body was recovered, intermingled with the remains of the two dray horses. Under the falling concrete Guernica's fire truck was flattened to a third of its original height.

Juan Silliaco picked himself up off the ground for the second time in thirty minutes and realized that Guernica now had no proper means with which to fight fires.

He ordered his firemen to pair off "and lend what assistance you can."

Above: The bombers go in. This remarkable photograph was taken by Father Eusebio Arronategui just as the first wave of Junkers-52s approached Guernica. If the Germans' target was the narrow Rentería Bridge, as they claimed, why were the planes flying three abreast? *(Photo: Authors' Collection)*

Below: The German planes attacked from the north, flying through the gap in the hills at the top of this picture and down the valley to Guernica. The main road leading south to Bilbao can be seen at center; parallel to it on the right is the railroad track. *(Photo: Authors' Collection)*

Above: The first bombs fall. *(Photo: Authors' Collection)*

Below: Faustino Pastor mans his machine gun in Guernica. Soon he would remove its legs in order to fire straight up at the attacking planes. *(Photo: Faustino Pastor)*

Above left: Interior of the Church of San Juan in flames. *(Photo: Authors' Collection)*

Above right: The gutted interior of the Church of San Juan after the attack. *(Photo: Informe Herrán)*

Below: Another view of the devastation of the Church of San Juan. *(Photo: Studio Pepe)*

Above: The Church of Santa María surrounded by flames. Just left of center is the Carmelite Convent, where Dr. Cortés and Teresa Ortuz were working in the operating room. *(Photo: Faustino Pastor)*

Below: The road from Guernica up to Luno. On this bend, many people were machine-gunned. *(Photo: Ataxi)*

Above: The remains of downtown Guernica, with the shell of the Bank of Vizcaya at center right. Nearly three-quarters of the town's buildings were reduced to rubble. *(Photo: Authors' Collection)*

Below: The Taberna Vasca, and a view of what was once Guernica's marketplace. *(Photo: Authors' Collection)*

Above: Guernica's wrecked *frontón*, or pelota stadium. *(Photo: Authors' Collection)*

Below: Basque troops search for survivors among the ruins. *(Photo: Faustino Pastor)*

Some thirty feet from the kitchen where he sat holding his wineglass, Isidro Arrién saw the front of his restaurant split open, as if in slow motion. Then the ceiling emitted a groaning noise. Dropping his glass, he ran from the kitchen.

Behind him the ceiling fell in with a crash as tons of masonry buried forever his prized cooking pots and the flans and cookies baking in the oven.

The next thing Isidro would recall was finding himself running through the marketplace. To reach there he must have completed a circle from the rear of his restaurant, a distance of some one hundred yards that he would never recollect covering.

Almost blinded now by sweat and close to exhaustion, the big man continued to run. He was one of the hundreds of men, women, and children now running in all directions through the town, aimlessly.

•29•

As Von Moreau's experimental squadron flew back to Burgos, at Vitoria airfield the ten HE-51s commanded by Captain Franz von Lutzow were about to start their engines.

Lieutenant Wandel was aware that he was being observed from the aircraft on either side of his. He hoped he had not given the wrong impression by the eager way he had checked his flaps and elevators and pulled himself into the cockpit.

Wandel was eager for combat; he wanted to show how sharp his reflexes and eyesight were, and that he had not "come all this way for nothing." But he did not want to be like some of the other new members of the squadron. On the way out to their planes they had spoken loudly about the feats they were going to perform. The more experienced pilots had been quiet and reflective in the presence of these brash newcomers.

Waiting for takeoff, Wandel again went over the route. From the moment he was airborne, he calculated, it would take sixteen minutes' flying before he would for the first time shoot to kill.

At Burgos airfield, the Junkers-52 coughed into life.

First Lieutenant von Knauer of No. 1 Squadron was the first to start his three engines. Then Lieutenant Hermann started his, and Sergeant Wienzek. Finally the sound of twenty-seven air-cooled BMW radial engines, each generating 725 horsepower, echoed around the base.

First Lieutenant von Beust's squadron of seven Junkers bombers carried out its engine tests. No. 3 Squadron started their preflight checks. Soon twenty-three Junkers-52s would be ready for action.

About 5:10 P.M., the aircraft dispatcher at Vitoria airfield raised and lowered his hand. One Heinkel aircraft engine after another sprang into life, and the fighter biplanes jockeyed into takeoff position.

Wandel followed Von Lutzow into the air, climbing to 5,000 feet, and then to the rendezvous point. The young flier found he had little time for sightseeing; he was busy keeping his position among the other HE-51s. He was relieved when Von Lutzow raised his hand and pointed northward.

At Burgos airfield, Wing Commander Fuchs watched as the remainder of No. 1 Squadron prepared to follow Von Knauer into the air.

Each bomber waddled into position, paused, spouted puffs of blue-gray smoke from the engine exhausts as its motors were boosted, and then commenced its takeoff run. As it gained speed, its tail lifted so that the aircraft was almost level with the ground, traveling on its two fixed wheels. Then, with a roar, it was airborne.

Fuchs could tell who was flying each plane by the way it took off. Sergeant Dous in 22-84 needed a lot of runway. Hampe, the NCO pilot of 22-91, flew like a carbon copy of Von Knauer. Chilla, the sergeant-pilot of 22-90, on the other hand, was better suited to flying a Heinkel. He took his bomber into the air with the daring of Von Moreau.

Sergeant Rasche, who flew 22-95, was the last of No. 1 Squadron to line up. Behind him came the fourteen planes of the other two squadrons.

At Vitoria airfield, an officer in flying control logged each fighter taking off. After the last one was airborne, he telephoned the news to the operations room in the Frontón Hotel.

As the Junkers bomber group assembled near Burgos, each of the HE-51s, having crossed the enemy line, fired a test burst of its twin machine guns. The ten planes flew on toward Guernica at 150 mph.

In Guernica, Lieutenant Gandaría succeeded in reaching GHQ in Galdacano by telephone. The military line from La Merced did not go through the town's telephone exchange. He reported the damage and asked for fighter plane and artillery protection "because there may be another attack." He was told the request would be considered.

"That means," said Captain de Beiztegi, "that nothing will be done."

The communications room in La Merced was now a makeshift damage-control center. Ever since Von Moreau's first bombs had fallen on the town, reports had been coming in from patrols sent to investigate the damage. By five-thirty, casualty figures were forty-two dead or missing, sixty-four injured. Serious cases had been admitted to the Carmelite Convent after Captain de Beiztegi had personally telephoned Captain Cortés and told him, "With the red cross on the roof anyone can tell you're a hospital. If you are going to be bombed, better to go down doing your job." There is no record of Cortés's reply.

The candy factory had been gutted. But surprisingly, there were no other reports of serious fires. Small ones were put out by bucket brigades.

To the men in the communications room, Guernica seemed to have survived its baptism of fire remarkably well. They turned their attention to the reports coming in from observation posts along the front: All afternoon, Italian and German aircraft had been attacking Basque positions between Marquina and Monte Oiz. Only six miles southeast, Múnditibar had been bombed and machine-gunned.

Captain de Beiztegi ordered the two thousand troops in and around Guernica to remain under cover, so as not to draw further attention to the town.

At the time that order was issued, the first soldiers were already fleeing. In ones and twos at first, then in small groups, and finally in large numbers, they stole away from the cemetery, from their positions on the west slopes of Guernica, and from La Merced. Those from the convent headed back down the Marquina road. Some of them told Juan Plaza they were looking for a place to ford the Mundaca south of the town.

"You're running away," Juan told them tearfully.

A soldier explained, "It's better to stay alive to fight another day with proper weapons."

As Juan approached the Rentería Bridge, "a mass of mad people came running from the town, over the bridge, and down the road toward me. One woman, her feet slashed by broken glass, was laughing insanely all the time. A man was carrying a caged bird and screeching for his wife to follow him. He didn't wait for anyone, just kept screeching."

Then, over the village of Arteaga, some miles from where he stood, Juan saw a sight that made him turn and join the fleeing mob.

Captain von Lutzow's HE-51s were coming in to attack.

Standing in the doorway of Unceta's bunker, José Rodríguez counted five pairs of fighters coming toward Guernica. He estimated they were flying at around 200 feet.

Near the Rentería Bridge they broke formation. Four pairs peeled off across the town; the fifth continued down the railway line, machine guns firing, toward the arms factory.

As the fighters reached the railway station plaza, some 400 yards from Rodríguez, they banked and released incendiaries.

Some of them started fires on Calle Fernando el Católico, a street leading to the arms plant. One struck a corner of the factory, bounced off the concrete onto the ground, and began to burn.

José Rodríguez and Luis Unceta rushed from the bunker to fight the fire. Water had no effect. Rodríguez grabbed a spade and shoveled sand over the flames, smothering them.

He and Luis ran back to the shelter. Choking from the acrid smoke of the incendiary, Rodríguez told Rufino Unceta, "It must have been a mistake. The bomb should have fallen elsewhere."

Augusto Unceta would recall how "Father just stood there, saying nothing, but radiating strength to everybody around him." The fourteen-year-old boy felt intense pride when he heard a workman say that Rufino Unceta's foresight in building the bunker had saved them all.

In addition to the 120 men in the huge cavern were their families, Victoria Arrién, and her daughters—all told, some 350 persons. It was uncomfortable for those at the back of the shelter, where the air was already stale. But for those grouped around Unceta and his family at the bunker entrance, there was a safe, well-ventilated view of the destruction of their town.

Antonio Arazamagni carried a young office girl, injured and suffering from shock, out of the Plazuela del Mercado. Antonio was taking her to the home of Jacinta Gómez on Barrencalle; he knew that the mother of three would look after the girl.

Jacinta saw Antonio coming down the narrow street and ran to meet him. Antonio could see her children standing in the doorway of their house.

At that moment, a Heinkel-51 began to machine-gun the street.

Antonio lurched into a doorway with the injured girl. He saw Jacinta knocked backward several feet by the force of the bullets.

Her three children ran screaming from their home toward their dead mother. A second Heinkel killed them all in one sustained burst.

Peering over the garden wall on Calle Allende Salazar, where he had remained since leaving the Taberna Vasca to look for his young brother, Juan Guezureya saw two HE-51s swoop on the market-place. To Juan it seemed as if their guns "systematically raked the whole area. The two planes just flew back and forth at about one hundred feet, like flying sheep dogs rounding up people for the slaughter."

When the planes finally climbed away, the dead included several members of the town band. Nobody had time to identify or to count the total number of bodies. Later, it was estimated that close to fifty people received injuries during this particular strafing.

María Ortuza waited for the Heinkels to fly away from the marketplace. Then she ran down Calle Adolfo Urioste past the Taberna Vasca and into the air-raid shelter under the Town Hall. The dash left her breathless, but mindful of her position as house-keeper to Señora Arriendiara, María did not lift her skirts above her ankles as she stepped down into the bunker.

About three hundred people were wedged inside. María found herself unable to move more than a few feet beyond the door. A man moved aside to give her a little more room. She smiled her gratitude to Mayor José Labauría.

About a quarter of a mile away, huddled between the pillars supporting the still-intact Rentería Bridge, a handful of people sheltered from the air attacks.

Francisco Lazcano could be forgiven for thinking that open though it was, the underside of the bridge was a safe place to be. So far not one plane had fired a single burst nor dropped a single bomb on the bridge.

Father Alberto de Onaindía—a canon of Valladolid Cathedral and close confidant of President Aguirre—was also under the bridge. The priest had been passing through Guernica from Bilbao en route to his family and birthplace at Marquina when the attack began. Sheltering by the water's edge, he took careful note of all he could see. Later he would offer the pope, and the world, his eyewitness account—and cause an international storm with his testimony.

Over five hundred people, mostly women and children, believed they were safe inside the Church of Santa María. Father Iturran was close to tears as many of them knelt and prayed before the high altar. Carmen Batzar, among them, prayed for Juan Dominguiz. Others crowded into the side chapels, counting their rosaries and asking for God's protection. Few noticed the neat pile of artifacts near the entrance.

Father Iturran abandoned the idea of leaving the church. Nor, he believed, would Lieutenant Gandaría now want to fortify the building. "The planes will avoid us," he kept repeating. "The pilots can tell this is God's house."

Pedro Guezureya, owner of the Taberna Vasca, would remember, "People were afraid to leave because of the unknown conditions outside. All we could hear were screams and shouts and bombs and guns. A mother placed her baby in the font. Another woman went into a confession stall with her child. People were kneeling in front of the holy statues, asking God to spare them."

For some reason, probably to go to her fiancé, Carmen Batzar left the church. She walked alone along Goyencalle, and must have just turned onto Calle San Juan when she was spotted by a fighter pilot. Like her fiancé, she was machine-gunned. But Carmen Batzar died where she fell.

José Rodríguez saw the fighters climb away from the town. He estimated later that thirty minutes had passed since their arrival.

Some 2,000 feet above Guernica, Captain von Lutzow waited until the last of his squadron had joined the circle. East of the town, two of the roads were empty. Along the third, the road to Marquina, figures were moving. Von Lutzow dived. The other planes followed.

Sheltering behind some rocks, Juan Plaza kept his eyes fixed on the aircraft. The first fighter passed overhead, and he realized their guns were silent. He lay on his back and started to "laugh like a madman, I was so relieved."

The fighters were probably not only out of ammunition, but also low on fuel. Von Lutzow had apparently led them in a valedictory swoop on the way back to Vitoria. As they climbed away out of the valley, smoke rose over Guernica.

Juan Guezureya waited until the smoke eddying from the lower part of the town had drifted to where he lay behind the garden wall. Then he vaulted it and sprinted northward along Calle Allende Salazar.

He did not see the viaduct in which his young brother, Cipriano, and fourteen other boys had taken refuge. In one of those bizarre flukes of the bombing, four incendiary bombs fell near the viaduct, creating a wall of flame across its mouth, cracking the cement rim of the pipe, and finally collapsing tons of earth on the boys. Two weeks would pass before a flash flood revealed their bodies.

In the packed air-raid shelter beneath the Town Hall, María Ortuza felt entombed. Mayor Labauría had ordered the shelter door shut after four persons standing by the doorway had been killed. Their bodies had been pushed aside so the door could be closed.

Even so, smoke was drifting in. María heard the "moans from the back of the shelter where people were half-choking. Some soldiers offered water bottles. The gesture was poorly received. People thought the soldiers should be outside, fighting back."

María heard a gasp, and a body slumped to the ground. A woman shouted hysterically, "My boy needs air! Give him air!"

It was almost 6:00 P.M. in Guernica, one and a half hours since Von Moreau had first flown over the town.

6:00 P.M.—Midnight

·30·

When Von Richthofen and Lieutenant Asmus reached the top of Monte Oiz, intervening mountains blocked their view of the target area. Disappointed, the two men descended.

No written record was made of their conversation on the way down; it is probably safe to assume, as Hans Asmus does, "that if we talked, it was undoubtedly about work. Von Richthofen didn't like social contact. You could not talk to him about the weather or a landscape unless it was directly linked with some strategic move."

By 6:00 P.M., the Condor Legion's main bomber force—twenty-three Junkers-52s—was streaming northward, spread over several miles of airspace north of Garay. Between them they carried the balance of 100,000 pounds of explosives with which to hit the still-intact Rentería Bridge.

In Guernica's Carmelite Convent, injured people filled the reception area and overflowed into ground-floor corridors already crowded with wounded soldiers brought from the upper floors.

Cortés and Teresa had moved out of the operating room to work in the casualty area. Teresa would remember Cortés "was like a demon, doing the work of five people."

Watching him work and make his decisions, she realized that "his hardness was no more than a shell. For months he had kept from us part of his character which now came out. It was easy for him to be brisk and tough with soldiers. But with civilians he was very gentle and patient. At times I thought he was close to tears at some of the injuries, especially among the children. He ordered that, whenever possible, they should be treated first."

Teresa followed the surgeon and tied a card to each victim; on it she wrote Cortés's diagnosis, the immediate treatment he had given, and his decision whether to operate or not. On some cards Captain Cortés drew a small circle. It meant they should not be resuscitated if they became unconscious.

Drums of compresses and instrument trays were everywhere. Doctors, nurses, and nuns had to step over the injured lying on the floor.

A man with legs smashed to pulp; a woman whose thorax was torn open; a youth with machine-gun bullets in the leg; a child with a mangled arm. Each victim had to be diagnosed, assessed, given immediate palliative treatment, and if possible, comforted.

The air, Teresa remembered, was "filled with cries of 'Get a priest. I am dying.' We didn't have a priest."

Mother Augusta and her nuns did their best to ease the suffering of those beyond help.

The dead were carried out to the mortuary.

Between operations Cortés would inspect new cases, deciding who should be saved first. Catching Teresa's eyes on him, he once growled, "I'm not playing God. I'm just trying to do what Solomon did—please everybody."

Sometime after 6:00 P.M., Mother Augusta reported that blood supplies were almost exhausted. She tried to contact Bilbao; the telephone was dead.

Cortés passed word to the other surgeons that they must exercise even more stringent control when contemplating transfusion.

Once, stepping away from the operating table, Teresa saw Captain Cortés stare at the sight of Mother Augusta bending over a wounded man and giving him sips from a brandy bottle. "Have a drink yourself," the surgeon urged her. Mother Augusta offered him the bottle. Cortés laughed and walked away.

Teresa later heard Cortés tell a doctor, "The old Superior had the nerve to get that bottle from my office!"

She was sure there was a note of admiration in the surgeon's voice.

Juan Plaza made another attempt to reach his grandmother's home by the Rentería Bridge. He spotted her walking down the road toward him, clutching a basket of eggs. It was, she said calmly, all she had been able to take before the flames from the candy factory had spread to her house.

She looked reprovingly at the loaf of bread Juan still clutched. In the course of the afternoon, it had become crushed and dirty.

"Have you been playing football with it?" she asked. Juan thought she was the most composed person he had seen since the air attack started.

During his training period with the Bilbao Fire Brigade, Juan Silliaco had learned that buildings destroyed by bombs present special problems. The instructing officer had used a number of photographs from World War I to illustrate his lectures. Silliaco also recalled a striking photograph taken after the San Francisco earthquake; it showed some of the city's firemen burrowing into a building.

This afternoon Silliaco saw numerous examples of the sort of bomb damage he had been taught to expect—and beware.

There were many buildings like the fire station, which as a result of a direct hit had totally collapsed in a heap of rubble. There was no point in searching them, for no one could survive under such wreckage. In other buildings only one wall had collapsed; they could safely be searched by somebody who knew what he was doing. Then there was the worst kind of all, the sort of building Silliaco now contemplated on Calle San Juan.

It had once been a rooming house, four floors high, filled with refugees. A bomb had penetrated the roof and plunged through to the ground floor. It had failed to explode, but the sheer force of its passage through the poorly built building had collapsed the inner supports. The upper floors had caved in, sending ceilings down on floors, floors down on ceilings. The building had been reduced to half its normal height. To an expert like Silliaco it was "a classic situation—terribly dangerous."

From inside came cries for help.

People were rushing forward to tear at the rubble when Silliaco ordered them to stand back.

"You'll kill them," he said, walking around the building, trying to establish where the people were buried. He called for silence. The voices seemed to be coming from a corner of the building, under the rubble. He guessed they were in an air pocket, a cavity created by a quirk in the way the building had fallen. He told the onlookers to fetch shovels, wood supports, and ropes.

As they rushed to do so, Silliaco picked at the rubble, determining where to start tunneling. A wrong decision would result in the collapse of the air pocket.

By the time the equipment had been produced, he had selected his approach route. He began to dig.

The fighter pilots landed at Vitoria about 6:10 P.M. While ground crews were busy refueling and rearming the HE-51s, the pilots gathered together to compare impressions of the action.

All agreed the dust and smoke were nuisances and that the roads east of the town had been surprisingly empty.

From this moment on, they would nevertheless insist that they had attacked genuine military objectives. The plausibility of this claim would be severely damaged thirty-seven years later, when former officers of the Condor Legion would say they did not know there were troops in Guernica. They still blamed "unexpectedly high winds" for carrying the bombs into the town.

Only a near-hurricane could have carried the HE-51s over the streets of Guernica.

And many in Guernica would later recall the absence of any appreciable wind; it gave the bucket brigades a chance to contain some of the fires in the town.

———————

Antonio Arazamagni headed a bucket brigade on Calle San Juan. A line of men stretched fifty feet from a hydrant, passing along pails of water to throw on flames licking at a burning building.

Antonio, after witnessing the killing of Jacinta Gómez and her children on Barrencalle, had kept moving. At some point he handed over the office girl he was carrying to someone; he would never remember to whom or where.

He next found himself working on the bucket brigade. People would later say the young baker displayed great courage in helping fight the fire.

Checking through the Convent of La Merced, Lieutenant Gandaría estimated there were less than two hundred troops left in the building. Hundreds had gone. He threatened to shoot the next man he saw leaving. When an officer said it was now more sensible to evacuate the convent, he turned on him. "What's wrong with our army is that it's filled with deserters."

Captain Juan de Beiztegi threatened to court-martial any officer who willingly let his troops go.

The garrison commander soon made other unpleasant discoveries. When Gandaría telephoned observation posts around Guernica, Arteaga did not answer. An officer in the monastery of the Augustine Fathers said some of his troops had "fallen back" farther westward; another officer near the town's cemetery reported his men had "extended" their positions "back into the hills." Gandaría angrily told him to bring them back to their original positions.

By the end of his telephoning, Gandaría was clear on one thing: Most of the troops he had counted on to turn the town into a Basque Alcázar had broken and fled. Virtually the only ones who remained were the headquarters staff of the Eighteenth Loyola Battalion, those whom he had successfully imbued with his own fierce desire to resist, and remnants of the Saseta Battalion out by the monastery. Even if he brought together all the troops, there would still be insufficient force for the last-ditch stand he had intended.

Bitterly, he told Captain de Beiztegi they had no alternative but to pull out from the town.

In La Merced Convent, Mother María told her nuns they must leave at once. First they would take the Marquina road, then walk south along the river until they found a place shallow enough to cross. From there they would go to Múgica and on to Bilbao.

Unwittingly, she had chosen the same route as many of the soldiers who were hastening out of the town.

During this break in the bombing, José Rodríguez made some calculations about the timing of the attacks. So far they had occurred at intervals of about twenty minutes.

On that reckoning, his watch told him if another attack was coming, it should begin in nine minutes.

Burrowing into the rubble, Juan Silliaco was trying to figure out the line of least resistance through the debris.

So far, he had excavated several feet of narrow tunnel. Using his shovel to dislodge the powdered plaster and brick, he passed handfuls of dirt to a man behind him, who in turn passed the debris back into the street. Then the process was reversed to bring to the tunnel head the wooden props needed to support Juan Silliaco's slow advance.

Juan knew that the greatest danger was in going too fast; every inch he dug had to be pretested or the burrow would collapse.

The trapped people cried out again. Silliaco was able to distinguish several voices, among them a child's. He shouted for them to be silent; he was concerned they might use up their air supply. From then on, there was no sound but the scraping of his shovel.

When he reached what he judged was ground-floor level, a door barred his way. It was still within its frame, but it leaned at a strange angle. Silliaco thought it might have fallen from an upper floor. Gently he pushed against it. It swung open. Below him in a cavern were a man, two women, and a girl about four.

A torch was passed down the tunnel. Silliaco inspected the hole and saw that the group had been saved by the way the beams had crisscrossed to create a roof holding back tons of rubble.

They moved toward him.

"Stay where you are," commanded Silliaco. "You'll disturb the roof."

They stood still.

"The child," continued the fireman. "Pass her to me." The man lifted up the little girl. Silliaco reached down and pulled her into the tunnel.

"Don't worry. I'll get your mother and father soon," Silliaco promised her. He edged his way back down the tunnel, taking the girl with him.

Juan Silliaco emerged into open air and handed the girl to one of the small crowd of watching people.

He was about to crawl back into the tunnel when the people around him shouted and ran away. When he saw what had frightened them, the fireman followed their lead.

Similar panic gripped the bucket brigade feeding water to Antonio Arazamagni. They dropped their pails and ran.

Earlier, as people had run for shelter from the air attacks, some of them had noticed an incongruous sight outside the Church of San Juan: a plate camera standing on a tripod before the church.

Father Eusebio had intended to photograph the church that afternoon, but when the first bombs fell, he had gone to the railway station plaza to give the last rites to the dying and spiritual comfort to the wounded. He took refuge when the machine-gunning started. After the fighters left, he heard that his own church had been hit. He ran all the way to San Juan and found it undamaged.

He was about to return to his ministering when he saw something that made him rush to his camera. At that moment, he would later say, his only thought was "to acquire positive proof of this terrible act of desecration of our holy town."

Father Eusebio tilted up the camera. In the viewfinder he could clearly see coming toward the town the first chain of three Junkers-52s.

Behind them, "as far as the eye could see," the evening sky was filled with bombers.

He took a picture, whipped out the plate, turned, and fled.

·31·

Some seven miles from Guernica, the planes in Von Knauer's No. 1 Squadron lowered their pots. The nine bombardiers climbed down into the cupolas to line up their bombsights. At two miles a minute the bombers flew toward the town.

Behind No. 1 Squadron, Von Beust's *Staffel* was circling the final turning point, Elanchove. Captain von Krafft's No. 3 Squadron was still flying north past Monte San Miguel.

The bomber crews had received no reports of Faustino Pastor's machine gun or of the riflemen in the Convent of Santa Clara. Both groups began firing when the first chain was about two miles away.

Julio Bareno lurched to his feet when he heard the gunfire. Exhausted from carrying the heavy mail pouch, he and his wife were resting by the Residencia Calzada. It took him a few moments to realize what the shooting was about. He turned and shouted to his wife, "Look at those planes!"

Over two hours had passed since the couple had reached the wall. Señora Bareno could not bring herself to leave her home and friends; she refused to go farther. Her husband had pleaded with her, but she had told him it was "madness to walk to Bilbao, and why should we do all this for the bank?" He could not explain "the special obligation" he felt as a branch manager.

When the air attacks had come, the couple had cowered against the wall, flinching as plane after plane flew overhead. In the intervals between raids, Bareno had tried to persuade his wife to move. Now, his patience exhausted, he screamed at her, "Can't you see what's coming?"

His wife opened her eyes and peered northward. Crying out in

horror, she got to her feet and ran down the road to Bilbao, leaving
her husband to stagger after her with the mail pouch.

The Junkers flew higher than the Heinkel bombers, so this time
Juan Plaza did not actually see the bombs being loosed from the
planes. But a good mile down the Marquina road, he and his
grandmother could hear the explosions reverberate through the
valley. They saw huge columns of flame and smoke rise into the air
above Guernica.

The lead bombers turned away. Juan later estimated that
between 500 and 1,000 meters separated each chain of three
Junkers.

The first salvo of bombs set fire to the huge, empty pelota *frontón*
behind the Arrién Restaurant. It also smashed Julio Bareno's Bank
of Vizcaya.

Juan Silliaco was near the bank just before it was hit. "The air
was alive with the cries of the wounded. I saw a man crawling down
the street, dragging his broken legs. He was saying, 'Help me, please
help me.' Then he just disappeared along with some cows who had
broken free from their pens at the market. They were literally blown
to pieces.

"Pieces of people and animals were lying everywhere. The
bombs were falling all around and the ground was rocking beneath
my feet."

Silliaco would not remember where, or how far, he ran. Then:
"There was a terrific crash. I was thrown on my face. From a great
distance I heard a voice screaming. Or maybe it was many voices
united in one common scream. From where I lay, it seemed far away.
It took me some time to discover I was trapped under a fallen
building. I was saved because before the building collapsed into the
street, the ground had cracked open, breaking one of the viaducts
carrying the town's main water supply. I had fallen into the viaduct
and was quite safe, but above me was a mass of timber and brick-
work. I could see daylight, and then I wished I couldn't see anything.
Close by, in the wreckage, was a young woman. I could not take my
eyes off her. Bones stuck through her dress. Her head had been

twisted right around her neck. She lay, mouth open, her tongue hanging out. I vomited and lost consciousness."

Julio Bareno and his wife were no more than a hundred yards beyond the Residencia Calzada when it received a direct hit.

They stood appalled as the home, filled with the elderly and orphaned, exploded before their eyes. Chunks of stone were hurled across the road and into the houses opposite. The shock waves blew the Barenos off their feet.

Very few inside the Residencia were to survive. It was estimated that forty-five old women and men, children, wounded soldiers, and the nuns caring for them died from the one bomb that hit the home. Neither the huge red cross on the roof nor the Residencia's reinforced *refugio* saved them.

Julio Bareno helped his wife to her feet, picked up the mail pouch, and they continued out of town.

It took each chain of bombers just thirty seconds to pass over Guernica and execute a standard 150-degree turn away from the target. By then a further 9,900 pounds of explosives, the collective load of each chain, were whistling over the town.

Antonio Arazamagni, his mind and body battered, swayed at the junction of Calle Santa María and Azoquecalle. He had no clear idea of how he had arrived there, or why.

Three hundred feet away—he would later measure out the distance—was the ugly air-raid shelter in the middle of Calle Santa María, filled with about 150 people. "A row of bombs fell along the street. One after another, in a line, like a pack of cards, the houses began to collapse. I saw them sway and fall with a roar that I could hear even above the sound of the planes. The shelter went, too. All the explosions fused together. The force of the blast threw three people out of the shelter."

Antonio turned and ran toward the Church of Santa María.

In the next street to the north, Father Eusebio was about 100 yards up the sloping Calle San Juan when he recognized a family that had recently arrived in his parish. Señora Urnganguru and her five daughters had returned from Shoshone in Idaho, following the death of Señor Urnganguru in the United States.

The priest had come to know the eldest daughter, twelve-year-old María, best; he had listened attentively to her stories of the United States. Now he watched the girl guiding her mother and younger sisters around the corner of Barrencalle and down Calle San Juan. He hastened to meet them.

María was relieved to find the priest beside her. She would remember, "He said our only chance was to get out of town. He began to lead us down the street. We had only gone a few yards when a bomb fell on the exact spot we had just passed. Farther down, another bomb hit a house and several bodies just flew through the air."

Led by the priest, the family ran down Calle San Juan. "Parts of houses were falling all around us. But we somehow managed to keep our feet. My mother kept shouting, 'Stay together, whatever we do, stay together.' I think she thought if we had to die, it was better we all died together. Once a wall fell, blocking the street. Father Eusebio did not hesitate. He pushed us up over the rubble and climbed over after us."

They were less than fifty yards from the Church of San Juan when it was hit by a cascade of incendiaries and burst into flames. The plate camera on its tripod was incinerated.

The bombs that destroyed San Juan had probably been dropped by the last chain of Von Knauer's No. 1 Squadron. A mile behind that chain, thirty seconds away, Von Beust's No. 2 Squadron now prepared to begin bombing.

In the gap between the departure of one squadron and the arrival of another, Father Eusebio managed to get the Urnganguru family past his burning church and onto the Rentería Bridge, which was still untouched.

He watched them turn onto the road to Arteaga, heading for the safest place he knew in all Spain—the Santimamiñe caves, four miles away.

Then the young priest sprinted back up Calle San Juan. He

passed his blazing church without pausing. He was now concerned only with getting to Santa María, a tempting target for any bomber pilot.

Squadron Leader von Beust, in 22-70, found it impossible to identify any target. He would remember, "I saw the bombs from the first squadron dropping. By the time we were over the target, the town seemed to be obscured by rising dust resulting from the first bombs. The air was very dry, and I suppose the roads were not paved. So we had to drop our bombs as best we could. There was no question that we wouldn't drop them—it would have been dangerous for us to land with a bomb load—but the navigator in the pot couldn't tell what he was hitting."

A Von Beust bomb may have been the one that reduced Antonio Arazamagni's prized Ford to a tangled scrap. A second one might have scored the direct hit on Antonio's bakery. Antonio arrived on Goyencalle in time to see the building bulge outward "and then fell right on top of my car."

Brokenhearted, Antonio headed out of Guernica, up the steep mountain road leading to the village of Luno.

The villagers of Luno had a panoramic view of the attack taking place several hundred feet below them in the valley. But gradually a blanket of smoke spread over Guernica, wiping out the view. By then, the first survivors of the raid had reached Luno, and the people of that hamlet were too busy aiding them to watch the hell that was happening almost at their feet.

Nobody would ever know how many victims were claimed by the smoke alone. In four days' time, a *refugio* would be opened in the basement of a house at the bottom of Calle Allende Salazar, and twenty corpses would be revealed, totally unmarked. A pathologist would establish that their deaths had been caused by suffocation.

In the Town Hall bunker, María Ortuza thought some of the people near her were about to choke to death. The heat in the shelter rose steadily as the air became more fetid. A group of women had cleared a little space for some children to squat, knee to shoulder blade, but everybody else had to stand.

Some sick, some hysterical, many near suffocation, all gasping for breath, the people in the bunker heard the raid outside increase in intensity. Then, immediately above, there was a sudden, terrifying explosion. A 550-pounder had hit the Town Hall.

María believed "we were being buried alive. The roof came down on us, and then the Town Hall was hit twice more. Three floors fell on our shelter. The air was filled with the smells of scorched plaster, wood, and flesh."

María dropped to her knees and crawled toward the shelter door. Her head stung from a glancing blow she had received. Ahead there was a sharp, splintering sound, and then daylight. Labauría had smashed open the door.

She closed her eyes tightly against the pain and scrabbled forward. Once she pushed aside a hand, but to her horror, she found it had caught in her belt and she was dragging a severed arm along with her. She thrust it away and continued to claw her way over the rubble.

Once in the open, she dragged herself to a corner of the Town Hall plaza. There, behind a pile of debris, María sheltered, biting her knuckles until they bled.

Others clambered out of the shelter and ran blindly. Then, with a crash, the Town Hall caved in, again sealing the shelter's entrance.

Rufino, Luis, and Augusto Unceta, José Rodríguez, and a score of workmen had formed themselves into a makeshift firefighting squad. Armed with shovels, buckets of water, and sand, they huddled between the bunker and the main factory building, ready to risk their lives to save the plant.

As the air attacks continued, Rufino Unceta carefully watched the path of the aircraft. All flew on a course that took them clear of the factory.

It was obvious that Unceta, with his calm demeanor, believed his loyalty to the Nationalists had been remembered; that the pilots had been ordered to avoid hitting his factory.

They had not.

The Condor Legion was unaware there was an arms factory in the town—let alone that its management was pro-Franco. The Unceta complex was saved because the bombers had orders to approach Guernica at an angle that carried them southwest over the town. The factory was due east of the railway line and some 400 yards south of the station. To have hit the Unceta works, the bombers would have had to follow a course farther east.

That the factory had not been machine-gunned was also explicable. There were better targets available for fighter pilots than a solid concrete building. Whether he knew it or not, Rufino Unceta had only to fear the odd stray spark crossing over the railway line and setting fire to his plant.

Out in the open, he and the other firefighters had an excellent view of the Unceta mansion, some 100 yards away to the west. Suddenly, explosions shook the house and sheets of flame gushed through the roof and windows.

The Uncetas watched in silence as their mansion collapsed, almost certainly hit by the last chain of No. 2 Squadron. They had lost all their private possessions. Rufino Unceta's only comment on the destruction of his home was "I will build again."

At that very moment, unknown to the Uncetas, Julio Bareno was hefting down the Bilbao road ledgers containing details of their deposits.

Lieutenant Gandaría waited until the last of Von Beust's squadron had cleared the town, and then shouted, "Go!"

At the command to go, Mother María and the nuns hurried past him, out of the Convent of La Merced, and down the Marquina road.

"Adiós," shouted Gandaría. The nuns made no reply. He looked at the soldiers crowding the central passageway of the convent.

When Captain de Beiztegi nodded, Gandaría waved the first soldier forward.

The troops ran past him after the nuns. The two officers followed them, leaving La Merced empty for the first time in centuries.

Behind Von Beust, Squadron Leader von Krafft led his bombers farther out to sea than the others had done; after he turned south again, the gap between him and the last of No. 2 Squadron was some five miles. Now, as he came in to attack, Von Krafft "could see nothing of the town, only smoke drifting southwest over it." But Von Krafft did spot the Rentería Bridge, standing well clear of the smoke.

"So the attack went ahead," Von Krafft would recall. "I felt my plane lift as the bombs were released, and I turned at once to look back at the target. The big bombs fell by the bridge. The incendiary bombs made a silver shower over the smoke above Guernica and dropped into the town."

Nine of the heavy bombs from Von Krafft's squadron fell in and around La Merced, just by the Rentería Bridge. They damaged a kitchen, part of the chapel, and uprooted the convent's orchard. But not one bomb hit the bridge itself.

Faustino Pastor and his team continued to fire at the bombers, too preoccupied to notice how many of their colleagues had left their positions.

The monastery of the Augustine Fathers was now empty. The monks had joined the soldiers fleeing the building; they eventually went to Bilbao and on to France, never to return to Guernica.

At the southern end of the town, most of the soldiers around the cemetery had also decamped. Those who remained were squeezed into the mausoleums, standing between the coffins.

Isidro Arrién felt he, too, was in a tomb, with thousands of men beating on its roof. He never knew when or how he had reached the shelter in the basement of the public school. His first clear memory was of his sons guiding him to a seat.

The Arriéns, with five hundred other children and parents, listened to the sounds outside. "The bombardment had gone on so long we grew accustomed to it, and terror in many cases simply gave way to total exhaustion," one of Isidro's children would remember.

Isidro found himself dozing, oblivious to the sound of hundreds of windows in the classrooms above being shattered.

A combination of rage and fascination had so far kept Juan Guezureya from breaking down.

He had reached the slopes to the west of the town, and was sheltering in a small cave about 400 feet directly above the now-deserted monastery of the Augustine Fathers. His vantage point afforded him a view of the family restaurant; on more peaceful afternoons he had come to the cave and dreamed of how, when the business was his, he would expand it "and give the Arrién Restaurant something to think about."

Now the Arrién Restaurant was gone. Juan could glimpse its shell through the smoke. But the Taberna Vasca, he could see, was still intact. Then came a series of crumping sounds and the Taberna Vasca went up in flames.

He wept. He did not raise his head from his hands until he heard the monastery of the Augustine Fathers explode, "blown to smithereens."

An overshoot, a sudden gust of wind, simple bad luck—nobody will ever be able to say with certainty what caused an incendiary to penetrate the roof of the Church of Santa María.

Father Iturran was in the pulpit, leading the packed congregation in prayer, when the bomb crashed into the side chapel of Our Lady of Begonia. Father Eusebio, standing at the rear of the church, grabbed a flower vase and rushed to dump the water over the smoking canister.

The incendiary was giving off clouds of smoke but no flames. It had left a gaping hole in the roof, knocked Our Lady's statue to the ground, and now rested on the chapel floor.

"Water! We need water," shouted Father Eusebio. "There is no danger if we get water."

From the pulpit, Father Iturran's voice came loud and clear. He commanded some of the men in the congregation to go to the sacristy and bring out the bottles of communion wine: "If our Lord could work a miracle by turning water into wine, then perhaps he will allow us to use wine as water."

Many people would later testify that only the old priest's words stemmed general panic. Water and wine were poured onto the incendiary, and it fizzled out without catching fire.

Some of the congregation later swore they had witnessed a miracle.

Soon after 6:30 P.M., the last three Junkers climbed away from the town, having rained down 9,900 pounds of mixed explosives.

About fifteen minutes had passed since Father Eusebio had taken his dramatic photograph of Von Knauer's JU-52 and the two others approaching Guernica. The priest still had the plate tucked into his cassock pocket. Later he would take it to Bilbao, where it would be developed and used for propaganda purposes.

During those fifteen minutes, over two hundred people had been killed and twice as many injured. Seven of every ten houses in Guernica—almost three-quarters of the town's buildings—had been destroyed, or soon would be, by the flames.

The Rentería Bridge, target of all this destruction, was still intact.

In the Church of Santa María, Father Eusebio counted silently. After sixty seconds he went outside. The sky to the north was empty.

He turned back into the church and told the people inside, "They have gone. But they may come back. We have little time." He issued orders: the infirm and elderly should make their way toward Luno; the remainder should run for the caves of Santimamiñe.

The people hesitated. Then from another part of the church came the commanding voice of Father Iturran: "Go, it is your only chance."

The people hurried from Santa María, some beginning the

climb to Luno, others streaming down Calle San Juan, across the Rentería Bridge, and up the Arteaga road. Nearly five hundred people eventually reached the caves.

Around 6:40 P.M., Knuppel's squadron of six Messerschmitts took off from Vitoria. The fastest fighters in the Spanish Civil War needed barely ten minutes to reach the town.

By then Santa María Church was empty; Mother María and her nuns were well south of Guernica. The soldiers from La Merced had overtaken them, but the nuns had caught up again because the soldiers had deliberately slowed their pace to that of the refugees. From the air it would have been impossible to tell the troops from the civilians.

Lieutenant Gandaría guessed there must be hundreds of people heading for the river crossing and on to Múgica. Years afterward he would recall their faces: "dark with smoke, coated with dust, and totally blank. They were alive, but all life had gone out of them."

He and Captain de Beiztegi trudged on, saying nothing "because there was nothing to say. The war was lost."

On the opposite side of the River Mundaca, Julio Bareno and his wife were about halfway between Guernica and Múgica when the Messerschmitts appeared. Bareno pushed his wife into a ditch, then jumped in beside her. Other people stood paralyzed, numbed by the noise of the planes racing toward them at almost ground level. The fighters banked toward Luno.

Antonio Arazamagni saw them coming, and he, too, rolled into a convenient ditch. "A group of men and women, and some soldiers, were coming up the road. They had no chance. They were all killed."

Later there would be some doubt as to how many swoops the Messerschmitts made over Guernica. Juan Guezureya saw them make one run, "low and steady, firing all the time, flying north to south over the town."

Above left: Eyewitness María Ortuza in 1975. *(Photo: Sigbert Butz)*

Above right: Eyewitness Juan Guezureya in 1975. *(Photo: Sigbert Butz)*

Below: The target that was missed: the Rentería Bridge. *(Photo: Sigbert Butz)*

Above: The new home of the Uncetas in downtown Guernica. *(Photo: Sergio Ferraris)*

Below: The summer home of the count of Montefuerte in Guernica. It was not damaged in the 1937 raid. *(Photo: Sergio Ferraris)*

Above left: Slightly battered but still standing, the Church of Santa María. *(Photo: Sigbert Butz)*

Above right: The Convent and Church of Santa Clara. *(Photo Sigbert Butz)*

Below: The Carmelite Convent. *(Photo: Sigbert Butz)*

Left: Close-up of the monument honoring those who died "under the banner of Francisco Franco." *(Photo: Sergio Ferraris)*

Upper right: Evidence of the 1937 attack can still be seen in Guernica. *(Photo: Sigbert Butz)*

Lower right: The cemetery at the outskirts of town. In the center is Guernica's sole memorial to those who died in the Civil War—but those of one side only. *(Photo: Sigbert Butz)*

Above: Guernica, as seen from one of the stations of the cross on the road to Luno. *(Photo: Sigbert Butz)*

Below: The Church of San Pedro at Luno, where many fled from the bombs in 1937. *(Photo: Sigbert Butz)*

Right: The rebuilt Town Hall and its Plaza de los Fueros. *(Photo: Sigbert Butz)*

Below: Because of the 1937 devastation, Guernica today is a remarkably new town in an ancient land. *(Photo: Sigbert Butz)*

Juan Plaza, almost two miles outside Guernica, believed he saw the ME-109s make two attacks before they flew off.

He may have confused them with Von Lutzow's HE-51s, which returned at about 7:00 P.M.

To José Rodríguez, still standing beside his fire bucket near the Unceta plant, it was "impossible to understand why they had come. The town was virtually flattened. Nothing stood between the market and the railway station."

Juan Silliaco, trapped in the viaduct, recovered consciousness at about the time the fighters began to strafe the ruins. Machine-gun bullets thwacked into the debris around him.

He knew his position was relatively safe, if unpleasant: The young woman's body a few feet away had begun to smell.

Machine gunner Faustino Pastor would also recall how low the planes flew. He could no longer fire at them—he was out of ammunition. But the fighter planes did not seem interested in attacking the machine-gun team. They concentrated on the town.

Juan Guezureya watched them "just going back and forth, back and forth, machine-gunning. Sometimes they flew in pairs, sometimes in a long line, sometimes in close formation. It was as if they were practicing new moves. They must have fired thousands of bullets in the process."

María Ortuza heard some of those bullets thudding into the dead donkey she hid behind. She closed her eyes, "so they would also think I was dead."

At seven-thirty, the HE-51s executed a final run over the town and headed back for base. The air attack on Guernica was over.

It was almost three hours since Von Moreau's pathfinding flight over the town. Those still alive were left with the fires to fight.

•32•

To Juan Guezureya, looking down from his cave on the stricken town, it was like "having a preview of the end of the world." From the heights of Luno, Antonio Arazamagni felt he was "witnessing Armageddon." Many others would express the sentiment that this had been their Day of Judgment, and that, in the words of Augusto Unceta, "God had chosen to spare some of us from this manmade hell."

In that hell, Juan Silliaco realized that if he were not rescued soon, he would be roasted alive. He was thankful his son was safe in Bilbao. He hoped the boy would never learn how his father had faced death without having made a proper confession and with sudden doubts about everlasting life.

Not far away, María Ortuza mustered enough courage to move from behind the dead donkey and make her way to the Church of Santa María. It was empty, its nave reeking of smoke. She turned back into the town, seeking "a sign of life to show I was not alone." She saw none as she passed the burning Taberna Vasca, the blazing marketplace, a dozen other burning buildings. The flames singed her hair; the smoke made her eyes smart.

At the corner of Artecalle, her path was blocked by the Bank of Vizcaya, its front collapsed across the street. She could see the bank's safe standing upright in the rubble. María could not know that the heat had incinerated all the paper money inside, but that the silver coins Julio Bareno had placed there would survive—and within a week would be used by the Nationalists.

She retraced her steps along the eastern edge of the marketplace. As she saw a horse move and then sag back into the flames, María shrieked. The beast had undoubtedly died some time before; and the intensity of the heat had caused its muscles to contract.

As she moved around another pile of rubble, a voice from inside called for help.

It was Juan Silliaco.

María saw some soldiers come out of the Convent of Santa Clara, the only troops to have remained in Guernica's center during the attack. She persuaded them to rescue Silliaco; they freed him in a short time and went on their way.

Silliaco himself began to search for other members of the town's volunteer fire brigade. He eventually located two sheltering by the River Mundaca. There were a number of bodies in the water.

"Don't bother with them," said Silliaco. "Concentrate on the living."

Those three men formed the nucleus of a rescue operation that in the hours to come would incorporate many other squads, some as large as forty men. They would fight the fires with any means available, free the trapped, and ultimately dig out the dead.

But now, Juan Silliaco was intent on completing a rescue he had begun almost two hours before. He and his two companions went back to Calle San Juan, to that pile of debris Silliaco had had to abandon when Von Knauer's bombers had arrived. He found the tunnel intact. When he shouted into it, a faint response came back. Silliaco crawled into the mound and brought out the two women and man who had remained unharmed during the world's biggest air raid to date on an undefended town. A few days later, they were reunited with the small girl Silliaco had saved earlier.

When darkness came, shortly before 8:00 P.M., Rufino Unceta decided that no further air attacks need be expected. He sent his sons and José Rodríguez into the town to assess the damage, and told his workers and their families they could leave the bunker. Then he entered his factory.

The soldiers had long since fled. "My only concern was what damage there was to the machines."

There had been none. The plant was ready to resume production. It would not, after all, be removed to Bilbao.

Luis and Augusto Unceta separated from Rodríguez outside the factory; the boys went to examine the damage to their home, the general manager to his.

No. 3 Calle de la Estación, Rodríguez's home, was "a smoking pile of stones." He counted a dozen blackened bodies nearby, another score in the railway station plaza.

By the time Rodríguez had walked the length of Calle Don Tello, he had counted a further forty corpses. He encountered another thirty-seven in his walk up Calle San Juan to the corner of Calle Ocho de Enero. The fiercely burning Church of San Juan made further progress dangerous.

He was undecided which way to go. "The difficulty was that apart from the church, there were no familiar landmarks. I was surrounded by ruins and death."

Profoundly shocked, he continued counting the dead. He had reached a figure of over two hundred "when the futility of counting dawned on me. Two, two hundred, two thousand—counting would not bring any of them back."

The Unceta boys, like many other people that night, were also busy with body counts. "Somehow," Augusto would remember, "the sheer number of corpses made it possible to look dispassionately at sights that on a smaller scale would have been overwhelming. One burned body is shocking; a hundred charred corpses lose their impact. I saw hundreds that night."

He and his brother Luis counted some 250 bodies in their walk up Calle de la Estación to Azoquecalle and back down part of Calle Santa María. They were stopped from going farther by the flames from the air-raid shelter, now surrounded by rescue workers trying to fight the fire with buckets of sand and water. Days would pass before the street was cleared, and Augusto would recall, "the biggest problem was matching up the bits and pieces of bodies. They did the best they could, and some people said that one hundred fifty died on that one street alone. But it was only a guess."

The Unceta boys would have another abiding memory of their walk through the town: "Some bodies lay in a pattern as if they were running away when hit. They were facedown and had been shot from behind."

When Juan Guezureya reentered the town from the northwest, he, too, noticed that corpses were facedown; they must have been machine-gunned as they fled out the Bermeo road. Juan forced himself to turn over some of the bodies, dreading he might identify any of his family. He did not. All had escaped to the Santimamiñe caves except fourteen-year-old Cipriano, buried in the viaduct with the other boys.

Juan reached Santa María Church, found it deserted, and went on to the Taberna Vasca. As he stood before it, openly weeping, he heard "a sound I never thought possible."

The bells of Santa María were tolling eight o'clock.

Fathers Iturran and Eusebio hoped, they told Juan, that those who heard the sound would take it as a signal that "from this moment, Guernica will begin its rebirth."

The two priests went into the nave and looked at the pile of relics Father Iturran had intended to move to Bilbao.

"There is nothing more to fear," said Father Eusebio. "Your church is safe."

He produced the camera film plate and explained about the picture.

"They will deny what they have done," he said. "The world must have proof. I must take this to Bilbao."

"I will stay here," said Father Iturran.

The two priests set to work, replacing Santa María's holy relics in their original places.

Around 8:30 P.M., Juan Plaza once more approached the town along the Marquina road. The smell of burning flesh carried strongly to the boy.

He reached the Rentería Bridge. Beyond, from Guernica, the heat rolled toward him in great waves. He scrambled down to the river bank and walked along it until he was across from the railway station. There he forded the river and entered the town.

"Everywhere people were carrying bodies to the Plaza Las Escuelas. The school had not been hit. When I reached it, there were already several rows of bodies, maybe a hundred laid out in the square. Dead animals were everywhere, terrible sights. The heat was unbearable."

He went up to Calle Allende Salazar, where he made a surprising discovery. All the large houses lining the road on either side of the Parliament Building were intact, apart from a few broken windows. Parliament itself was untouched, as was the sacred oak tree on its grounds. The Convent of Santa Clara, near the oak, had also escaped damage.

Juan heard two men state as fact a rumor that became commonplace in the days to come. "These were said to be the homes of Franco sympathizers which had been intentionally spared in the bombing."

No such orders had been given to the pilots. It was pure chance that their northeast-to-southwest bombing run across the town had taken them on a course that precluded their hitting the homes of the wealthy on Guernica's western slopes.

But the rumor grew. Further "proof" was provided by the "fact" that "everybody in those houses, fearing the people's revenge, ran away to await the arrival of the Nationalists."

Groups of townspeople searched those houses, looking for the "traitors." María Ortuza watched a group of vigilantes force open the door of the count of Montefuerte's residence. The young housekeeper was close to collapse from her experiences; that, she later admitted, could be her only excuse for what followed.

"I went after them into the house. I couldn't believe my eyes. A hundred feet away, on the other side of Calle Allende Salazar, everything was gone. My friends, my town, everything. But here in this house, the pictures on the wall were straight. The silver on the sidetables gleamed. The flowers in their vases were freshly watered.

But there were signs of a quick departure. Clothes were scattered around. The dining table had not been cleared. One of the men who had broken in said the Montefuertes fled after the raid ended and that the house was now a *refugio* for refugees. I went upstairs, going from one room to another. Finally I found myself in a big bedroom with a four-poster bed. I flopped on it and fell asleep."

María would sleep in the count of Montefuerte's bed for fifteen hours.

By 9:00 P.M., a record number of operations had been performed by the surgical teams in the Carmelite Convent. The doctors and nurses had time only to sip scalding coffee prepared by Mother Augusta before they plunged back into work that, thirty-seven years later, Teresa Ortuz could recall only as "an endless routine of cutting and sawing and slicing."

After the air raid ended, Cortés had reoccupied the upper floors of the convent.

Lieutenant Juan Dominguiz was one of those carried back upstairs. Under his pillow were the diaries Carmen had left with him. Lying in the darkened ward lit only by the glare from the town, he waited patiently for Carmen to appear. He still believed she was working somewhere in the hospital.

Dominguiz would learn of her death in Bilbao, where he was taken in an ambulance late that night. He would eventually recover from that shock; his physical recovery would be completed in the Basque country in France. There he would stay, with his memories of Carmen and her diaries.

At nine-thirty, Captain Cortés, at the urging of Mother Augusta, went to inspect the morgue. In it were crowded some fifty corpses, flies and insects crawling over the bodies.

"They should be buried at once," said Cortés.

"Not without a Christian service," insisted Mother Augusta.

The surgeon said he did not see what difference a "proper funeral" would make. "They're dead, and no amount of praying will change that." He returned to his work. When Teresa saw the surgeon's face, "I realized that I must have looked dead myself. All that sustained any of us was the knowledge that if we stopped, more would die."

They continued with short breaks for the next twenty-four hours. By then, the military patients had been evacuated to Bilbao. Cortés, his surgeons, and the orderlies of the field unit went with them, while Mother Augusta and her nuns remained to nurse the civilian casualties. Teresa, torn between the desire to find her own family and her professional responsibilities, in the end was persuaded by Mother Augusta to search for her loved ones. Eventually she found them, safe in Bilbao. Later, she insisted on returning to the convent.

Faustino Pastor was "too emotionally upset by all the destruction, too tired after all the shooting," to join the troops arriving in the town to help with the rescue work.

By 10:00 P.M., it was estimated that about four hundred soldiers were engaged in the task. And about that time, Juan Plaza would later claim, he heard "people say that the number of bodies recovered was over three hundred." Soon that figure would be doubled, trebled, even quadrupled by some of the journalists then heading for the town.

The spectacle of the burning town brought in civilian help from the surrounding countryside. But it was not until eleven o'clock, when the Bilbao Fire Brigade trucks arrived, that a determined attack could be made on the flames.

Juan Silliaco and his men teamed up with the Bilbao firemen, but there was little they could do. The water soon ran out. Sixteen hours would pass before the last flame died, leaving the town smoldering.

On Calle Allende Salazar, close to where Cipriano Guezureya and fourteen other boys lay buried, Antonio Arazamagni discovered a cat inside a water pipe. Sometime earlier, possibly during the raid, she had given birth to kittens. He scooped up the mother and her litter, placed them inside his jacket, and went in search of food for them. In Luno, Antonio persuaded a farmer's wife to give him some milk. The kittens all survived and eventually became inseparable from the baker.

In Guernica, the arrival of the press was viewed with disfavor by some people. Juan Guezureya would recall a mood of "not wanting reporters, but rescue workers. If only they had sent planes to defend us, everything would have been different."

The Condor Legion bomber and fighter pilots were debriefed at Burgos and Vitoria. Both Asmus and Von Beust would remember the sessions as "routine."

By midnight a party was going on in the lounge of the Frontón Hotel. Fighter pilots sang bawdy songs. The brothels were open; while the Legionnaires waited their turn, most agreed it had been one of the busiest afternoons since their arrival in Spain.

Shortly before midnight, Von Richthofen completed his customary stroll among the aircraft at Vitoria airfield. He could see that the piles of bombs in their guarded dump had been depleted. There were plenty more available.

He returned to his room and his diary.

Much later, after he had learned in detail what had happened, *Freiherr* von Richthofen stated in a secret report to Berlin that "the concentrated attack" on Guernica "was the greatest success."

Tuesday,
Wednesday,
Thursday

·33·

Throughout the night the fires worsened in Guernica. The heat became so intense that most people moved back to the western slopes overlooking the town. They stood in small groups, most watching in silence, some weeping quietly. Sometimes they saw policemen with hoses and soldiers with buckets working alongside the firemen. Everyone knew their task was hopeless. The fires raged out of control.

About 8:00 A.M. on Tuesday, a fine drizzle began to fall over Guernica. Later it began to rain steadily, helping the firefighters.

During the morning a passenger train arrived from Bilbao and stopped outside the town. It was soon filled with refugees. During the day the train would shuttle back and forth between the town and port, carrying hundreds behind Bilbao's "ring of iron."

Most of the soldiers departed, as did many of the sightseers from other towns who had come to watch Guernica burn.

The day after the raid, the Condor Legion was grounded by the weather, apart from a small action near Durango. Nevertheless, there was plenty for the airmen to talk about. News filtered through of the fall of Marquina; Nationalist ground troops were pressing toward Guernica.

In Berlin, the Nazi minister of war, Field Marshal von Blomberg, sent the Legion High Command repeated cables demanding to know who had bombed Guernica. According to Sergeant-Telegraphist Kurt Albrecht, he was ordered to reply: "Not Germans."

Years later, Squadron Leader *Freiherr* von Beust said that it was about this time that "we were suddenly told to 'hush up' about the raid."

That evening the Nationalists issued the first of a long series of disclaimers. On his regular nightly broadcast over Radio Seville at 10:00 P.M., General Queipo de Llano told listeners in Spain, France, and from them to the world, that the "reports that Guernica was bombed by our planes are completely false." He suggested that the Basques themselves had destroyed the town with dynamite. That same night, the Nationalist Press Office in Salamanca repeated the lie.

And so was the legend born that Guernica was burned by its own people.

·34·

Guernica's conquerors came early Thursday morning—Spanish, Italian, and Moroccan troops first entered the town about eight-thirty. They met some resistance; five Nationalist soldiers were killed and twenty-eight were wounded. But by ten-thirty, Franco's flag flew over the Parliament Building. The Moors were accorded the honor of guarding its entrance.

According to all accounts, the troops behaved well; they even set up field kitchens to dispense food to anyone confident enough to approach them.

Their entrance into Guernica was easy. Every Nationalist soldier in the town crossed over the still-standing Rentería Bridge.

Epilogue

For the rest of the Spanish war Hitler continued to secretly support Franco, sending troops to the Condor Legion for one-year tours of duty. They would return to Germany tanned and wealthy.

Rudolph von Moreau, who dropped the first bombs on Guernica, returned in the spring of 1937 and became a test pilot in the Luftwaffe. On March 26, 1939, he was killed on a test flight.

After the Spanish Civil War ended on March 29, 1939, among the tributes to Franco received were messages of congratulation from Adolf Hitler and Pope Pius XII.

When the Condor Legion returned to Germany on May 31, 1939, the troops were greeted in person by Reichsmarshal Hermann Göring, who promised that each "volunteer" would receive a special medal in bronze, silver, or gold.

On June 6, the entire force of some fifteen thousand men, with Sperrle and Von Richthofen at its head, paraded through Berlin. Hitler told his heroes that their success in Spain "was a lesson to our enemies."

Despite Franco's debt to the Condor Legion, when Hitler, in 1940, invited Spain to ally itself with Germany and Italy, Franco skillfully declined.

Some of those who had been in the Condor Legion in Spain at the time of Guernica went on to satisfying military careers.

Hugo Sperrle, in 1940, was commander in chief of Air Fleet III, an armada of some fifteen hundred bombers and fighters that Germany used in the Battle of Britain. On the eve of battle, Sperrle was promoted to field marshal. Toward the end of the war, he went into hiding. An American patrol unearthed him in southern Germany in 1945. Sperrle protested he was now "a retired private citizen." He was put on trial at Nuremberg in 1948 for war crimes.

Two years earlier, the court had refused an appeal by the former Basque minister of justice, Jesús Leizaola, that the destruction of Guernica be included in the charges, ruling that the tribunal was concerned exclusively with World War II crimes. Sperrle was acquitted of all charges. He retired to his birthplace, Ludwigsburg, near Stuttgart, where he died in 1953.

Wolfram, *Freiherr* von Richthofen, given command of Air Fleet VIII, a new close-combat unit composed principally of Stuka dive bombers, led the assault on Poland with spectacular results. Ultimately, Hitler made him the youngest field marshal in the Luftwaffe. He was forty-seven years old.

In May 1945, on his way to Hitler's redoubt in Bavaria, Von Richthofen was captured by an American patrol, but had to be transferred to a military field hospital, where he died just two months after the war ended in Europe.

The leader of No. 2 Squadron during the attack on Guernica, Hans Henning, *Freiherr* von Beust, became, at twenty-five, the youngest captain in the Wehrmacht. During World War II he survived 480 bombing missions, including some thirty over London.

Von Knauer, who led the raid on Guernica, used his experiences in Spain to prepare a manual for Luftwaffe bomber pilots, with particular emphasis on low-level attacks. He, too, survived the war, and like Von Beust and the leader of No. 3 Squadron, Von Krafft, was by 1975 retired from the German armed forces.

Captain Franz von Lutzow received two Iron Crosses before he was killed over the English Channel by a Spitfire.

Lieutenant Hans Asmus, shot down over London, survived, though wounded. He eventually returned to flying as a NATO pilot and rose swiftly in that organization to become commander in chief, NATO Air Force, Baltic. His wife is a Basque.

General Sperrle's adjutant at the time of Guernica's bombing, Heinz Trettner, had a meteoric rise in the Luftwaffe, and straight into controversy. He was accused of attacking Rotterdam after it had capitulated. He denied the charge, claiming that he had attempted to stop the blitzkrieg. At the end of the war in Italy, he was held responsible for atrocities committed by the troops under his command, a charge he also rejected.

In 1964 the KGB, the intelligence arm of the Soviet Union, fed through Bonn's diplomatic pipelines "hard evidence" that Trettner, by then inspector general of the Federal Armed Forces of West Germany, was a "war criminal" who had led the attack on Guernica. It wasn't true—and Heinz Trettner, now comfortably retired, doesn't care what the Russians say about him.

The rebirth of Guernica probably dates from Saturday, May 1, 1937, when the Nationalists established a field kitchen in what had been the town's marketplace. People came out of the hills to eat their first warm food in almost a week.

Father Iturran lived to see the Church of Santa María completely repaired. He died in 1946, and is buried in Guernica. Father Eusebio made his way to France, where he would spend the rest of his life.

On Monday, May 3, 1937, the Unceta plant was back in production—making weapons for the Nationalists.

In 1939, Teresa Ortuz became a postulant nun. In 1974, she celebrated thirty-five years in the Carmelite Order.

The Sisters of Penance, in the Convent of Santa Clara, no longer make wedding gowns for the town's favored brides.

The ruins of the Church of San Juan were fenced in to stop children from playing among them.

The Bank of Vizcaya, of course, reopened. The ledgers that Julio

Bareno had carried to the bank's head office in Bilbao enabled business to be transacted smoothly.

Today, Guernica is a thriving town of 15,500 people. It shows few signs of the bombing.

The Unceta factory now employs over five hundred, exports over 200 million pesetas' worth of guns to over seventy countries each year. Rufino Unceta is fond of presenting heads of state with hand-tooled weapons. The late President Dwight D. Eisenhower received a set of exquisite silver-tooled pistols; his letter of gratitude has a special place in the company's archives in Guernica.

Notes

PROLOGUE

Based partly on personal interviews with eyewitnesses who lived in Guernica during the Civil War, including Augusto Unceta, José Rodríguez, Juan Silliaco, Juan Plaza, Teresa Ortuz, Antonio Arazamagni, María Ortuza.

Details of German involvement in Spain were provided by Hans Asmus, Heinz Trettner, Hans Henning, *Freiherr* von Beust, Hannes Trautloft, among others.

Gotz, *Freiherr* von Richthofen, made available hitherto unpublished details from his father's diaries, showing how and why the Condor Legion went to the Basque country.

Details of the Nonintervention Pact and the strength of the Republican forces came from British and German government official documents; Hugh Thomas's *The Spanish Civil War;* George Steer's *The Tree of Gernika; House of Commons Report on Parliamentary Debates.* Refugee atrocity stories are mentioned in *The "Military" Atrocities of the Rebels,* published by the British Labour Party, and *Spain at War,* published independently. Mola's proclamation: Steer, p. 159, et al.

SUNDAY, APRIL 25, 1937

1. Based mainly on personal interviews with Sister Teresa Ortuz.

2. Largely based on personal interviews with Hans Asmus, who pro-

vided supplementary material on Von Richthofen as well as a detailed description of life at Vitoria; also based on lengthy interviews and documentation provided by Baroness von Richthofen and *Freiherr* von Richthofen.

3. Sister Teresa Ortuz provided the hospital details. The arrival of retreating troops in the town was revealed by one of them, Faustino Pastor, in a personal interview with one of the authors. Evacuation of the arms factory from Guernica was revealed by Augusto Unceta during a lengthy personal interview with the authors. The refugees' attempt to hijack the train was described by Ramón Gandaría. Details of the fires in the town and Guernica's fire service were given during several interviews with Juan Silliaco as well as with members of the present fire service in the town; further corroborative details came from José Rodríguez and Juan Plaza. Personal interviews with Antonio Arazamagni provided details of the cat-stealing gangs and the remainder of the chapter.

4. Based on interviews with Baroness and *Freiherr* von Richthofen, Hans Asmus, *Freiherr* von Beust. Written sources include: Militärgeschichtliches Forschungsamt Leitender Historiker archives at Freiburg; Hans Henning Abendroth's *Hitler in der Spanischen Arena;* Manfred Merkes's *Die Deutsche Politik im Spanischen Bürgerkrieg 1936–1939.*

5. Sister Teresa Ortuz provided material on her relationship with Captain Cortés in this and subsequent chapters. Augusto Unceta and José Gandaría provided the bulk of the remainder of the chapter on Rufino Unceta, his attitude toward the Nationalists, and the dangerous cat-and-mouse game he played with the Republicans. Direct quotes were provided by Rufino Unceta himself.

6. Hans Asmus provided details of the reconnaissance flight, Von Richthofen's attitude toward the Legion's official brothel, and toward his aircrews. Additional and confirmatory details were provided by Baroness and *Freiherr* von Richthofen, and *Freiherr* von Beust, among others.

7. The Basque retreat was recorded by Juan Dominguiz, whose diaries,

as well as those of his fiancée, Carmen Batzar, were made available to the authors and provided the material for the first part of this chapter. Additional material was provided by former colleagues of Dominguiz, including Ramón Gandaría. In Guernica the authors were able to see Father Iturran's papers; additional material on the priest came from Juan Plaza, Juan Silliaco, Antonio Arazamagni, Augusto Unceta, Ramón Gandaría, Father Alberto de Onaindía, María Urnganguru, María Ortuza, and the priest of Santa María in 1974, who made available to the authors the church records covering the period of the war. Juan Silliaco's story emerged during personal interviews. Carmen Batzar's story comes mainly from her diaries.

8. Hans Asmus provided the source material for the actual workings of the operations room. He also described the various German personnel there and provided the authors with a copy of the TSI map used to plan the attack. Written sources: The military archives at Freiburg provided much material, including Von Richthofen's thoughts included in "Auswertung Rügen," written by him in 1938, countersigned by Sperrle, of which the authors have a copy. In it he sets out many of the complaints and orders the chapter refers to. The few direct quotations by those involved in the Marquina raid were recalled to the best of his knowledge by Hans Asmus.

9. Sister Teresa Ortuz and Ramón Gandaría provided the bulk of the material for this chapter. The character and attitudes of Mayor José Labauría were recalled in personal interviews with the authors by people who had observed him at work, including Jesús Leizaola, Juan Plaza, Father Alberto de Onaindía, Antonio Arazamagni, Frank Ellere, Ernst Borchers, Juan Guezureya, and Mother María, the Superior of La Merced Convent. President Aguirre's decision is recorded in Talón's *Arde Guernica*. The theft of flour comes from firsthand recollection of Antonio Arazamagni. Juan Dominguiz's diaries provided the source material for the closing scenes of the chapter.

10. The church services were recreated through personal interviews with members of the congregations, including Juan Plaza, Augusto Unceta, José Rodríguez, members of the Arrién family, Juan Silliaco, Juan

Guezureya. Written sources consulted include the papers of Father Iturran and the diaries of Carmen Batzar. María Ortuza contributed details of her lunchtime dilemma with the rabbit. Gandaría's attempts to telephone Marquina were recalled by him.

11. The events leading up to the wounding of Dominguiz were recalled by himself and another survivor, Frank Ellere, during personal interviews with the authors. Carmen Batzar's diaries provided most of the source material for her behavior that day. Sister Teresa Ortuz provided a number of details about life in the hospital. Isidro Arriéb's son-in-law, Ortis, his wife, and other members of the family pooled their recollections, papers, and menus to provide the fullest possible picture of the Arrién restaurant, and of Isidro Arrién's thoughts and actions. The meeting between José Rodríguez and Rufino Unceta emerged during interviews with José Rodríguez and was corroborated by Augusto Unceta.

12. Hans Asmus searched his memory and his files to provide portraits of the debriefing and the meeting of the Target Selection Committee. Other German written sources (see Bibliography) provided additional data.

13. Sister Teresa Ortuz, Mother Augusta, and Carmen Batzar's diaries provided the main source material for the hospital scene. Juan Silliaco and Antonio Arazamagni are the sources for the scenes in Guernica.

14. Part of this chapter is based on personal interviews with Hans Asmus and with Baroness and *Freiherr* von Richthofen. Details of the meeting in Burgos came from Von Richthofen's own papers, both those in the possession of his family and those at the military archives in Freiburg. Manfred Merkes's *Die Deutsche Politik im Spanischen Bürgerkrieg 1936–1939* provided additional information. The biographical details of Von Moreau came partly from his *Help for the Alcázar*. The flight over Bilbao was partly recreated from the writings of Count Max Hoyos, who flew on the raid. Further details were provided by personal interview with Trautloft and a study of his *Als Jagdflieger in Spanien,* arguably one of the most informative

books written by a German flier in Spain. See also Steer, Thomas, and Talón; and "Auswertung Rügen," and the Von Beust report (Freiburg).

15. Father Iturran's reactions are indicated in his papers; later, he discussed them with Juan Plaza's father, who passed them on to his son, who was interviewed by the authors. María Ortuza and María Urnganguru were just two of several eyewitnesses who recalled the band playing and the troops coming into the town.

Juan Plaza and Ramón Gandaría provided separate detailed accounts of Father Iturran's clash with Gandaría; Mother María, Superior at La Merced Convent, provided corroborative details. Carmen Batzar's diaries revealed the existence of the chapel of prayer at the Convent of Santa Clara, which the authors visited. José Rodríguez provided the account of the soldiers "cavorting about."

Rufino Unceta was one of several people who saw troops in the Convent of Santa Clara. Further confirmation came from nuns now living in the convent.

Personal testimony from María Ortuza revealed her reactions to the troops; she was interviewed on four separate occasions before her full story emerged. Members of the Arrién family provided the details about their restaurant. Additional information came from Juan Guezureya, in 1974 owner of the Taberna Vasca, who gave the authors several long interviews, as well as documentation and photographs. Ramón Gandaría, Juan Plaza, Juan Silliaco, and Sister Teresa Ortuz were among some thirty eyewitnesses who told the authors about the presence of troops in the town, their location and behavior. The encounter between Antonio Arazamagni and Gandarí was recollected by Arazamagni and confirmed by Gandaría.

16. The opening scene was recalled by Sister Teresa Ortuz. Juan Silliaco described the scene in his bar. The reactions of Father Eusebio, indeed most of the story of the parish priest of San Juan, is drawn from one prime source: Antonio Arazamagni. A close bond later existed between the baker and the cleric. Father Eusebio, according to the testimony of Arazamagni, whom the authors found a reliable witness in all matters which they could

corroborate, discussed openly his relationship with Father Iturran. Some corroboration over the conflict between the two priests came from Ramón Gandaría, Father Alberto de Onaindía, and the diaries of Carmen Batzar. María Ortuza told us of her visit to Santa Clara; corroboration came from Arazamagni. The Radio Salamanca broadcast was remembered by Juan Plaza, José Rodríguez, the Arrién family, and others.

17. Hans Asmus revealed Von Richthofen's preoccupation with the weather. Baroness von Richthofen made available, for the first time, relevant portions of her husband's diary, quoted here. The brothel and party descriptions came from various former Legionnaires whose names have not been mentioned. Those mentioned by name in other contexts were personally interviewed by the authors. The description of Vigón and his intelligence report were recalled by Hans Asmus, who knew Vigón well, and Baroness von Richthofen, who knew of him from her husband. *Freiherr* von Beust contributed details about life at Burgos and the idiosyncrasies of a JU-52 bomber, as did various other former Legionnaires.

MONDAY, APRIL 26, 1937

18. Ramón Gandaría and Sister Teresa Ortuz provided details of the early hours in Guernica on Monday. Additional material came from Antonio Arazamagni and María Ortuza. The principal written source was Carmen Batzar's diary.

19. Hans Asmus provided the bulk of the material. Additional information came from written German sources listed in the Bibliography, including the diary of Hans Joachim Wandel, part of which the authors have seen.

20. Lazcano's arrival and subsequent behavior were carefully noted and documented by Juan Silliaco, among others. Additional information came from Sister Teresa Ortuz and Ramón Gandaría, who also furnished details of the meeting with Mother María and Father Eusebio. Juan Plaza described the market scene. María Ortuza and Rafael Herrán told the

authors the story of the cooking clubs and other market details, Arazamagni contributed data about his customers. Gandaría is the source for the air alert. See also Talón, Steer, Aguirre.

21. The basis of this chapter comes from a compilation of: *Kampfflieger* by Von Knauer, countersigned by Sperrle; part of "Auswertung Rügen" by Von Richthofen, and also from his personal diary, Von Beust's report, and other documents at Freiburg. Additional material came from former Legionnaires listed in the Appendix.

22. Ramón Gandaría provided details of the morning conference at La Merced. His visit to the factory was confirmed by José Rodríguez. The Bank of Vizcaya's staff in Guernica in 1974 included Ramón Larrinaga Levereguo, who had served under Bareno, and was able to reveal the story. Details of the bank's reactions to Bareno was also provided by the branch's 1974 manager, José Aboitiz Garechama.

23. The sole source for this chapter is Von Richthofen's personal diary.

24. Lazcano's tour through the town was observed by Juan Plaza, María Ortuza, and Juan Silliaco, who between them helped to recreate it; see also Talón. José Rodríguez revealed his premonition to the authors. Carmen Batzar's diaries provided the other material.

25. Hans Asmus provided the bulk of the material for this chapter. Supplementary material came from Condor Legion documents at Freiburg, from Wandel's diary, from information provided by Ehrhart von Krafft, and an interview with *Freiherr* von Beust.

26. Based on interviews with Sister Teresa Ortuz, Arazamagni, Gandaría, Silliaco, Juan Guezureya, Rodríguez, Larrinaga, and María Ortuza.

27. The basis for this chapter is a compilation similar to that outlined for Chapter 21. Additional material came from Juan Plaza, Faustino Pastor, Arazamagni, María Ortuza, Silliaco, members of the Arrién family,

Guezureya, Herrán, Gandaría, Rodríguez, Augusto and Rufino Unceta. See also Steer and contemporary newspaper accounts.

28. Material for the scenes in Guernica came mainly from interviews with eyewitnesses mentioned in the text. The Condor Legion scenes are based on material from the archives at Freiburg, with some background information from Hoyos's *Pedros y Pablos*.

29. Sources are similar to those for preceding chapter. For the Legion scenes, additional information was provided in interviews, particularly by *Freiherr* von Beust, and from Wandel's diary. Certain background information was culled from Trautloft's book, and in an interview with him. The scenes in Guernica came mainly from personal interviews. See Talón and Steer.

30. Based almost exclusively on testimony drawn from eyewitnesses mentioned in the text, with a small amount of additional information from contemporary newspaper accounts.

31. Bareno scenes as in Chapter 22. The escape of the widow Urnganguru with her five daughters was described by one of her daughters, María. The view of Guernica being bombed as seen from Luno was recalled by two elderly residents of Luno who preferred to remain anonymous, and by Arazamagni. The scenes in the Town Hall shelter were later reported by Mayor Labauría in the pamphlet *Guernica,* and in personal interview by María Ortuza. Apart from interviews with eyewitnesses, the scenes within, and bombing of, the Church of Santa María (and San Juan) are mentioned in the church records.

TUESDAY, WEDNESDAY, THURSDAY

32. Again, the sources are mainly interviews with eyewitnesses. Important written sources include Steer's *Tree of Gernika* and contemporary newspaper accounts in *The Times* of London and *The New York Times*.

33. Based mainly on eyewitness accounts, including interviews with Father Alberto de Onaindía and passages from his book *Hombre de Paz en la Guerra,* plus contemporary reports in German, British, Spanish, French, and American newspapers. See also Steer, Thomas, and Talón.

34. Based on eyewitness accounts of those who saw the conquerors arrive, plus corroborative reports in German, French, and British newspapers.

EPILOGUE

Based mainly on interviews, including one with the president of the Basque Government-in-Exile, Señor Jesús Leizaola. Written sources include part of Wandel's diary; *Hansard,* vols. 323–326; *The Trial of German Major War Criminals at Nuremberg; German Foreign Policy Documents; Guernica, The Official Report of a Commission; House of Commons Parliamentary Debates,* February 7, 1938. See also Steer, Aguirre, Thomas, Talón, and contemporary newspaper accounts.

Appendixes

---

1. INTRODUCTION

Twenty-seven months of research went into this book. In that time we traveled thousands of miles and amassed some 4.5 million words of material already written on the subject. Much of it turned out to be suspect. Some, as we have indicated, was fabricated by government agencies, such as the KGB.

From the outset we knew that getting to the truth would be difficult. Guernica continues to be a source of embarrassment, particularly to the West German and Spanish governments. Nor are the French and British administrations anxious to be reminded of their countries' roles in the Spanish cockpit.

In the summer of 1974 a State Department source in Washington told us that the "truth about Guernica could rock the boat. It could make people wonder why we have bases in Spain, where such a thing like Guernica happened. And Franco would get mad at any reopening of the Guernica episode."

Though thirty-eight years have elapsed, in 1975 the Franco regime was still refusing to cooperate with any impartial inquiry into the event.

Nevertheless, we went to Guernica. It is a cheerful town in spite of the secret policemen and Civil Guard constantly on the lookout for Basque separatists, who enjoy chalking slogans and the movement's initials—ETA—on public buildings.

Guernica's mayor suggested we leave as soon as he learned of our presence. Señor Gervasio Guezuraga insisted, "There is nothing here for you. Nothing for tourists. Why come here? Go to Madrid or Bilbao."

The secretary of the Parliament Building became even more hostile when he learned of our visit. "On instructions from Madrid," he refused us facilities, and his assistant, Charo Zubelalia, the twenty-year-old daughter of a Spanish officer, threatened we would be "sued for copyright" if we even photographed the Tree of Guernica. It was she who also told us that the police could make our life "difficult" if we continued to ask questions.

Despite the official strictures, we found many persons willing to talk. When we told one of them that, on the surface at least, the town seemed very peaceful, he replied, "Everything is also quiet in Sing Sing prison! And remember, no one hears much about what is happening in Hell!"

Our search for eyewitnesses was worldwide. Some had moved to Australia, where they tended sheep in Queensland, or kept bars in Melbourne or Sydney. One runs a delicatessen in Los Angeles. A few live in Miami. Still others have settled in Idaho, a state that now has some ten thousand Basques. Some live as close as the French side of the Pyrenees. A few reside in the Italian Dolomites. Many went to England, found it difficult to settle there, and moved on to Portugal, Canada, and even Alaska.

In our lengthy interviews with eyewitnesses, we found that following the air attacks, many of them had jotted down their recollections. Almost none of them we talked to had been previously interviewed. Many were unaware of each other's existence. Yet there was almost unanimous agreement among them as to what actually had happened.

We are especially grateful for their time, their patience, their desire to be totally honest; their wish, in the words of one, "that you tell it as it was."

We have tried to do so. If we have succeeded, it is in large measure due to those who spoke to us about their experiences:

A. EYEWITNESSES

We have respected the wishes of some who preferred that their names were not mentioned; they are not included here or elsewhere in the book.

Alcibar, Mother Superior Augusta	Arrién, Engartze
Arazamagni, Antonio	Arrién, Felipe
Astoreca, Félix	Arrién, Isabel
Arrién, Castor	Arrién, Victoria
Arrién, Celestina	Artugi, María

Bengoechea, Juan de Arana
Borchers, Ernst
Dominguiz, Juan
Ellere, Frank
Ellere, María
Gandaría, Ramón
Garachema, José
Guezureya, José
Guezureya, Juan
Guezureya, María Concepción
Hernández, Miguel
Herrán, Rafael
Icazeriaga, Julián
Irriondo, Mother Superior María
Jauregui, Juan Antonio
Levereguo, Ramón

Molares, Basilio
Onaindía, Father Alberto de
Ortis, Augustino
Ortuz, Sister Teresa
Ortuza, María
Pastor, Faustino
Plaza, Isabel
Plaza, Juan
Plaza, Victoria
Rodríguez, José
Silliaco, Juan
Silliaco, Pedro
Tellería, Angeles
Unceta, Augusto
Unceta, Rufino
Urnganguru, María

B. CONDOR LEGION

Most members of the Legion who were involved in the planning and execution of the raid on Guernica died in World War II. We talked to many of those who survived; they, too, were anxious that at last the truth, however painful, should emerge. Some of the evidence to support their recollections has been destroyed by war, and sometimes they said they could not totally trust their own memories. But during the year when we conducted interviews in person and by post with the Legionnaires listed here, a great deal of original material emerged.

Some were anxious that we understand that their actions over Guernica did not occur in a vacuum, but were related to preceding events in the war. While they saw Guernica as a catalyst, they insisted it must be viewed in perspective.

We hope we have provided that perspective. In terms of the German involvement, we owe a great deal to:

Albrecht, Kurt
Asmus, Hans, Generalmajor a.D.
Berger, Gerhard

Beust, Hans Henning,
  Freiherr von, Oberst I.H.a.D.
Krafft, Ehrhart von Dellmensingen

Krauth, Joseph
Munkel, Rudi
Patzewitz, Walter
Rahn, Lothar

Trautloft, Hannes,
    Generalleutnant a.D.
Trettner, Heinz, General a.D.
Weiser, Franz

C. OTHERS

We consulted many individuals who, althought not directly involved in the raid on Guernica, have claim to specialist knowledge.

Above all we should like to acknowledge our debt to the wife of Wolfram von Richthofen, Jutta, the Baroness von Richthofen, and her son, Gotz, *Freiherr* von Richthofen. Over five months of interviews by mail and in person, they allowed us to consult the field marshal's unpublished private papers and diaries and helped to paint a portrait of a remarkable man. Today, as in the past, they maintain Von Richthofen behaved correctly in every aspect of the attack. We respect their right to their beliefs; we know they will accept our duty to present the facts as we unearthed them. If at times we differ in interpretation, it does not mean we are any less in their debt.

Señor Jesús María de Leizaola took time off from his duties as president of the Basque Government-in-Exile to give us two lengthy interviews and also to provide considerable material describing the destruction of Guernica as seen by the Basques. Again, if there are any aspects of the story where our version of events does not tally with his, it does not mean our gratitude to him is diminished.

We owe particular thanks to Herr Wolfgang Mischnick, leader of the FDP party in the Bundestag, who smoothed our passage in Germany and directed us to the authorized sources of information.

Finally, we should like to record our thanks to Mac Slee, who provided us with hitherto restricted American military material on the Condor Legion, and to Bill Moloney, who enlightened us on the finer points of bombing.

2. ACKNOWLEDGMENTS
A. INDIVIDUALS

Beascoechea, Xavier
Butz, Sigbert

Ferraris, Sergio Arfino
Mena, Carlos

Moloney, Karen
Montagu, Ivor
Peet, Stephen

Saisseval, Guy Coutant de
Thomas, Hugh
Tolstoy, Count Nikolai Miloslavsky

B. ORGANIZATIONS, INSTITUTIONS

Most of the small amount of contemporary material still extant relating to the Condor Legion's involvement at Guernica is deposited in the West German government's military archives at Freiburg. Klaus Maier spent a good deal of time dealing with our queries, both during our visits to Freiburg and in correspondence. It should be noted that although it has been suggested in some quarters that the Italians were involved in the attack, we found no hard evidence to substantiate this claim.

Bundesarchiv, Militärarchiv,
    Freiburg i. Br.
Cabinet Office, Historical
    Section, London
Delegation Euzkadi
Foreign Office Library, London
Hammersmith Books, London
    (Ronald Bray)
Imperial War Museum, London
National Archives, Library of
    Congress, Washington
New York Public Library
Public Records Office, London
Wiener Library, Institute of
    Contemporary History,
    London

Guernica:
Bank of Bilbao
Bank of Vizcaya
Casa de Juntas
Church of Santa María
Convent of La Merced
Convent of Religiosas Carmelitas
Convent of Santa Clara
Fire Department
Office of the Mayor
Post Office
Registro de la Propriedad
Residencia Calzada
Tourist Board

C. TRANSLATORS

Creff, Martine
Cruft, Sebastian
Heald, David
Ide, Gisela

Kraner, Joachim
Urwick, Alan
Van Dijk, Frank
Weigall, Michael

Bibliography

A. BOOKS

To our knowledge, there are two books worthy of special mention that deal mainly with the destruction of Guernica. The first, published in 1938, is the account by George Steer, special correspondent of *The New York Times* and *The Times* of London. The second, by Vicente Talón, first published in 1970, is similar to many others in that it is largely a compilation of the many millions of words that had already appeared in diverse form.

For the entire war in Spain, the standard work is by Hugh Thomas.

Most of the books on this list tend to put forward one or the other of the two "classic" points of view: either that Guernica was destroyed in a "terror attack" or that Guernica was destroyed in an act of self-destruction.

Abendroth, Hans Henning. *Hitler in der Spanischen Arena.* Paderborn, F. Schoningh, 1973.

Acier, Marcel, ed. *From Spanish Trenches.* New York, Modern Age Books, 1937.

Aguirre y Lecube, José Antonio de. *Escape via Berlin.* New York, Macmillan, 1944. British edition: *Freedom Was Flesh and Blood.* London, V. Gollancz, 1945.

Aldecoa, Ignacio. *The Basque Country.* Barcelona, Editorial Noguer, 1963.

Allan, Ted, and Gordon, Sidney. *The Scalpel, the Sword.* London, Hale, 1954.

Alvarez del Vayo, Julio. *Freedom's Battle.* Trans. by Eileen E. Brooke. London, W. Heinemann, 1940. New York, A. A. Knopf, 1940.

Ansaldo, Juan Antonio, *Para Qué . . . ?* Buenos Aires, Editorial Vasca Ekin, 1951.

Atholl, Katherine Marjory (Ramsay) Stewart-Murray, Duchess of. *Searchlight on Spain.* Harmondsworth, Penguin Books, 1938.

Azpilikoeta, Dride, ed. *Le Problème Basque.* Paris, B. Grasset, 1938. *The Basque Problem.* New York, The Basque Archives, 1939.

Belforte, Francesco. *La Guerra Civile in Spagna.* Milan, Instituto per gli Studi di Politica Internazionale, 1938.

Beumelburg, Werner. *Kampf um Spanien.* Berlin, G. Stalling, 1940.

Blunt, Sir Anthony. *Picasso's Guernica.* London, Oxford University Press, 1969. New York, Oxford University Press, 1969.

Bolin, Luis A. *Spain: The Vital Years.* Philadelphia, Lippincott, 1967. London, Cassell & Co., Ltd., 1968.

Bolloten, Burnett. *The Grand Camouflage.* London, Pall Mall, 1968. New York, Praeger, 1968.

Borkenau, Franz. *The Spanish Cockpit.* London, Faber and Faber, 1937. Ann Arbor, University of Michigan Press, 1963.

Bowers, Claude Gernade. *My Mission to Spain.* London, Gollancz, 1954. New York, Simon & Schuster, 1954.

Cardozo, Harold G. *March of a Nation.* London, Eyre & Spottiswood, 1937. New York, McBride, 1937.

Cleugh, James. *Spanish Fury.* London, Harrap & Co., Ltd., 1962.

Colodny, Robert Garland. *Struggle for Madrid.* New York, Paine-Whitman, 1958.

Cowles, Virginia. *Looking for Trouble.* London, H. Hamilton, 1941. New York, Harper & Row, 1941.

Deschner, Karl Heinz. *Abermals Krahte der Hahn.* Stuttgart, Hans Günther Verlag, 1968.

De Wet, H. Oloff. *Patrol Is Ended.* New York, Doubleday, 1938. British edition: *Cardboard Crucifix.* London, Blackwood & Sons, 1938.

Díaz-Plaja, Fernando, comp. *La España Política del Siglo XX.* 2nd ed. Barcelona, Plaza & Janés, 1971.

Douhet, Giulio. *The Command of the Air.* Trans. by Dino Ferrari. New York, Coward-McCann, 1942. London, Faber and Faber, Ltd., 1943.

Eby, Cecil De Grotte. *The Siege of the Alcázar.* New York, Random House, 1965. London, Bodley Head, 1966.

Galland, Adolph. *The First and the Last.* London, Methuen, 1970.

Gallop, Rodney. *Book of the Basques.* New York, Macmillan, 1930.

George, Robert Esmonde Gordon. *Spain's Ordeal.* New ed. London, Longmans, Green & Co., 1940.

Gerahty, Cecil. *Road to Madrid.* London, Hutchinson, 1937.

Göring, Hermann. Testimony recorded in *The Trial of German Major War Criminals. Proceedings of the International Military Tribunal Sitting at Nuremberg* . . . London, H. M. Stationery Office, 1946–50.

Gomá Orduña, José. *La Guerra en el Aire.* Barcelona, Editorial AHR, 1958.

Gordon, Sidney, jt. author. See Allan, Ted.

Guttmann, Allen. *The Wound in the Heart.* New York, Free Press of Glencoe, 1962.

Hoyos, Max, Graf. *Pedros y Pablos.* Munich, F. Bruckmann, 1941.

Jellinek, Frank. *Civil War in Spain.* London, Gollancz, 1938. New York, Ryerson Press, 1938.

Jerrold, Douglas. *Georgian Adventure.* London, Collins, 1937. New York, Scribner, 1938.

Jolly, Douglas Waddell. *Field Surgery in Total War.* London, H. Hamilton, 1940. New York, Harper & Row, 1941.

Kemp, Peter. *Mine Were of Trouble.* London, Cassell, 1957.

Kindélan, Alfredo. *Mis Cuadernos de Guerra.* Madrid, Editorial Plus-Ultra, 1945.

Kirsch, Hans Christian. *Der Spanische Bürgerkrieg in Augenzeugenberichten.* Düsseldorf, Rauch, 1967.

Kohler, Klaus. *Kriegsfreiwilliger 1937.* Leipzig, Günther Heinig Verlag, 1939.

Larracabal, J. S. *Das Flugzeug im Spanischen Bürgerkrieg.* Stuttgart, Stalling Verlag, 1969.

Lent, Alfred. *Wir Kampften für Spanien.* Berlin, G. Stalling, 1939.

Lerma, José Larios Fernández de Villavicencio, Duque de. *Combat over Spain.* New York, Macmillan, 1966. London, Neville Spearman, 1968.

Madariaga, Salvador de. *Spain.* London, J. Cape, 1942. New York, Creative Age Press, 1943.

Maier, Klaus A. *Guernica 26.4.1937: Die Deutsche Intervention in Spanien und der "Fall Guernica."* Freiburg, Verlag Rombach, 1975.

Mattioli, Guido. *L'Aviazione Legionaria in Spagna.* Roma, L'Aviazione, 1938, 1940.

Merkes, Manfred. *Die Deutsche Politik im Spanischen Bürgerkrieg.* Bonn, Rohrscheid, 1969.

Merry Del Val, Alfonso, Marqués de. *Spanish Basques and Separatism.* London, Burns Oates and Washbourne Ltd., 1939.

Mosley, Leonard. *The Reich Marshal.* New York, Doubleday, 1974.

Moss, Geoffrey. *Epic of the Alcázar.* London, Rich & Cowan, 1937. United States edition: *Siege of Alcázar.* New York, A. A. Knopf, 1937.

Onaindía, Alberto de. *Hombre de Paz en la Guerra.* Buenos Aires, Editorial Vasca Ekin S.R.L., 1973.

The Reconstruction of Spain. Madrid, Publicaciones Españolas, 1947.

Regler, Gustav. *The Owl of Minerva.* London, Hart-Davis, 1959. New York, Farrar, Straus & Cudahy, 1960.

Rowe, Vivian. *The Basque Country.* London, Putnam, 1955.

Sencourt, Robert, pseud. See George, R.E.G.

Sesmero Pérez, Francisco. *Vizcaya.* Léon, España, Editorial Everest, 1969.

Southworth, Herbert Rutledge. *La Destruction de Guernica.* Paris, Ruedo Ibérico, 1975.

——— *Le Mythe de la Croisade de Franco.* Paris, Ruedo Ibérico, 1964.

Stache, R. *Armee mit geheimen Auftrag.* Bremen, H. Burmester Verlag, 1939.

Stackelberg, Karl Georg von. *Legion Condor.* Berlin, Heimbücherei, 1939.

Steer, George Lowther. *Tree of Guernika.* London, Hodder & Stoughton, Ltd., 1938.

Talón, Vicente. *Arde Guernica.* Madrid, San Martín, 1970.

Thomas, Hugh. *The Spanish Civil War.* London, Eyre & Spottiswood, 1961. New York, Harper & Row, 1961.

Tinker, Frank Glasgow. *Some Still Live.* New York, Funk and Wagnalls, 1938.

Toynbee, Arnold Joseph (with Boulter, V. M.). *Survey of International Affairs, 1936–1937.* New York, Oxford University Press, n.d.

Trautloft, Hannes. *Als Jagdflieger in Spanien.* Berlin, A. Nauck & Co., 1940.

Watkins, K. W. *Britain Divided.* London, Nelson & Sons, 1963.

Yeats-Brown, F.C.C. *European Jungle.* London, Eyre & Spottiswood, 1939. Philadelphia, Macrae Smith, 1939.

Zeitz, Carl Hermann. *Soldaten retten Spanien.* Berlin, Die Wehrmacht Verlag, 1939.

B. PERIODICALS, PAMPHLETS, REPORTS, POLEMICS

The Basque Country and European Peace. London, Autonomous Government of Euzkadi, 1938.

British Medical Aid in Spain. London, *The News Chronicle,* 1936.

Bulletin of Spanish Studies. Liverpool, Institute of Hispanic Studies. Vol. XIII, No. 52, to Vol. XVI, No. 62, 1936–1939.

Catholic and Protestant Priests, Freemasons, and Liberals Shot by the Rebels. London, Spanish Embassy Press Office, 1937.

The Crime of Guernica. New York, Spanish Information Bureau, 1937.

Crónica de la Guerra Española, Vol. LXII. Buenos Aires, *Arde Guernica,* Codex S.A., 1967.

Deutsche Kampfen in Spanien. Berlin, Wilhelm Limpert Verlag, 1939.

Durango, ville martyre. Paris, Comité franco-espagnon, 1937.

Estudios Socio-Económicos Comarcales: Guernica-Bermeo. Bilbao, Cámara de Comercio, Industria y Navigación, 1974.

Foreign Wings over the Basque Country. London, The Friends of Spain, 1937.

German Foreign Policy, Documents on. Series D, Vol. III, Germany and the Spanish Civil War (1936–39). London, H.M.S.O., 1951.

Guernica—The Official Report of a Commission Appointed by the National Government to Investigate the Causes of the Destruction of Guernica on April 26–28, 1937. London, Eyre & Spottiswoode, 1938.

Guernica. Bilbao, Government of Euzkadi, 1937.

Hansard. Vols. CCCXXIII–CCCXXVI. London, H.M.S.O., 1937.

History of the Second World War, Blitzkrieg. London, Purnell & Sons Ltd., 1974.

History of the World Wars, Bombers 1914–1939. London, Purnell & Sons Ltd., 1974.

La Legión Condor Se Despide. Santander, Aldus, 1939.

The London Mercury and Bookman (Guernica, by G. Steer). Vol. XXXVI, No. 214, 1937.

The National Review (London). Vol. CIX, No. 654, pp. 253–254, 1937.

The National Review (New York). Vol. XXV, No. 35, 1973.

Preliminary Official Report on the Atrocities in Spain. London, Eyre & Spottiswoode, 1936.

Report of a Religious Delegation to Spain, April 1937. London, Victor Gollancz Ltd., 1937.

Student (A. H. Farrar-Hockley). New York, Ballantine Books Inc., 1973.

C. UNPUBLISHED DOCUMENTS, DIARIES, RECORDS

Even these must be consulted with caution: In a confidential report written in 1955, doubtless in good faith, *Freiherr* von Beust, while recalling that wind blew the bombs into the town, also remembered the bridge as being to the south of Guernica—when in fact it was to the north.

Auswertung Rügen, Anlage 1 zu Lw Gr Kdo 3, Nr. 7179/38 gKdos (Ausertestab R. Luneburg) (Militärarchiv/Freiburg) -Oberst v. Richthofen. Heft 1/2, Fuhrung (1938)-Hptm. v. Knauer. Heft 3, Kampfflieger (1938) -Hptm. v. Lutzow. Heft 4, Jagdflieger (1938)

Batzar, Carmen. Diary, Guernica, 1937.

Bestandsmeldungen K/88, Stabskompanie K/88, Spain, 1937 VB/88, 1937; VJ/88, 1937; 4J/88, 1937; AS/88, 1937; J/88, 1937; S/88, 1937 (Militärarchiv/Freiburg)

Beust, Hans Henning, *Freiherr* von. Die Deutsche Luftwaffe im Spanischen Krieg, Lw 107/1, Stuttgart, 1955 (Militärarchiv/Freiburg).

Church of San Juan, Guernica. Records (in Church of Santa María) 1941.

Church of Santa María, Guernica. Records, 1946.

Convent of Religiosas Carmelitas, Guernica. Records, 1937.

Die Kampfe im Norden, RL2/V 3188, 1. Exemplar, 8. Kriegswissenschaftliche Abteilung der Luftwaffe, Abteilung "Spanienkrieg," Luneburg 1938, revised and reissued Berlin 1940 (Militär-archiv/Freiburg).

Dominguiz, Juan. Diary, Spain/France, 1937.

Handbook on German Military Forces. U.S. War Department, Intelligence Division, 1943.

Foreign Office, London. Records, in files 371/21290 to 21294, and 21333, 1937 (Public Record Office).

Iturran, Father José. Papers/diary, Guernica, 1937.

Richthoften, Wolfram, *Freiherr* von. Diary, Spain, April 1937.

Wandel, Joachim. Diary, Germany/Spain, April 1937.

D. NEWSPAPERS

George Steer's reports in *The Times* of London and *The New York Times* caused the greatest stir. Among other newspapers consulted for the period from the end of April to approximately mid-May 1937, when Guernica was most in the news, were:

France—*Ce Soir, La Croix, L'Aube, L'Echo de Paris, Le Monde, L'Humanité;*

Germany—*Berliner Tagesblatt* and *Nachtausgabe, Die Wehrmacht, Frankfurter Allgemeine Zeitung;*

Spain—*ABC* (Seville and Madrid), *Aspa* (Salamanca), *Unidad* (San Sebastián), *Euzkadi* and *Gudari* (Bilbao);

United Kingdom—*The Daily Express, Daily Telegraph, Manchester Guardian, News Chronicle, The Sunday Times, The Star;*

United States—*The Christian Science Monitor, New York Herald Tribune, Washington Post.*

Interesting accounts of the Condor Legion's exploits in Spain were published at the time of its return, notably in Germany's *Illustrierter Beobachter* (Munich), *Berliner Illustrierte,* and in *Die Wehrmacht,* published by Oberkommando der Wehrmacht, especially in *Sonderheft: Wir Kampften in Spanien:*

—Sperrle, "Condor Legion."

—Von Moreau, "Hilfe für den Alkázar" and "Mit Bomben Kreuz und Quer durch Spanien".

A report on Señor Leizaola's appeal to the Nuremberg Tribunal to include in its charges the destruction of Guernica, particularly against Göring as head of the Luftwaffe, is to be found in *Euzko Deya,* published in Paris, April 30, 1946.

Index